D1475391

Alexander Strahan
Victorian Publisher

Alexander Strahan
Victorian Publisher

Patricia Thomas Srebrnik

THE UNIVERSITY OF MICHIGAN PRESS
Ann Arbor

Library of Congress Cataloging-in-Publication Data

Srebrnik, Patricia Thomas, 1950–
  Alexander Strahan, Victorian publisher.

  Bibliography: p.
  Includes index.
    1. Strahan, Alexander, 1834?–1918.   2. Publishers
and publishing—Great Britain—Biography.   3. Publishers
and publishing—Great Britain—History—19th century.
4. English periodicals—Publishing—History—19th
century.   5. Great Britain—Intellectual life—19th
century.   I. Title.
Z325.S887S68   1986   070.5'092'4 [B]   85-20954
ISBN 0-472-10072-6 (alk. paper)

To Henry

Acknowledgments

My first thanks must go to the Department of English and the Horace H. Rackham School of Graduate Studies of the University of Michigan for generous financial support over a number of years.

My research was begun with the help of the staff of the Graduate Library of the University of Michigan. In Great Britain I was assisted by many librarians and archivists. I am most grateful to the staffs of the British Library and the Institute of Historical Research of the University of London. I wish also to thank, in addition to the staffs of the institutions mentioned in the Bibliography, the librarians and archivists of the British Library Newspaper Collection at Colindale; the British Library of Political and Economic Science; the Royal Commission on Historical Manuscripts; the Westminster City Libraries; St. Bride's Printing Library; Bishopsgate Institute; and St. Deiniol's Library, Hawarden, Wales. I owe particular thanks to Mr. D. E. Hayward of the Central Reference Library in Lincoln, who provided me with photocopies from the Tennyson Research Centre. I also received photocopies from the Humanities Research Center at the University of Texas and the Huntington Library in San Marino, California.

For their hospitality, interest, and reminiscences I owe heartfelt thanks to Mr. and Mrs. Alexander Strahan and to Mr. and Mrs. Ralph Strahan Soames. Mr. and Mrs. Soames also entrusted me with a number of family letters and photographs. Commander Alexander Strachan Watt responded to my queries swiftly and graciously.

I have benefited from conversations with Professors Donald L. Hill and Earl J. Schulze of the Department of English and with Professor Stephen J. Tonsor of the Department of History of the University of Michigan. My debts to many other scholars are, I hope, evident in the notes to this volume. The comments from readers for the University of Michigan Press were also helpful. Thanks to Anne Craft for compiling the index and for assistance in the proofing process.

For their warm interest during the final stages of this project, I wish to express sincere thanks to my colleagues in the Department of English at Gettysburg College. I am particularly grateful to Professor Mary Margaret Stewart, Chair of the Department.

I owe my deepest appreciation to Professor R. H. Super, who has commented exhaustively upon several drafts of the manuscript. His guidance and the exemplary rigor of his scholarship have been an inspiration to me.

Finally, I thank my husband Henry for support emotional, financial, and intellectual. From his own researches into twentieth-century British politics, he has taken the time to become an aficionado of Victorian literature and its publishers.

Contents

Chapter

CHAPTER I

Introduction

Compared to the enduring publishing dynasties of the Blackwoods, the Constables, the John Murrays, or the Macmillans, the various publishing firms established in the 1860s and 1870s by Alexander Strahan (1834?–1918) seem ephemeral indeed. But during those decades, Strahan's name and his publishing device—the *Anchora Spei*, or "Anchor of Hope"—were familiar to hundreds of thousands of readers throughout the British Empire and in the United States. His highly eclectic publishing lists included volumes by such well-known Anglicans as A. P. Stanley, the dean of Westminster; Henry Alford, the dean of Canterbury; and Samuel Wilberforce, the bishop of Oxford, alongside volumes by Presbyterian and dissenting ministers who were Strahan's personal friends. His imprint appeared also on the works of such Victorian best-sellers as George MacDonald, Robert Buchanan, Dinah Mulock, Alexander Smith, Amelia B. Edwards, Dora Greenwell, Edward Jenkins, Sarah Tytler, and "A.K.H.B." (Andrew Kennedy Hutchison Boyd). At the peak of his career, Strahan published essays by W. E. Gladstone and fiction by Anthony Trollope; in 1869 he became the exclusive publisher to the poet laureate, Alfred Tennyson.

Strahan's greatest significance, however, is as the founder, publisher, and in large part conductor of several of the most important and innovative periodicals of the nineteenth century. These included *Good Words*, a sixpenny monthly that in the late 1860s was the best-selling magazine in the English-speaking world; *Good Words for the Young*, which featured the "faerie-allegories" of its editor, George MacDonald; and the *Contemporary Review*, a half-crown monthly that included articles by such notable figures as Gladstone, Ruskin, T. H. Huxley, and Matthew Arnold on matters "Theological, Literary, and Social."

Strahan began his career as a publisher convinced that given "the rapid progress in common education which was certain in the near future," it was necessary to provide the people with inexpensive literature, and that unless "our chief authors" could be persuaded to "descend to the magazines," periodical literature would become a force for ignorance and viciousness rather than for progress and good. In the popular literature of the 1850s Strahan perceived "a chilling narrowness, an absence of anything like a broad, warm humanity." He was appalled by the spectacle of high-priced, "exclusive" periodicals, "avowedly opponents, all fighting . . . for hostile views in religion and politics."[1]

Strahan was remarkably effective in securing for his own more broadly based periodicals contributions from the great names of the day. He made the periodicals as successful as they were partly by making extensive use of the names of his contributors, partly by carefully identifying and to some extent creating a market for his wares: in the case of *Good Words,* for example, he achieved high circulation figures by consciously amalgamating a variety of reading audiences— readers of fiction and readers of sermons, English readers and Scottish readers, readers from the middle classes and readers from the lower classes, Anglican readers and Nonconformist readers. In this way he created a new type of magazine that did not always meet with favor: the editors of rival, sectarian periodicals complained that the "religiose-comic *Good Words*" was "a curious mixture" of *Temple Bar,* which specialized in serial fiction; of *Chambers's Journal,* which emphasized soberly educational essays; and of the *Penny Pulpit,* a periodical whose name is self-explanatory.[2] For those readers who steadfastly refused to tolerate such a "mingle-mangle," particularly on the Sabbath, Strahan provided the *Sunday Magazine,* which became nearly as successful as *Good Words.* For those who preferred to take their essays and fiction without any admixture of piety, Strahan launched the *Argosy;* in 1869 he acquired another secular monthly, *Saint Pauls Magazine,* which at the time was edited by Anthony Trollope.[3] Meanwhile, in the *Contemporary,* Strahan promoted the development of yet another new type of periodical literature: the monthly review which provided a platform for the expression of diverse opinions.[4] As Mark Pattison wrote in 1877,

> Those venerable old wooden three-deckers, the *Edinburgh Review* and the *Quarterly Review,* still put out to sea under the command, I believe,

of the Ancient Mariner, but the active warfare of opinion is conducted by the three new iron monitors, the *Fortnightly*, the *Contemporary*, and the *Nineteenth Century*. . . . The monthlies . . . form at this moment the most characteristic and pithy part of our literary produce.[5]

But although Strahan's periodicals were deliberately nonpartisan and nonsectarian, it is true that Strahan was guided in his endeavors by a set of interconnected beliefs which he explained in numerous prospectuses, advertisements, and essays. In religion he was a broad-minded evangelical; in politics, he was a Gladstonian Liberal and a fervent populist. He believed in the power of the printed word to educate the masses and thus effect a transformation of society. Strahan's keen interest in social reform led him to publish the work of such "Christian Socialists" as Charles Kingsley, J. M. Ludlow, and F. D. Maurice.[6] His zeal to provide "wholesome" literature for children led to the appearance in *Good Words for the Young* and on his general publishing list of stories, poems, and essays by Jean Ingelow and by William Brighty Rands, as well as by George MacDonald.[7] And because Strahan believed that illustration could serve to enhance the improving literature he published, his magazines featured the work of the leading artists of the 1860s, including W. Holman Hunt, Edward Burne-Jones, Herbert Herkomer, Arthur Boyd Houghton, and J. E. Millais.

Many of these attitudes and opinions had their roots in Strahan's Scottish origins, for Strahan, like so many other Scots in the London publishing world, was inspired by the cultural values of his Presbyterian background, as a brief outline of his career will indicate.

Born in the Highlands, Strahan was raised in the Calvinist theology of the "Free Church" which separated itself from the Church of Scotland during the "Disruption" of 1843. When he went to Edinburgh in his teens, it was to become an apprentice in a religious publishing house which served the Free Church cause. Within a few years, Strahan established his own publishing firm. He also left the Free Church to become a congregant of the Church of Scotland. But the Free Church emphasis on social reform and on the political claims of "the people" remained a part of Strahan's philosophy even after his religious opinions became more moderate. By force of personality, Strahan also managed to retain many of his Free Church associates, even as he made friends within the Church of Scotland who were more useful socially, such as the Reverend Norman Macleod, a queen's chaplain who became the editor of *Good Words.*

Strahan's religion and his nationality were both a help and a hindrance when he moved his business and his periodicals to London in 1862. He quickly made friends and found business associates among other Scots who had preceded him to the English capital. But *Good Words* came under attack by Scottish Calvinists in London who were inclined to rehearse indefinitely the differences between the Church of Scotland and the Free Church. And even though Strahan went out of his way to make *Good Words* and his other periodicals acceptable to English readers by including contributions from as many Anglican writers as possible, Anglican ministers fretted that *Good Words* was conducted, after all, by Presbyterians. *Good Words* also came under scrutiny on at least two occasions by the *very* English *Saturday Review,* which pretended in 1870 to be offended by the characterization of an Anglican clergyman in a story published in *Good Words:* "Even the Order to which *Good Words* owes so much is treated here with flippancy. . . . These witticisms may gratify the tastes of a Presbyterian editor, but what are our bishops and archbishops about to allow it?"[8]

Strahan might have had an easier time of it if he had become an Anglican himself. It was a step taken by many other transplanted Scots, for reasons often as much social as religious. As one London journal remarked in 1873, Presbyterianism, "however it might answer on the other side of the Tweed," was traditionally regarded as "un-English . . . it was felt that Presbyterianism was not the religion for gentlemen in the south."[9] But although Strahan seems to have made the transition from Free Church to Church of Scotland with no great difficulty, he was either unable or unwilling to enter the Church of England. Perhaps he feared that he would not be at ease there: what we know of his personality suggests that, like the typical Scottish immigrant to England as described by Robert Louis Stevenson in the 1882 essay, "The Foreigner at Home," Strahan was "vain, interested in himself and others, eager for sympathy"—a sharp contrast to the typical Englishman who, again according to Stevenson, "is self-contained. . . . Compared with the grand, tree-like self-sufficiency of [the Englishman's] demeanour, the vanity and curiosity of the Scot seem uneasy, vulgar, and immodest."[10] Strahan seems to have compensated for his own social disadvantages by securing for the *Contemporary* Anglican editors—Henry Alford, E. H. Plumptre, James Thomas

Knowles—who moved at ease in social circles that were not so ready to receive him.

Despite these problems, Strahan and Company thrived in the 1860s, or so it must have seemed to observers unaware of yet another personal handicap of Strahan's: his extremely poor business judgment, a fault closely connected to the unbridled enthusiasm that he brought to every publishing project. Although Strahan spent lavishly on payments to authors and on advertisements, he was usually deeply in debt to the firms which printed and supplied the paper for his publications. At various times Strahan's long-suffering creditors insisted on taking part in the management of his company. In 1872, they seized *Good Words* and the *Sunday Magazine* and forced Strahan to retire from the business. In dire need of cash to continue the *Contemporary Review,* Strahan made the mistake of turning to English associates whose religious and political views were very different from his own. When the inevitable conflicts developed and Strahan found himself heavily in debt to his new partners, he compounded his error by appealing, through his Scottish evangelical connections, to a group of ministers and laymen who constituted the most theologically conservative faction within the Congregational Union of England and Wales, and who were in search of periodicals that might be used to express their theological opinions. Thus Strahan, who in earlier years had thrown in his lot with a milder theology and emerged unscathed from the quarrels between various Presbyterian factions, now became allied with the Calvinist faction within Congregationalism—an alliance which had unfortunate consequences for the reputation of the *Contemporary.* In 1882, Strahan was once again forced to retire as a result of financial difficulties; this time, he lost the *Contemporary.*

Strahan's story, then, can be understood only in its social and cultural context, and this volume constitutes a study, not merely of the commercial and editorial decisions of an individual publisher, but also of the successive milieus in which he lived and worked. Chapter 2 begins with a discussion of Scottish authors, editors, and publishers in London in the late eighteenth and early nineteenth centuries. Then the Calvinism of Strahan's part of the Scottish Highlands is described. In both chapters 2 and 3 the differences between the Free Church and the Church of Scotland have been delineated in order to provide a background for the controversies that enveloped *Good Words* and Strahan's other periodicals in the 1860s. In chapters 4, 5, and 7 there are references to Strahan's interest in the schemes for Christian social reform propounded by his friends within the Congregational Union, references intended to explain Strahan's eventual business partnership with these same friends in the 1870s; and in chapter 8 it has been necessary to discuss in some detail the intradenominational politics of the Congregationalists.

But although Strahan's career was shaped and then undermined by religious controversies which are for the most part long forgotten, enough has been said already to suggest that it would be a mistake to dismiss him as primarily a "religious" publisher who operated outside the cultural mainstream of Victorian Britain. In 1870 he was identified by the *Athenaeum* as one of several publishers "especially concerned with the literature of the people."

> The Messrs. Low, the Messrs. Strahan, the Messrs. Cassell, the Messrs. Nelson, the Messrs. Routledge and others . . . have *grown* into their present position. They did not start with it. . . . We may say of them now that they are not so much men as systems.[11]

Through the books and periodicals that Alexander Strahan published, and through the other periodicals which sprang up in imitation of *Good Words* and of the *Contemporary Review,* the central ideas of the age were brought before the new mass readership, and public opinion was formed. In the words of Strahan himself, "No publisher could enter on more glorious work."[12]

CHAPTER II

A Highland Prelude

> . . . records left
> Of persecution, and the Covenant—times
> Whose echo rings through Scotland to this hour!
>
> —Wordsworth, *The Excursion*, 1:174–76

In 1829, Thomas Carlyle sat in an isolated farmhouse in Scotland, pondering what he took to be the "Signs of the Times." He deplored the fact that "every little sect among us, Unitarians, Utilitarians, Anabaptists, Phrenologists, must have its Periodical, its monthly or quarterly Magazine." He regarded it as no less dangerous that

> the true Church of England, at this moment, lies in the Editors of its Newspapers. These preach to the people daily, weekly . . . inflicting moral censure; imparting moral encouragement, consolation, edification; in all ways, diligently "administering the Discipline of the Church."

Literature no less than philosophy, according to Carlyle, had come to depend upon "its Paternoster-row mechanism, its Trade-dinners, its Editorial conclaves, and huge subterranean, puffing bellows; so that books are not only printed, but, in a great measure, written and sold, by machinery." Carlyle neglected to acknowledge that he himself was one of the "new Preachers" of the periodical press: the *Life of Friedrich Schiller* appeared originally in 1823 in the *London Magazine;* in 1827, his study of Jean Paul Friedrich Richter was the first of many contributions to the *Edinburgh Review;* "Signs of the Times" would appear in the *Edinburgh* for June 1829. Nor did Carlyle mention that whatever praise or censure may have been due to the editors, contributors, and publishers of such magazines and reviews, the lion's share of it must have gone to Scottish compatriots of his own.

The *Edinburgh Review*, founded in 1802, was the first of the great quarterlies which so shaped public opinion in the nineteenth century.

Three of its founders—Francis Horner, Henry Brougham, and Francis Jeffrey, who served as editor until 1829—were Scots. The Englishman in their midst, Sydney Smith, never tired of pretending that his northern friends regarded oatmeal as the greatest possible delicacy, and claimed to have urged that their *Review* should adopt as its motto, "*Tenui musam meditamur avena*" ("We cultivate literature upon a little oatmeal").[1] The *Edinburgh* favored Whig policies. In 1809, the *Quarterly Review* appeared to champion the cause of the Tories. The *Quarterly* was based in London; but it was published by John Murray, who boasted Scottish descent, and its editor from 1824 to 1853 was John Gibson Lockhart, the son of a minister of the Church of Scotland and the son-in-law of Sir Walter Scott. In the same year that Lockhart began his editorship, James Mill, who in his native land had been licensed as a minister of the Scottish church, assisted in establishing the *Westminster Review* to serve as the organ of the Benthamite Radicals. A decade later his son, John Stuart Mill, would serve as editor of the short-lived *London Review*, and then stay on to edit the amalgamated *London and Westminster* between 1834 and 1840.

Meanwhile, *Blackwood's Edinburgh Magazine* served as the model for lighter miscellanies from the time of its establishment in 1817. One London imitator, the *New Monthly Magazine* (founded 1821), was edited by the Scottish poet Thomas Campbell. Another, the *London Magazine* (1820), brashly proclaimed itself a rival to journals emanating from "secondary towns of the Kingdom," i.e., Edinburgh; so deadly was the rivalry that the *London*'s first editor, John Scott, was killed in a duel with a member of the staff of *Blackwood's*. Scott was, ironically enough, a native of Aberdeen. The *London Magazine* ceased publication in 1829. But its place was filled in 1830 by *Fraser's Magazine*, which poached its editor (William Maginn) and many contributors from *Blackwood's*, and which serialized Carlyle's *Sartor Resartus* in 1833–34. James Fraser, the magazine's founder, was one of many Scotsmen who made their livelihoods as London publishers.[2]

At half a crown each, *Blackwood's* and *Fraser's* were well beyond the reach of the average workingman; the *New Monthly Magazine*, at 3s.6d., was even dearer. Edinburgh publishers took the lead in providing cheap yet "wholesome" literature for a wider readership. Archibald Constable, who is remembered as Sir Walter Scott's publisher, determined to publish books "so good that millions must wish to have them, and so cheap that every butcher's callant may have them." Constable's grandiose schemes reduced him to bankruptcy, but his "Miscellany," founded in 1827, survived to include editions of such recent nonfiction as Lockhart's *Life of Burns*.[3] Cheap reprints were also to be had from William and Robert Chambers, who published such didactically minded series as *Chambers's Information for the People, Chambers's Miscellany of Useful and Entertaining Information*, and *Chambers's Repository of Instructive and Amusing Tracts*. In 1832, they launched their famous *Edinburgh Journal*, a three-halfpenny weekly that would continue to appear far into the twentieth century.

Another "mechanism" to provide educational nonfiction for the working classes was the Society for the Diffusion of Useful Knowledge (SDUK). From the time of its establishment in 1827, its productions were greeted enthusiastically by the *Edinburgh Review*—perhaps because the society was the project of Henry Brougham, one of the founders of the *Edinburgh*. Brougham was confident that education would serve to make workingmen pious as well as sober and industrious. Many upper-class Anglicans disagreed: they suspected that the society would spread only irreligion and political sedition. Even William Cobbett, a leader of the workers whom Brougham sought to assist, found the wealthy philanthropist's zeal to be inherently distasteful, and derided the "brilliant enterprise to make us '*a*' *enlightened*' and to fill us with '*antellect*,' brought, ready bottled up, from the north of the Tweed."[4] But Brougham found an ally in Charles Knight, an idealistic English publisher who served as "superintendent" of the publications of the SDUK, and who issued his famous *Penny Magazine* (1832–45), as well as a variety of weekly and monthly serials, under the society's auspices. Another supporter was George Lillie Craik, a Scottish apostle of the philosophy of "self help" who in 1865 would become a partner in Macmillan and Company; *The Pursuit of Knowledge Under Difficulties* (1830) was the first of several works by Craik published by the society.

Other Scotsmen, resident in London, dispensed instruction in their capacity as editors of the weekly and monthly journals that sprang up with ever-increasing frequency as the century progressed. Sectarian journalism could hardly have developed without them. It was natural that Scotsmen should control Presbyterian organs such as the *Weekly Review* and the *British and Foreign Evangelical Review*. They were also prominent as editors of and contributors to the many periodicals representing the most influential of the English Nonconformists, the Congregationalists: the *British Banner*, the *Christian Witness*, the *Patriot*, the *Fountain*, the *Christian's Penny Magazine*, the *Eclectic Review*—these thers were conducted by such earnest Scots as John Brown ., John Kennedy, and John Campbell, men more famous in their time than in ours. They were in no doubt concerning their mission. Campbell, who shared the typically Scottish concern for a ministry to the masses, advocated "light postage, quick transit, cheap Bibles, and cheap Periodicals for the Millions of England!"[5] James Grant, a staunch Calvinist who edited the *Morning Advertiser* from 1850 to 1871 and then the short-lived *Christian Standard,* prefaced his three-volume survey of the press by announcing that it was the responsibility of newspapers and magazines "to Enlighten, to Civilize, and to Morally Transform the world."[6] The pretensions of such Nonconformists to serve as the conscience of Victorian England were bitterly disputed by the notorious *Record,* the organ of the most theologically narrow Evangelicals within the Establishment, and an enemy to dissent no less than to more latitudinarian believers within the church. For many years the *Record* was conducted by its Scottish founder and proprietor, Alexander Haldane.

Secular journalism as well owed much to its Scottish practitioners. Robert Stephen Rintoul, a zealous crusader for political reform, edited the *Spectator* for nearly thirty years following its establishment in 1828. James Wilson became the first editor of the *Economist* in 1843. John Douglas Cook, a Scottish Episcopalian, edited the *Morning Chronicle* from 1852 until in 1855 he became joint proprietor with Anthony Beresford Hope, and editor for its first thirteen years, of that most English of institutions, the *Saturday Review.* By then, the *North British Review* was proudly calling attention to the fact that "London is full of Scottish literary men, and Scottish editors of newspapers." The anonymous author of these words, David Masson (1822–1907), was a native of Aberdeen who had studied for the ministry and then been employed in Edinburgh by the Chambers brothers before coming to London in 1847.[7]

London had long been filling with Scottish publishers. Andrew Millar, who established himself in the Strand in 1729, published Dr. Johnson's *Dictionary* and became the subject of more than one celebrated remark recorded by Boswell; Millar had dealings also with Fielding and with James Thomson. His partner from 1739 was William Strahan, a native of Edinburgh who later published the work of Hume, Gibbon, and Adam Smith. John Murray, who changed his name from McMurray in an attempt to deflect anti-Scottish prejudices, arrived in London in 1768. In 1859, John Murray III would publish Samuel Smiles's *Self-Help* and Charles Darwin's *Origin of Species* on the same day. George Smith and Alexander Elder set up shop as booksellers and stationers in 1814; the second George Smith became head of the business in 1847. The Blackwoods, Chamberses, Blacks, Constables, Collinses, and many other firms based in Edinburgh or Glasgow maintained London offices. Those who did not were represented in the south by such massive wholesalers as Hamilton, Adams and Company or Groombridge and Sons.

Considering these pedigrees, the famous Macmillan brothers were relative latecomers to the London publishing world. Daniel arrived first from the Highlands in 1833, carrying a list of friends who already worked on Paternoster Row, and speaking a dialect so incomprehensible to English ears that his landlady called immediately for a Scottish interpreter.[8] One of Daniel's friends arranged eventually for him to be employed by the publishing firm of Seeley and Company, and in 1839 Alexander joined him there. During the years in which they saved up the money necessary to go into business for themselves, the brothers kept their spirits high by reading aloud *Sartor Resartus* as they dressed and breakfasted each morning. By 1843 they were able to purchase a bookshop in Cambridge. Daniel died in Cambridge in 1857, but Alexander returned to London in 1858 as an established publisher. In 1859 he launched *Macmillan's Magazine,* a shilling monthly that was characterized by an earnest desire to instruct and improve its readership. The magazine was edited by Macmillan's countryman, David Masson; remarked the publisher, "these things have considerable influence, and ought not to be left wholly in hands that use that influence unworthily."[9] In 1865, Macmillan's imprint appeared on the title page of *Ecce Homo,* the controversial life of Christ written anonymously by John Robert Seeley, the historian; Seeley was the son of the publisher who had given the Macmillans their start. In 1869, when both the prime minister of Great Britain (William Ewart Gladstone) and the archbishop of Canterbury (Archibald Campbell Tait) were men of entirely Scottish descent, Arthur J. Munby would record in his diary that on a London street he had encountered

> Macmillan the publisher, rosy and plump, making thousands, son at Eton, & all that. He came up smiling and cordial, offered me [his] card, so glad to see me at his country house at Streatham, would I come tomorrow? Talking of his original business at Cambridge, "Do you know" says

he "I regret all that: I am not at all ambitious!" "Just so" I replied: "but some men have greatness thrust upon them." Par exemple![10]

Contemporary observers did not fail to attempt an explanation of the preponderance of Scottish writers, editors, and publishers. Many pointed first to the differences between English and Scottish systems of education. Francis Jeffrey of the *Edinburgh Review,* for example, asserted that the Scottish curriculum, at the parish level no less than at the university, emphasized general studies and philosophical dispute far more than did the English.[11] Walter Bagehot, writing in 1855, distinguished between the English "education of facts" and that "education of speculation" which fostered "the genius of the Scottish people . . . a power of reducing human action to formulas or principles." In other words, "the teaching of Scotland seems to have been designed to teach men to write essays and articles."[12] Perhaps he was again thinking of the Scottish curriculum when he came to discuss, in 1869, "The Uses of Scotch Liberalism."

> The Scotch Liberal . . . is essentially a rationalist, a man who looks directly from cause to effect, who reasons out his principles in his own mind, and once satisfied applies them unflinchingly. . . . The Englishman . . . is not so impressed with the *necessity* of the action following the thought.[13]

Another frequently remarked feature of Scottish education was its egalitarianism, which had its origins in the theology of the Reformation: as early as 1560, John Knox's *First Book of Discipline* asserted the church's responsibility to ensure that every individual should have the learning necessary to read and understand Scripture. Education at the parish level may often have fallen short of this ideal, especially in poorer areas; Dr. Johnson remarked of eighteenth-century Scots that "their learning is like bread in a besieged town: every man gets a little, but no man gets a full meal."[14] Yet Francis Jeffrey took particular pride in the intellectual attainments of the laboring poor, and it seems certain that the Scottish peasant or laborer was, on the average, better educated than his English counterpart. An obituary notice for William Chambers makes the point.

> Thanks to that wise and benevolent provision common in Scotland . . . the boy was enabled to pick up . . . the elements of a more liberal

education on terms which to English people appear ludicrous. . . . On these terms even the poorest Scotch lads enter upon the race of life; no wonder at so many succeeding.[15]

It was an advantage that, once these poor lads arrived in London, probably counted for more on Paternoster Row than on any other street in the city. For a publisher, more than most businessmen, could profit from just such an education, whereas many an Englishman of a class to enjoy the same education would have regarded himself as superior to the work of retail bookselling or, even worse, job print-ing—two occupations inextricably bound up, in the nineteenth cen-tury, with the business of publishing.

A reverence for egalitarian learning—which frequently translated into a zealous interest in the provision of cheap literature—was not, however, the only value Scotsmen acquired in an educational system controlled by the Presbyterian Church. They themselves proudly be-lieved that what has been termed, despite vigorous sectarianism, "the folk or national religion of Scotland"[16] had forged an ethos which differed fundamentally from that of the Anglicans to their south. In his *North British Review* article of 1854, for example, Masson suggested that the English and the Scots, who had differed to some extent even when they shared the Roman Catholic faith, had diverged more and more widely since the Reformation, as in Scotland "Calvinistic the-ology, the theology of a rigid logic . . . had been worked . . . into the very blood and brain of the people."

> Always a more fervid, emphatic, opinionative, and speculative being than the Englishman . . . the Scotchman felt these differences from his neighbour greatly increased after he had embraced Presbyterianism, and especially after he had learned to fight for it.[17]

Political no less than temperamental differences were to be traced to the respective religions of the two countries, according to Masson: for while the Church of England was Episcopalian, the Church of Scot-land and its offshoots were "administered not by bishops, but by democratic assemblies of mixed clergymen and laymen," a fact that allegedly predisposed the Scottish people to sympathize with the dem-ocratic movements that emerged in the early nineteenth century.

Writers, editors, and publishers raised in such an atmosphere may be suspected as well of a predisposition to certain forms of literature.

One modern critic has written of "Puritan liberalism" generally that, based as it was upon "faith in democratic rule and in the priesthood of all believers," it assumed that familiarity with the Divine might be granted to even the most humble of believers, and that assimilation of the Divine into everyday concerns was a goal to be sought actively. Such attitudes often gave rise to a mode of speaking and writing that struck those less accustomed to viewing daily life sacramentally as tasteless and impious cant.[18] These attitudes were also likely to persist even after the specific tenets of Calvinist theology had been discarded. The Macmillan brothers, for example, attended Baptist and Congregationalist chapels in England before ridding themselves of what Daniel termed "Calvinistic cobwebs" and entering the Church of England. But to the end of his brief life Daniel believed that his "daily task-work" was "noble and holy and spiritual because of His appointment whose we are and whom we serve."[19] Alexander regarded Frederick Denison Maurice, the Christian Socialist who had more to do with bringing the Macmillans into the Anglican fold than did any other minister, as a prophet raised up by God "to stem the tide of infidelity that I felt coming on us." And so, even though they knew that Maurice's notoriously abstruse musings on God and society could never earn them a profit, the brothers published book after book by their hero, until the list filled a page and a half in their catalog.[20] In the late 1860s, Maurice would find another platform in Alexander Strahan's *Contemporary Review*.

While the Macmillans were establishing themselves in the south, Alexander Strahan was growing up in the Highlands, imbibing the same values and cultural assumptions that guided so many other Scottish writers, editors, and publishers.

Strahan was born in the early 1830s in Tain, Ross-shire, a town of about two thousand on the southern shore of the Dornoch Firth, in the synod of Moray and Ross. He was the sixth of nine children and the first to be born in Tain, for his father, John, who spelled his last name "Strachan," had only recently moved the family from Forres, Moray.[21] John Strachan was a "messenger-at-arms" and "sheriff's officer," which could not have been an entirely agreeable occupation during the 1830s and 1840s, as thousands of Ross-shire peasants were being evicted by their landlords in order to make room for the new sheepwalks; perhaps it was so disagreeable that the officials of Tain preferred to employ officers who did not have long-standing ties of kinship and friendship with the local populace.[22]

The entire synod was a center of perfervid Calvinism. Tain had reputedly been the first town north of the Grampians to embrace the doctrines of the Reformation,[23] and the evangelical revivals of the early nineteenth century had little to teach the impoverished residents of Moray and Ross: according to one witness, "the people were accustomed to hear the doctrines of grace explained, and the offer of salvation pressed upon the heart and conscience by Gospel ministers."[24] A childhood friend of Strahan's, Alexander Taylor Innes, would in old age recall that

> in the early half of the nineteenth century, as in the early half of the fifteenth, the religious peculiarities of my native country or district stood out as the most remarkable thing about it. Within living memory the Highlands of Scotland were filled with ideas of religion, and penetrated with a reverence for the divine, to an extent which I have nowhere else found. . . . It was a religion characterised by great inwardness and tenderness, both of them enveloped in a brooding melancholy—the same racial melancholy, no doubt, of which Matthew Arnold tells us that in *Ossian* "all Europe felt the power."

Innes also attributed to his countrymen "an overweening passion for the doctrinal and deductive system of Calvinistic theology."[25] During his and Strahan's first years the people were given cause to act upon their convictions, for in 1833 there commenced the "Ten Years' Conflict," a period of struggle between parties within the church, and between church and state, that would lead in 1843 to what has been termed "the most momentous single event" of nineteenth-century Scotland—the Disruption of the Established Church.[26]

The Disruption had its genesis in the eighteenth century. Then there had emerged, within the general assembly which governed the church, two rival factions. The "Moderates," who constituted the more powerful party, were a cultured and well-educated lot, with as keen an interest in history and philosophy as in theology. So far removed were they from the passions of the sixteenth-century reformers that one among their number went so far in his zeal for moderation as to describe John Knox as a boorish ruffian.[27] The "Evangelicals," in contrast, clung doggedly to the strictest Calvinist orthodoxy, regarding themselves as the spiritual heirs of the Covenanters who had fought, not only against the forces of "the Roman anti-Christ," but against those of the English kings who sought to impose episcopacy and the Anglican liturgy on the Scottish church. In the eighteenth century, the Evangelicals believed that the Moderates, by insisting that the church must be subject to the state and its civil courts even in matters ecclesiastical, were surrendering the hard-won right of the Scottish people to maintain their own church. For the laws to which the Moderates would subject the Scottish church were promulgated by a parliament in which the majority of members were English and Anglican.

The Evangelicals found their primary rallying cry in the issue of patronage, that is, the right of the crown, local landowner, or other patron, many of whom were not even members of the Church of Scotland, to "present" a minister to a pastorless congregation. Patronage had long been a source of conflict. Abolished in 1690, it was restored by the British Parliament in 1712, a mere five years after the union that deprived the Scots of their own legislature. During the years of Moderate ascendancy, even the right of the local presbytery to accept or reject a candidate presented to it was reduced to little more than a formality. The result was a series of schisms that the minority Evangelical party was helpless to prevent.

In the early part of the nineteenth century, however, the tide turned against the Moderates, who had taken so much pride in being in tune with the intellectual currents of the Enlightenment. The Evangelical party gained strength rapidly, not only as a result of the waves of revivalism which heightened religious feeling throughout the British Isles, but also as a result of the growing demand for political reform, a demand which accorded ill with the Moderates' emphasis on obedience to existing laws and structures of government. By 1834, the Evangelicals had a substantial majority in the general assembly, and they were determined to settle once and for all the troubled issue of patronage: they passed a "Veto Act" which guaranteed to individual congregations the right to reject a patron's nominee to any living. Soon, however, the Evangelicals learned that even though they might gain control of their church's assembly, it was all for naught unless the state could be made to understand that the Church of Scotland must govern itself in all matters ecclesiastical. In one case after another, a rejected clerical nominee appealed to the civil courts and was placed in the living over the veto of the congregation. The protests of the church were rejected out of hand at all levels of government. The Moderate party counseled patience and submission. The Evangelicals threatened a greater schism than any of those which had disrupted the church in the eighteenth century. It all came to a head when in 1842 the general assembly declared once again, in a "Claim of Right," that the Church of Scotland must be spiritually independent, and that when Parliament or the civil courts overturned the acts passed in the general assembly, they acted in violation of the terms of the union of the two kingdoms. Parliament, led by the Tory prime minister, Sir Robert Peel, considered the church's claim and then rejected it.

Englishmen, be they Whig or Tory, inside Parliament or out of it, had difficulty understanding what all the fuss was about. The Anglican church, which was governed technically by the monarch in council, and whose own convocations had been suspended since 1717, presented no relevant parallel to the claim of the Scottish church to govern itself by means of an elected assembly. John Douglas Campbell, the seventh duke of Argyll, struggled vainly in the House of Lords in 1841–42 to explain the position of the Church of Scotland; years later his son, the eighth duke, would assert in his memoirs that he had never met an Englishman "who could understand, or even conceive, that idea of the relations between Church and State which was embedded and embodied in the Constitution of Scotland."[28] Sydney Smith of the *Edinburgh Review*, who had himself entered the Anglican clerisy through lack of any better opportunity for advancement, wrote to a correspondent in 1841 that

> it is in vain that I study the subject of the Scotch Church. I have heard it ten times over from Murray, and twenty times from Jeffrey, and I have not the smallest conception what it is about. I know it has something to do with oatmeal, but beyond that I am in utter darkness.[29]

Whig and Tory alike took comfort in the mistaken idea that if only Parliament stood firm, the crisis would soon blow over. It was a stance certain to exacerbate matters: the Evangelicals won popular support by depicting themselves as national heroes, engaged in a struggle against those traditional enemies of the nation and religion of Scotland, the English Anglicans. They were to charge ever after that it was the British Parliament, and not themselves, that must shoulder the blame for rending their church in two.

In 1843, the annual meetings of the general assembly were scheduled to commence on 18 May. English politicians fully expected a
small number of firebrands to stage a protest. They were astonished
when word came that no fewer than 474 ministers (of 1,203) had
marched from the assembly, forfeiting their parish churches, their
endowments, their manses and glebes, to establish the Free Church of
Scotland. With a single exception, every missionary of the church
went with them. So did approximately 40 percent of the laity, a fact
that made it necessary for the Free Church to open nearly a hundred
more churches than on the first Sabbath following the Disruption it
had ministers to fill. Led by the great Thomas Chalmers (1780–1847),
and full of righteous indignation against those who, although expressing sympathy for the Evangelicals, had elected to remain behind,
the seceders energetically set about building up an ecclesiastical struc-
ture which would soon rival that of the Establishment itself.

In the Highlands, Calvinist fervor on behalf of the Evangelicals was
powerfully blended with anger over the fact that the established
church had done little to protest the progress of the clearances. The
Moderates were widely regarded as allies of those landowners—com-
municants themselves, in many cases, of the Episcopalian church—
who had driven their tenants from the lands they had farmed for
generations. The Evangelicals did not hesitate to present themselves
as champions of the peasantry, and when the Disruption came, the
Highlanders seceded almost to a man, woman, and child.[30]

The residents of Tain were not exceptions. In 1839 they were
visited by Thomas Chalmers, who drew an audience of nearly a thousand for his address. "A marvellous day meeting in so small a place,"
he commented. "Much pleased with the antique and simple air of
Tain."[31] As the Disruption drew near, the Tain presbytery nervously
petitioned the government to keep its gunboat in the nearby Firth of
Cromarty "till after the present excitement shall have subsided."[32]
Such measures were to little avail. The dramatic exodus from the
general assembly had its counterpart in Tain, where the Sunday
morning congregation marched from its parish church, led by their
minister, who said he "walked on air."[33] Within weeks a wooden Free
Church building was erected while the parish church stood empty.
There, the town magistrates had been accustomed to enter in procession and occupy seating directly across from the pulpit. They followed the same practices in the new Free Church until word came all

the way from Edinburgh that their official endorsement of the secession was of questionable legality.[34] The bitterest scorn was entertained for those few who remained in the Establishment; according to one woman who grew up in Ross-shire, even as late as the 1860s,

> no really sincere Free Churchman would have anything to do with a member of the Established Church, and I can remember as a child being made to cross the road because the minister of the Established Church was coming towards us, and we were not allowed to speak to him.[35]

Little wonder, then, that the *North British Review* would be of the opinion in 1854 that "those who were children in Scotland between 1834 and 1843, will bear the marks in all their subsequent career."[36] Alexander Taylor Innes remarked of Ross-shire that as a result of the Disruption controversies,

> for men born there during the last century the Scottish history most present to the imagination was—not the woes of Queen Mary, or the snapping of the White Rose in the Forty-Five but—the Puritan and religious side, and in particular the long struggle of the persecuted Cameronians.

"If one wishes to have an idea of our part of Scotland," continues Innes, "he should read Hugh Miller; not so much the geologist, or the Churchman and editor, as the son of the soil, in his *Schools and Schoolmasters,* and his *Scenes and Legends.*"[37] Miller, who was born in Ross-shire in 1802, was a personal friend of the Innes and Strachan families. He was also an example of that archetypal figure in Scottish legend, the poor but self-educated mechanic.[38] Apprenticed to a stonemason at the age of seventeen, he studied geology while at work in the quarries, and soon was indulging in that hobby dear to the hearts of nineteenth-century amateurs and professionals alike: the reconciliation of geology with Revelation. He was destined to achieve fame, however, not as a man of science, but as a controversialist on behalf of the Evangelical party. In 1839 there appeared his *Letter to Lord Brougham,* a strongly worded attack on the institution of patronage and on the decisions of the civil courts upholding it. The pamphlet made his name and brought him to the notice of a group of Evangelicals, including such future leaders of the Free Church as

James Begg, R. S. Candlish, and Thomas Guthrie, who had decided to found a newspaper to express their views. They brought Miller to Edinburgh to serve as its editor; there he became a member of Guthrie's congregation. The *Witness* made its debut in January 1840 under the imprint of John Johnstone, who had published Miller's *Letter,* and whose publishing firm more than any other was identified with the cause of the Evangelicals.[39]

W. G. Blaikie, an Evangelical minister who in the 1850s edited the *Free Church Magazine* under Johnstone's imprint, would later recall that "it looked like infatuation to bring a stone-mason to edit a metropolitan paper. Were the party reduced to this, that an uncouth Highland mechanic should be called to give expression to the voice of the Church in genteel, aristocratic Edinburgh?"[40] But Miller was at the beginning of a highly influential career; and his success was based on earnest sectarianism. Thomas Guthrie would come to regard him as "that mightiest champion of truth" who was, with the single exception of Thomas Chalmers, "by much the greatest man of all who took part in the 'Ten Years' Conflict.' "[41] In 1863, the *Weekly Review,* a Presbyterian paper based in London, would approvingly summarize the record of the *Witness:* "For three-and-twenty years that paper has advocated Free Church principles with a singleness of aim which might be thought narrow, and, on the whole, with remarkable ability. If any paper was ever printed, in which the authority of God's word was maintained, and the Calvinism of the Westminster Standards professed, such a paper is *The Witness.*"[42]

The *Witness* was not so narrow, however, as to be limited to the exposition of abstract theological views. Hugh Miller's writings demonstrate clearly the social, political, and nationalistic overtones to the Ten Years' Conflict. His fervent belief that the Scottish church was the property of "the people," "a patrimony won for them by the blood of their fathers, during the struggles and sufferings of more than an hundred years," impelled him to charge that the enemy of the people in these struggles was the Tory party—an "irreligious" collection of aristocrats, many of whom had become so Anglicized that they adhered not to the Scottish church, but to the Episcopalian communion. Their political opponents, the Whigs, should have been the natural protectors of the people and the church. Instead, the Whigs had subjected church to state, which meant, ultimately, to the British Parliament. At this point the abused church had made a fatal error:

"Offended by the usage which she had received at the hands of the Whigs," she had "thrown her influence into the Tory scale. . . . The people, however, though they might, and did, become quite indifferent enough to the Whigs, could not follow her into the Tory ranks." Miller hailed the Evangelicals as a group dedicated to restoring to the people their ecclesiastical patrimony. The role of the *Witness* was to be a paper "that, without supporting any of the old parties in the State, should be as Liberal in its politics as in its Churchmanship."[43]

Just two months prior to the Disruption, Miller published in the *Witness* a gloomy article entitled "A Vision of the Railway"—a vision which foresaw the decay of distinctively Scottish religious traditions as a result of the new mode of travel, linking Scotland with the Erastian south.[44] In 1845 Miller himself, unable to resist the lure, paid his first visit to England. The result was a series of articles in the *Witness,* later collected under the title *First Impressions of England and Its People,* which was thoroughly disparaging of just about everything Miller had seen south of the Tweed. Miller's basic theme is that the English and Scottish characters are completely different; he assumes that such differences arise from the respective religions of the two countries. The English are a "country of insulated men . . . detached particles" because their church fails to promote a sense of community. "But while the Englishman is thus detached and solitary, the Scotchman is mixed up, by the force of his sympathies, with the community to which he belongs. . . . That adhesive coherency of character in the Presbyterian Scot, which so thoroughly identifies him with his country, and makes the entire of his Church emphatically his, gives to the Erastian principle a degree of atrocity, in his estimate, which, to the insulated English Episcopalian . . . it cannot possess." The English have also been rendered, as a result of their eclectic theology and ritual, incapable of sustained logical thought: "Religion, in its character as a serious intellectual exercise, was never brought down to the common English mind, in the way in which it once pervaded, and to a certain extent still saturates, the common mind of Scotland. . . . Calvinism proves the best possible of all schoolmasters for teaching a religious people to think. I found no such peasant metaphysicians in England as those I have so often met in my own country."[45]

With such a heady mixture of earnest Calvinism, liberal politics, social zeal, and Scottish nationalism, it is not surprising that the

Witness during Hugh Miller's editorship became a vehicle for the expression of the pride and aspirations of those Scots who were Evangelicals and, after 1843, Free Churchmen.

The Strachan family of Tain were most certainly regular readers of the newspaper edited by their friend. They seem to have won among their neighbors a reputation for exceptional intellect: Alexander Taylor Innes would later recall that at the Tain Academy, where sound instruction in the classics and the sciences was available to even the poorest child, the elder Strachan brothers had been the "despair" of all others, as they carried away prize after prize for their feats of scholarship.[46] John Strachan's great-grandchildren repeat even today stories of how the large family would crowd around a single candle in order to pass the long winter evenings over their reading; "Alick" Strachan would one day tell, as one of his "earliest recollections," how "as a little boy in a far-away country-house" he had pored over the inexpensive monthly volumes published "For All Readers" by Charles Knight.[47] By the time of the 1851 census, sixteen-year-old Alexander was a "bookseller's apprentice." But he was not to remain in the Highlands. In May 1853, John Strachan died, and Alexander's future career was determined by Hugh Miller, who took him to Edinburgh and arranged for him to become an apprentice, at an annual salary of £70, to what was now the firm of Johnstone and Hunter, Free Church publishers of the *Witness* and many other books and periodicals.

Strachan was probably gone by the autumn of 1853, when Tain had an illustrious visitor, one who was to become a revered leader to those Free Churchmen, English as well as Scottish, who sought a new political party to replace the Whigs. The visitor was William Ewart Gladstone, already Chancellor of the Exchequer under Lord Aberdeen. Gladstone was no stranger to the synod of Moray and Ross. His maternal grandfather was provost of the nearby town of Dingwall and he had visited the area many times before. Gladstone's father had moved from Scotland to Liverpool to make his fortune as a merchant; there he also became a leader of the local Whig Radicals. But despite having left the Presbyterian church to become an evangelical Anglican, the elder Gladstone was always made to feel an outsider in England, and during every election campaign, the Tory lampooners caricatured his Scottish origins. About 1830, after nearly forty years in Liverpool, John Gladstone returned to his native land. But he was determined that his sons should be Englishmen, and he insisted on sending William Ewart to Eton and Oxford as the necessary prelude to a political career.[48]

Alexander Strachan, who was to become a devoted follower of Gladstone and the publisher of many of Gladstone's periodical writings, did not enjoy the social advantages of inherited wealth or of an English public school education. Nonetheless he seems to have had ambitious plans. Soon after his arrival in Edinburgh, he dropped the *c* from his last name—apparently in order that one day it might roll all the more readily off an English tongue.[49]

CHAPTER III

Periodicals as Pulpits: Doing Good in Edinburgh, 1853–62

> This dark city . . .
> And gray metropolis of the North.
>
> —Tennyson, "The Daisy" (1853)

Edinburgh in the 1850s was still a center of literary culture. Sir Walter Scott had been dead less than twenty years; his monument had been erected as recently as 1844, and the two-hundred-foot spire must not yet have been entirely blackened by soot. Francis Jeffrey of the *Edinburgh Review* lived until 1850. The essayist and poet John Wilson ("Christopher North," 1785–1854) and the "common sense" philosopher Sir William Hamilton (1788–1856) were nearing the ends of their careers at the university, lecturing on moral philosophy and on logic and metaphysics, respectively. Dr. John Brown (1810–82) was a member of the medical faculty; his first published work, a series of notices of paintings exhibited at the Royal Scottish Academy, had been solicited by Hugh Miller for the *Witness* in 1846, but his most famous essays, concerning *Rab and His Friends,* would not appear until 1859. John Stuart Blackie (1809–95), a fervent nationalist who was not yet as famous as he was to become for his long flowing white hair and his habit of dressing regularly in kilts, arrived in 1852 to teach Greek at the university; he devoted at least as much of his time to promoting what has been termed "the cult of Scottishness."[1] Thirty years later an article in the *Cornhill Magazine* would recall how Blackie put "uncouth, umbrageous students . . . fresh from the heather . . . at their ease with ready human geniality"; the author of these words, Robert Louis Stevenson, was born in the New Town in 1850.[2] Thomas De Quincy, who took up residence in Edinburgh as a result of his friendship with John Wilson, would continue until his death in 1859 to impress all who heard him with the brilliance of his conversation. Proud Edinburghers supposed that the fame of their city was being

enhanced by the efforts of John Wilson's son-in-law, William Ed-
monstone Aytoun (1813–65), author of *Firmilian,* no less than by two
of the "spasmodic" poets he satirized, Sydney Dobell and Alexander
Smith, who arrived in tandem in 1854. No fewer than five major
newspapers catered to various religious and political constituencies:
the *Courant* and the *Advertiser* for Tories and Established Churchmen;
the *Witness* and the *Caledonian Mercury* for Liberals, Nationalists, and
Evangelicals; the *Scotsman* for worldly anti-ecclesiastics—but then,
huffed some devout Presbyterians, a high proportion of contributors
to the *Scotsman* were drawn, after all, from the ranks of "London
hacks."[3] The London *Times* might grumble in 1856 that "Edinburgh,
indeed, continues to affect literary airs, and a coterie of writers live
together on terms of mutual admiration."[4] But to those on the inside
it must still have seemed, as one historian has written, "a pleasant and
witty society" that "retained the stimulus of immemorial associations
and of historic names, not yet whirled away to the great vortex of
London."[5]

Life was not so pleasant in the alleys and back lanes of old Edinburgh where, as in Glasgow, an influx of population from the rural
areas had resulted in fetid, overcrowded slums. Many of the new-
comers were Highlanders who had been forcibly uprooted and who
left behind not only the lands their families had farmed for generations, but also, in many cases, the daily discipline and the patterns of
religious observance which had been carefully inculcated by parish
churches and schools. Ironically, considering that the Free Church
Evangelicals tended to regard themselves as champions of the people,
the Disruption of 1843 had undermined those institutions which
should have assisted the urban poor. The educational system, for
example, lost many of its most dedicated teachers, ordained ministers
who prior to the Disruption had been unable to find clerical positions,
but who now filled Free Church pulpits. The Poor Law, which had
been administered by the church, became unworkable after the Evangelicals seceded and threw up their own parish system alongside that
of the established church. A new Poor Law was passed in 1845 to
transfer the power of granting relief from the established church to a
central board which retained the old parochial boundaries as admin-
istrative units; but the new system, at least in its early years, worked
creakily at best.

Free Churchmen, however, were confident that they could now battle irreligion, illiteracy, pauperism, and social vices far more effectively than they had when their best energies were absorbed by the struggle against the Moderates and the state. The miserable condition of working-class housing, for example, concerned many Free Churchmen: William Garden Blaikie was responsible for the formation of a "Model Dwellings Company" in Edinburgh while James Begg, who was one of the founders of the *Witness* and whose theology was regarded as ultra-Calvinist even by some of his fellow Evangelicals, was thought by local Tories to be a dangerously radical "ecclesiastical demagogue" because his outrage over poor sanitation frequently erupted in bitter diatribes against upper-class landlords.[6] Thomas Guthrie, another founder of the *Witness* and author of *The City: Its Sins and Sorrows* (1857), worked closely with the seventh earl of Shaftesbury to establish "Ragged Schools" for the poor. Thomas Chalmers was horrified by the widespread drunkenness in his Glasgow parish; he was even more distressed that few among the working-class poor ever bothered to attend a religious service.

Few Free Churchmen, however, were sympathetic to the Chartist agitation of the 1840s, for whereas the Chartists, as Hugh Miller complained over and over again in the *Witness*, made not the slightest effort to relate their schemes for economic and social improvement to God's scheme of salvation, the Evangelicals believed that all urban social problems were the result of man's estrangement from God. W. G. Blaikie expressed their sense of mission in his autobiography.

> The peculiarity of the position of the Free Church seemed to me to be this, that it was the true representative of the ancient Reformed Church of Scotland, and that Knox and the other founders of that Church had set before themselves a glorious national ideal, which the Free Church was bound to prosecute—the Christian transformation of the whole country, the elevation of the masses, intellectually, morally, and socially, and the bringing of all classes into friendly relations, so that under the influence of a living Christianity, all should live happily amid the comforts of this life, and die in the hope of a better life to come.[7]

Or, as the *British and Foreign Evangelical Review* would put it in 1861, "the preaching that the time requires . . . resembles missionary preaching."[8]

Blaikie, Begg, and Guthrie were noted for their eloquence; a contemporary has named Guthrie, under whom Hugh Miller sat, as "by far the most popular preacher in the city during his day."[9] But so long as the working classes stayed resolutely away from their churches, such ministers sought to develop more effective channels through which to preach their gospel doctrines. Blaikie conducted prayer meetings in the home of a bookkeeper of an iron works "but two or three hundred yards from my church." His work there provided him with material for a sixpenny tract, *Six Lectures to the Working Classes on the Improvement of their Temporal Condition*, which was published by Johnstone and Hunter in 1849.[10] And increasingly, the urban evangelists found new pulpits in the cheap and not-so-cheap periodicals which flourished from mid-century.

By the time Alexander Strahan arrived at Johnstone and Hunter in 1853, that firm was publishing several of the most popular and influential periodicals that spread the Free Church message. The *Witness* was theirs, of course; so was the *Free Church Magazine,* a sixpenny monthly edited from 1849 by Blaikie. The Reverend Andrew Cameron, who was general secretary of the Religious Tract and Bible Society in Scotland, edited two periodicals for Johnstone and Hunter: the quarterly *British and Foreign Evangelical Review,* which at its peak achieved a circulation of about a thousand copies; and the famous *Christian Treasury,* "a Family Periodical for Sabbath Reading," which sold for one penny weekly, and which achieved a circulation of thirty thousand by serving up, in each issue, a number of mini-sermons with such titles as "Prayer and Effort Rewarded," "The Lord Liveth," and "A Ministry for Home Evangelizing."[11]

Young Strahan, who was already saving from his annual salary of £70 the money he would one day require to go into business for himself, learned at Johnstone and Hunter how such periodicals were edited and produced. He also met a number of men who were to be his associates for many years to come. Two of his fellow apprentices were William Isbister, who would be his partner in Edinburgh and then in London, and William Gellan, who would work as a subeditor in their firm.[12] Peter Bayne, who was, like Strahan, a native of Rossshire, and who served as one of Hugh Miller's assistants on the *Witness,* would be a contributor to periodicals published by Strahan and Isbister. Thomas Guthrie would edit one of these, assisted by W. G. Blaikie. But even before his apprenticeship came to an end,

Strahan seems to have determined that he would not be limited to the confines of Free Church, sectarian publishing; and one of the periodicals he studied during these years was the *Edinburgh Christian Magazine,* which had been edited since its founding in 1849 by a "fiery Celt" from the Highlands who was fast becoming the most famous minister within the established church: Norman Macleod.[13]

The Church of Scotland had not, on the whole, demonstrated as keen an enthusiasm as the Free Church when it came to mounting an evangelical ministry to the urban poor; indeed, one of the reasons for Norman Macleod's popularity was the exceptional interest he took in such activities. But while Free Churchmen expended their energies in the slums, the ministers of the established church, dazed by the calamitous outcome of the Ten Years' Conflict, turned their attention to effecting a theological renewal. The departure of many of the more rigid Calvinists had minimized opposition to the spread of a milder, Arminian theology, which assumed that Christ had died for the salvation of all who believed in him, and not merely for the elect. By the 1850s, many ministers had been influenced by such Scottish thinkers as Thomas Erskine of Linlathen and John Macleod Campbell—men who rejected the doctrine of predestination. Another milestone was the publication in 1853 of Frederick Denison Maurice's *Theological Essays,* which reinterpreted traditional concepts of eternal life and eternal punishment, triggering vicious attacks on Maurice by Calvinists within his own Church of England. Many Scottish Presbyterians were sympathetic to Maurice's thought, however; and the result was the emergence within the Church of Scotland of a "Broad Church" party which was more earnest concerning religious faith than had been the eighteenth-century Moderates, but less Calvinist in its theology than were the nineteenth-century Evangelicals.[14] Two leaders of this group were to achieve considerable academic influence: John Tulloch (1823–86), who in 1854 became principal of St. Mary's College, St. Andrews; and John Caird (1820–98), who in 1862 would become professor of theology and in 1873 principal of the University of Glasgow. One of the more popular preachers of the Broad Church party was Dr. Robert Lee, who taught from his pulpit at Old Greyfriars, Edinburgh, that if the church was to retain its hold upon the intellectual classes, it was essential that there should be a greater freedom of belief.[15] The greatest crowd-pleaser of them all, however, was Macleod, of the famous Barony Church, Glasgow, who seems to have been gifted with immense eloquence, irrepressible mirth, and unflagging energy, as well as with great physical size and strength. Lady Augusta Bruce, who in 1868 would become the wife of A. P. Stanley, dean of Westminster, wrote to a friend in 1856 that she had just heard Macleod preach "with the ease and grace of a Highlander—and one the very opposite of sectarian. All were delighted."[16] Macleod was no less popular among those parishioners who attended his Sunday evening services for the poor, to which none were admitted unless wearing working clothes.[17] He was also one of the few ministers within the Establishment to work as tirelessly on behalf of foreign missionary endeavors as did the scores of Free Churchmen who were prominent in the various missionary societies.

Yet Norman Macleod, even though he shared many of their enthusiasms, was one of the Establishment ministers most resented by Free Church Evangelicals. Their hostility dated back to the Ten Years' Conflict. Then, they had regarded the young Highlander as one of their own. The son and grandson of Evangelical ministers, Macleod had been raised in an atmosphere of strict Calvinism, and early letters from his parents are full of injunctions that the youth should make a greater effort to bridle his high spirits and cultivate a more seemly piety.[18] He had been a student of Thomas Chalmers, the leader of the Evangelicals, and he sympathized with their protests against patronage. But under the influence of his cousin and friend John Macleod Campbell, Norman Macleod gradually turned away from hellfire-and-brimstone theology, and in later years he would become fond of saying that although his ship was anchored, it swung with a free cable.[19] He began to be repelled by the narrow truculence of the Evangelicals, and to fear that their claims on behalf of the church's spiritual independence savored of "ultramontane pretensions" that might ultimately replace "presbyter" with "priest writ large"; he was particularly wary of "fanaticism in Ross-shire."[20] Above all, he came to agree, with many Moderates, that an established church was too essential to the Christian life of the nation to be torn asunder for any other than the gravest of issues.

And so in 1842, as it became apparent that a crisis was imminent, Norman Macleod threw in his lot with a "middle party" of about forty ministers who thought like himself. This group—reviled by the Evangelicals as "the Forty Thieves"—undertook a desperate, twofold campaign to preserve the church: on one hand they urged the Evangelicals to adopt a policy of compromise and conciliation; on the other, they encouraged parliamentary leaders to suppose that a compromise might be forthcoming. Many outraged Evangelicals would later insist that it was this act of betrayal and cowardice that confirmed the government in its erroneous belief that the Evangelicals would yield if the government stood firm, thus making inevitable the Disruption. Nor were the seceders impressed by the fact that as they filed out of the general assembly on the day of the Disruption, the "Forty Thieves"—with the exception of Macleod, who was, ironically, occupying the chair of the moderator of the assembly during this crucial year—rushed across the assembly hall to throw themselves upon the deserted benches, vowing to continue the struggle against patronage. Macleod, on his part, was outraged that certain seceding ministers insisted that "the Lord Jesus Christ will have left the Church when we go!" and asserted that the Devil was preparing a cradle in hell for those who stayed behind. "Yet I daresay," wrote Macleod in a rare display of bitterness, that

> in a century after this, we shall have some partisan historian writing whining books about these persecuted, self-denying, far-seeing saints, and describing all who oppose them as lovers of the fleece, dumb dogs, and all that trash.[21]

In the years following the Disruption, many honors came to Macleod. The greatest of these was his appointment in 1857 to be one of the royal chaplains in Scotland; soon he became a trusted friend and the favorite spiritual advisor of Queen Victoria. Free Churchmen, who had given up all hope of worldly advancement when they left the established church in support of principles Macleod had once seemed to espouse, resented him all the more as his fame increased; and when they referred to him, they preferred to dwell, not upon his Sunday evening services for the poor, but upon the nights he allegedly passed on the terrace of Windsor Castle, smoking and drinking whiskey with the Prince of Wales until "ungodly hours."[22]

Macleod's name would have been a black one to those Free Churchmen who frequented the offices of Johnstone and Hunter. He himself had feared "anathemas loud and deep from the *Witness*" as he anticipated, on the eve of the Disruption, that his own "simple vote as Moderator" would "decide the game one way or another."[23] When

Macleod complained, immediately following the Disruption, that the seceders had kindled a fire and then left it for those who stayed behind to put out, Thomas Guthrie retorted that in fact, the seceders had "taken away well-nigh all the fire along with us."[24] Hugh Miller was notorious for being one of those spiritually proud Free Churchmen who regarded all those who remained within the Establishment as living outside the pale of true Christianity. But Strahan seems to have harbored different ideas. He was never to forget that one afternoon, before coming to Edinburgh, he had caught his first glimpse of the famous Norman Macleod, advancing down a lonely Highland road "with a tread that seemed to grip the ground and nearly shake it," and swinging an umbrella so large that Strahan was put in mind of "a beneficent giant brandishing his club in glee at having just slain some monster."[25] As for the Free Church itself, Strahan would one day write to a minister who was leaving that communion to enter the Establishment, "I cannot say I am surprised. . . . The Free Church . . . never did appear to me to be a catholic institution, or one in which an open inquiring mind could find satisfaction."[26]

Strahan was not long obliged to accommodate himself to the theological views of his friends and employers. In 1856, the firm of Johnstone and Hunter, despite the popularity of its periodicals, went bankrupt with little prior warning. On Christmas Eve, Hugh Miller shot himself to death. He had long suffered from severe depressions; he had been anxious over the failure of his publishers; some contemporaries speculated that he had been unable to adjust to life in Edinburgh, or to account for the manifold evils he witnessed there; others suggested that he had recognized the futility of his attempts to reconcile the findings of science with the Calvinist tenets of his faith.[27]

Strahan rented a room at 42 George Street, doubtless with an eye to the fact that his near neighbors at Number 45 were the famous firm of Blackwood and Company, and proclaimed himself a publisher. He seems soon to have become a congregant of the established church, but no Free Churchman could have had a keener sense of mission. His childhood friend from Tain, Alexander Taylor Innes, was also in Edinburgh, studying law and writing for the periodical press; Innes would later recall how, about this time, Strahan burst into his rooms one evening, "already planning the great publishing enterprises . . . which did so much to unite orthodoxy and thought in one onward movement."[28] Strahan would describe himself, more than once in the course of his career, as a proud "follower in the footsteps of Charles Knight," the publisher to the Society for the Diffusion of Useful Knowledge, and would suggest, in passages that echo the social concern of the Free Church, that before the appearance of Knight's *Penny Magazine,*

> nothing in fact had been done to draw the humbler classes out of the slough of despair in which drunkenness had landed them; the upper classes rather exulted in the example they gave of hard-drinking; and the result was a society sharply divided into classes with directly opposing interests, all alike given up to sensual indulgence, heartily hating each other.

Strahan would express his ambition to "carry on the work of his master, by supplying such literature as will not ignobly interest nor frivolously amuse, but convey the wisest instruction in the pleasantest manner."[29] Strahan went far beyond even Knight's idealism, however, in the utopian claims he made on behalf of their common calling.

> We shall find that in the writings of our best authors we possess all we require to strike our grappling-iron into the working people's souls, and chain them, willing followers, to the car of advancing civilization.[30]

Meanwhile, Strahan was joined on George Street by William Isbister, his fellow apprentice from Johnstone and Hunter. No less a judge than Anthony Trollope would one day describe Isbister as one who understood paper and printing, but who was "altogether astray" when it came to judging whether or not a given book would earn a profit.[31] That would be no problem as long as Isbister remained in partnership with Strahan, who was soon to acquire the reputation of possessing, in the words of W. G. Blaikie, "a remarkable instinct" for "what would take the public taste"; others would say that Strahan "needed only . . . to sniff at an author's manuscript to realize its worth."[32] Strahan and Company's earliest book lists were heavily weighted with such pious titles as *Revival Lessons* (price 6d.; also issued as tracts, 1s. per 100); *Ten Years of a Preacher's Life* (4s.6d.); and *The Power of Prayer* ("Fine Edition," 2s.; "Cheap Edition," 1s.). Some of these works had been published previously by Johnstone and Hunter, and were perhaps available at bargain-basement rates to that firm's former apprentices. Other volumes were reprints of American publications that cost the fledgling publishers little or nothing in copyright fees: in November 1858, for example, Strahan and Company advertised editions of *The Autocrat of the Breakfast Table* by Oliver Wendell Holmes, a title that was being pirated by many British publishers; and of *Life Thoughts,* a volume of selections from the poetry of Henry Ward Beecher, for which the author was paid no fee whatsoever.[33] By April 1859, Strahan and Company was able to advertise a reprint of a recent best-seller: John Lothrop Motley's *History of the Rise of the Dutch Republic* (1856), a classic of mid-nineteenth-century democratic nationalism that in its first year of publication sold fifteen thousand copies in London alone.[34] Strahan and Company issued Motley's *History* both in a two-volume edition which cost 10s.6d., and in nine monthly shilling parts. In the fall of 1859 they advertised *Heroes of Childhood: A Hearty Book for Boys and Girls* "With Numerous Illustrations" (3s.6d.); *Prevailing Prayer,* an account of a Boston prayer meeting "and the Remarkable Instances of Conversion Related at it," with an introduction by Norman Macleod (1s.6d.); and a Christmas edition of Beecher's *Life Thoughts,* "printed on toned paper, with richly ornamented borders."[35] By this time they had acquired the *News of the Churches and Journal of Missions,* a six-penny monthly established by Johnstone and Hunter in 1854 to record philanthropic and religious endeavor at home and abroad. The times were propitious for the success of such a journal: from about 1859 to 1865 the United Kingdom, and particularly Scotland, Wales, and Ireland, experienced a wave of revivalism which gave great impetus to evangelical activity.[36]

Strahan's lifelong interests—in evangelical religion, in democratic political movements, in children's literature—were already apparent in these early lists; so, too, was his concern for tastefully produced volumes. But he placed his greatest faith in the power of general literature to transform the world socially and morally, and he was already planning a magazine with which he intended to advance this cause. As he would later recall, he set out to remedy the "deficiencies" of the periodical literature of the day, deficiencies which he traced back to "a distinct division . . . between what purported to be secular and religious, Sunday and weekday reading; with this practical result, that the one kind was made largely repellent and the other left hugely maimed."[37] The belief that only religious works were fit reading for the Sabbath, and religious works that were, at that, of the precise theological narrowness endorsed by whatever happened to be a given reader's religious denomination, was one held with conviction by many evangelicals. But Strahan, along with many of the men who were to be his associates, urged that all of life might be viewed sacramentally, and thus become fit for consideration on the Sabbath: their goal was "to provide a Periodical *for all the week*," which would not merely "blend 'the religious' with 'the secular,' " but rather "*yoke* them together without compromise."[38] Strahan aimed to restore "religion and literature to one another" by publishing sermons alongside stories and essays, and ministers alongside secular writers. But it was not the inclusion of nonreligious literature that was bound to provoke controversy so much as Strahan's plan to draw his contributors from various schools of religious thought, and to bill the result as a magazine appropriate for Sunday reading, which was "enough," as he later put it, "for the fanning of a hundred prejudices."[39]

In 1858, however, Strahan had a more immediate problem: "I, then a young man of twenty-four and utterly unknown, had necessarily to look around for an editor, less youthful it might be expected, more experienced it was to be hoped, but at any rate much less obscure."[40] He did not intend to set his sights too low. Counting heavily on the Highland background they shared, Strahan made an appointment to discuss his ideas with the newly appointed royal chaplain for Scotland, Norman Macleod.

Strahan could hardly have chosen more astutely. Macleod, who in the spring of 1858 entered his tenth year as editor of the *Edinburgh Christian Magazine*, had been consciously guided in this work by Dr. Arnold's call for a periodical that would utilize as "vehicles of good" not merely the usual "comments on Scripture, or essays on Evidence," but also "History and Biography" and other "articles on common subjects written with a decidedly Christian tone."[41] The *Edinburgh Christian Magazine* thus included papers on social and scientific subjects, not to mention pious fiction written by the editor himself. Unlike the magazine Strahan planned, the *Edinburgh Christian Magazine* was intended for members of the Church of Scotland, and most of its articles were signed by ministers of that denomination. Macleod, who was not by temperament a man to endure with equanimity the hostility and scorn that had come his way as a result of sectarian conflict, may well have felt some apprehension concerning Strahan's plan to solicit contributions for the new magazine from ministers of various denominations. Soon, however, he was persuaded by the enthusiastic young publisher that such a publication could serve, in Macleod's own words, as "a medium of communication between writers and readers of every portion of the Church of Christ."[42]

Still Macleod hesitated to take on the editorship himself. The *Edinburgh Christian Magazine* had never achieved a circulation much above four thousand, and by 1858 its publishers, the firm of Paton and Ritchie, were growing impatient concerning the losses they had been incurring. Macleod also realized that between the claims of his parish and the claims of his new friends, the members of the royal family, he would have little time or energy to spare for such work in the future. But one of Strahan's most pronounced personal characteristics was that, "sanguine and buoyant to a degree," as Blaikie put it, "he never seemed to fear any exhaustion of resources";[43] and Macleod, who was to become an intimate friend of Strahan's despite the twenty-two-year difference in their ages, was eventually won over by the younger man's promise that he himself would undertake most of the day-to-day work of conducting the magazine: "I will become the captain," consented Macleod, "provided you become the sailing-master."[44] As for the question of Macleod's salary, enough confidence already existed between the two Highlanders that it was agreed "there was to be no agreement"; rather, Strahan would pay Macleod whatever he felt the magazine could afford as it progressed.[45] And so, the final issue of the *Edinburgh Christian Magazine*, dated March 1859, included a rueful note of farewell signed by "the Editor."

> He has always been alive to the fact, that it never has attracted any public attention, or occupied any position of the slightest eminence in the literary world, but, month after month, has passed in silence from the press to apparent oblivion. Yet the Editor has been induced to continue it, hitherto, solely by the thought that it was doing good.[46]

A month earlier, Macleod's name had appeared, not as "Editor" but as "Reviser," on the title page of Strahan and Company's new venture, the *Christian Guest: A Family Magazine for Leisure Hours and Sundays*, which made its debut in February 1859.

Publisher and editor might have been expected to realize that if their new magazine were to be any more successful than the *Edinburgh Christian Magazine*, it would be necessary to attempt a new and certainly bolder editorial strategy. But their first efforts were cautious indeed. The self-proclaimed goal of the *Christian Guest* was "to give the Families of our country a weekly sheet richly freighted with the great truths of Salvation and the interests of the Redeemer's Kingdom"; its motto, from Luke 2:10, was "Behold I bring you tidings of great joy"; its staple fare was inspirational essays on such topics as "Missionary Work in China," "The Probabilities of Conversion," and "What Death Brings to the Christian." There were a few pious stories and poems, including, in the first issue, five sonnets by Elizabeth Barrett Browning ("Tears," "Comfort," "A Thought for a Lonely Deathbed," "Substitution," "Work and Contemplation"); but Macleod's earlier magazine had dared as much as this. True enough, although many of the articles were unsigned, Strahan and Macleod did manage to include in their tables of contents the names of ministers who belonged to different schools of thought—Thomas Guthrie of the Free Church, for example, along with John Caird, the "Broad" Churchman. But this innovation seems to have gone unnoticed, perhaps because, in this *annus mirabilis* of periodical publishing, when 115 new publications were started in London alone, including *All the Year Round* (30 April) and *Macmillan's* (November), the *Christian Guest* attracted very little attention whatsoever.[47] The most dramatic claim it could make on its own behalf was that its price would not exceed "the half of that charged for any similar production": a monthly issue of forty-eight pages cost 3d.; weekly numbers, on poorer quality paper, were to be had for a mere 1/2d. But its extreme cheapness seems to have resulted in financial losses rather than in high circulation, and by the time the *Christian Guest* concluded its first and only annual volume, Strahan and Macleod had decided that a fresh start was in order.

In November 1859, G. H. Lewes was writing to John Blackwood, "What days these are for furious speculation in the periodical world!"[48] Events would prove that the best was yet to come. The final issue of the *Christian Guest,* dated December, announced that toward the end of the month there would appear, along with the other periodicals dated January 1860, a new magazine, which would call itself *Good Words.* The *Publishers' Circular* of 1 December duly announced this newest entry in the periodicals sweepstakes, noting that the prospectus promised contributions from "many of the best-known writers of the day." But the *Circular* was clearly more excited by the idea of "Mr. Thackeray's forthcoming Magazine. . . . We believe it will include nearly every writer of eminence in the literary world; in fact, that it will prove a determined effort to make it *the* Magazine of this country."[49] Two weeks later, the advertising pages of the *Circular* included the breathless announcement that Thackeray's magazine would be published "at NINE o'clock A.M. on Friday, the 23rd instant";[50] and Strahan himself, when he came to write his recollections of these heady days, would find it remarkable that the famous *Cornhill Magazine*—which was to be the most inspiring model and, in the early years, the stiffest competitor to Strahan's magazine—had "happened to publish its first number on the day when the first part of *Good Words* appeared."[51]

The first issue of the *Cornhill* lived up to the advance publicity. Its 128 pages included no fewer than five of the type of serious, educational essays that had hitherto been the specialty of the ponderous and costly quarterlies, as well as the first installments of three serials that could scarcely fail to please: *Lovel the Widower* and *Roundabout Papers* by Thackeray, and Trollope's *Framley Parsonage*, which would soon achieve immense popularity. It was an impressive package, for only a shilling; and it sold an amazing 120,000 copies.

The first sixty-four-page monthly issue of *Good Words* was weak fare in comparison. Macleod himself had objected to the magazine's title until Strahan won him over by producing, from George Herbert's *Outlandish Proverbs,* the motto that appeared on the title page: "Good Words are Worth Much and Cost Little"—in this case, 6d. monthly or 1-1/2d. weekly, a figure that would have put *Good Words* just out of the reach of many working-class readers who would have been able to afford the *Christian Guest.*[52] On the inside cover of the first number, Macleod indicated the special function of the magazine by asserting that the " 'good words' " of Christ "have become as 'household words' in our Christian homes." Macleod also promised that in "this new and catholic enterprise" he would be assisted by writers from various denominations. Nonetheless, editor and publisher apparently deemed it the better part of valor to omit the signatures of contributors, at least for the present, and to commence by extending an olive branch to the Free Church: the second article, following a New Year's greeting from Macleod, chronicled certain good deeds performed by Dr. Thomas Chalmers, leader of the Evangelicals at the time of the Disruption. Other articles, which averaged less than two pages in length, discussed such subjects as "Protestantism in France," "Joy among the Angels," "True Stories of God's Providence," and "A Journey by Sinai to Syria." There was as yet no fiction, nor illustrations.

Although scoffers would soon be referring to the *"Goody Two Shoes Magazine,"*[53] the first issue sold a highly respectable thirty thousand copies, prompting the *Bookseller* to congratulate *Good Words* for surpassing at once the circulation of its supposed competitors, Edinburgh-based miscellanies such as the *Christian Treasury* (twenty-nine thousand sold monthly) and the *Family Treasury* (twenty-five thousand). The *Bookseller* also took the opportunity to direct a few well-chosen words to those firms that might have been expected to provide similar reading matter for Anglicans.

> What can the Parkers, and Hatchards, and Rivingtons be about to let their Presbyterian brethren—no, not brethren, church-people don't recognize others—well, their opponents—why do they let their dissenting opponents beat them?[54]

But Strahan—who would soon be denying that *Good Words* was in any way a "dissenting" periodical unsuited for Anglican consumption—was far more ambitious than the *Bookseller* could have guessed. It was no comfort to him that *Good Words* had outsold the *Cornhill* in Scotland, racking up six thousand sales in Macleod's home of Glasgow alone, for example, in contrast to the *Cornhill*'s sales of four thousand in Glasgow and two thousand in Edinburgh.[55] For Strahan was already eyeing that far greater reading public south of the Tweed, a public clearly enamored of serial fiction; and the evidence is that he studied the *Cornhill* carefully for clues as to how he might overcome the division, not merely between "religious" and "secular," but also between "Scottish" and "English."

The first issue of the *Cornhill* included two full-page illustrations. Strahan would maintain in his autobiographical essays that he had all along intended that *Good Words* should be illustrated: "Only in a most meagre and mean, or else in an utterly base, way did popular literature avail itself of the helps which I believed it could rightly obtain from Art for the purpose of adding to its own attractiveness and heightening its proper delights."[56] His opinions were not as uncontroversial as they might appear today. Scottish Evangelicals often distrusted illustration no less than they did fiction: according to a writer in the *Contemporary Review* in 1867, "some of the most successful Scottish painters" of the time had in their youth "daily to do battle against peasant prejudices in such a way that up to this hour the memory of their outset in art-study is painful to them to recall."[57] Knight's *Penny Magazine,* based in London, had featured woodcuts in the 1830s; but Chambers's *Edinburgh Journal* was still unillustrated in the 1860s. While the first issue of *Good Words* was still being sold, however, Strahan began advertising the fact that the second issue would commence a series of "Illustrations of Scripture" by "the well-known J. B." (Mrs. Blackburn).[58] The best-remembered artist to appear in the volume of *Good Words* for 1860 would be W. Q. Orchardson; soon Strahan would enlist the aid of a group of young Scottish artists including John Pettie, Tom Graham, Frederick McWhirter, John McTaggart, and John Dawson Watson. Their work would help to make the early volumes of *Good Words* famous in the annals of art history, and Strahan would be proud until the end of his life that he had advanced and in some cases even initiated their careers.[59]

The February 1860 issue of *Good Words* also featured the first installment of a serialized story. *Lady Somerville's Maidens,* by an unidentified author, seems never to have been republished in volume form. Set in Edinburgh at the time of the Union of the Two Kingdoms, it assumed extensive knowledge of Scottish history and of the geography of old Edinburgh, as well as an understanding of Scottish dialect. The main characters are identified as Presbyterians; but Episcopalians and even Roman Catholics—at least, Roman Catholics who are native Highland peasants—are treated sympathetically, and the narrator is critical of those "more zealous after Presbyterianism than Christianity."[60] The most appealing characters are a family of French Huguenots who succeed better than many of the Presbyterians in tempering their piety with a sense of fun. It was the first of many stories that would reflect the latitudinarian intentions of publisher and editor.

Strahan and Macleod were also beginning to make use of the names of their contributors. Although, as Macleod explained in the February issue, it was "not thought advisable at present, to adhibit to each article the name of its author," lists of those authors began to appear in advertisements and in each issue, in order, as Macleod put it, to suggest the magazine's "catholicity." The early lists consisted for the most part of ministers of the Church of Scotland, occasionally punctuated by the name of a Free Churchman, Scottish Baptist, Scottish Congregationalist, Wesleyan, or, more rarely, evangelical Anglican. Professor Blackie was perhaps the most colorful of the lot; Caird and Tulloch, the two "Broad" Churchmen, were probably the most controversial. Tulloch would become a personal friend of Strahan's; so, too, would other early contributors such as the Reverend Donald Macleod (Norman's younger brother) and the Reverend W. Fleming Stevenson, a minister of the Church of Scotland whose parish was in Dublin.

These names would have had less appeal for English readers than for Scottish ones. But that was about to be remedied. Urged on by Strahan, Macleod had begun to address his requests to such "Broad" Anglicans as A. P. Stanley, who would become dean of Westminster in 1864; and to members of what Strahan termed "the striking group of social reformers and religious Liberals . . . commonly spoken of as 'the Maurice school,' " a group which included the Reverend Charles Kingsley, as well as John Malcolm Ludlow, a barrister who was the leading theoretician of these "Christian Socialists."[61] Ludlow was the first to respond: his series of papers on "Aspects of Indian Life During the Rebellion" commenced in the issue for April 1860.

By June, the Edinburgh-based *Caledonian Mercury* was asserting that "not even the *Cornhill* itself—can shew a better list of contributors than 'Good Words.' "[62] The evangelical newspaper's praise was excessive, at least at this early date. But by December, the London *Bookseller* was remarking that *Good Words* was "undoubtedly the best and cheapest of the religious monthlies, and has attained a great success. We hear the impression of the new number will be forty thousand."[63]

Not everyone was so well pleased. The issue of *Good Words* for December 1860 included a "Note from the Editor" which indicates that Macleod, who many times in the future would quake before criticism, was already becoming alarmed over the response from some extremely narrow believers. He defended the policy of "blending" the religious with the secular in order "to provide a periodical for *all the week*," and pointed his arguments with an anecdote concerning an old Scotswoman who demanded of her son, when she found him reading a "religious" book on a weekday, "O Sandy, Sandy! are ye no' frichtened to read sic a guid buik as that, and this no' the Sabbathday?"[64] It must have pleased Macleod to be able to advertise on the same page that the volume of *Good Words* for 1861 would include a series by Thomas Guthrie, the Free Church leader who had been hostile to Macleod at the time of the Disruption, but who had known Strahan as a protégé of his congregant Hugh Miller, and as the employee of his publishers, Johnstone and Hunter. There was greater news even than this, however, for lovers of fiction: the year-long serial was to be "A NEW STORY, by the Author of 'John Halifax, Gentleman.'" The author in question, Dinah Maria Mulock, had long-standing ties to the Free Church through her father, a minister-turned-journalist named Thomas Mulock: in the 1840s, as editor of the *Inverness Courier,* he had condemned the Highland Clearances; in the 1850s he wrote on urban social problems for the *Witness.* His daughter's rags-to-riches story, *John Halifax* (1857), was a recent best-seller when Strahan began to advertise widely the information that she would be the major forthcoming attraction in *Good Words.*[65]

Strahan was also combing the roster of the *Cornhill* for potential contributors. One of these was John Hollingshead, who in 1868 would become manager of the Gaiety Theatre in London. In the early 1860s, Hollingshead was describing scenes of London working-class life in the *Cornhill* and in Dickens's periodical, *All the Year Round.* Strahan's letters to Hollingshead demonstrate that he did not anticipate any insurmountable difficulty in securing from such a secular writer fit fare for the more pious reading public of *Good Words;* they also demonstrate that although Macleod occasionally exercised his right of veto over manuscripts submitted to the magazine, it was Strahan who performed the bulk of the actual editorial work. Strahan wrote to Hollingshead to suggest topics that reflected his own interest in social amelioration: "the over-crowding of the London lower-class houses, about which so much is being said and written just now," for example; or "Dives . . . a good subject, [that] would afford you fine scope for hitting at luxury of all sorts, and at the universal race in this age for roast beef and plum pudding."[66] Strahan also suggested titles, such as "What there is in London to vex and to cheer a man's righteous soul," or "Ten Shillings a Week," for an "unvarnished" tale "of the lowest life . . . treated as if it was a chimney sweep who was holding the pen. It will be healthy of course, but let it be as directly Christian as circumstances will admit of." He was careful to explain to Hollingshead that there existed a "line of distinction" between *Good Words* and *All the Year Round:* "With us, everything must have a purpose. To interest and amuse are not enough in themselves. . . . Not that I would wish or expect you to turn parson, but there is a great need of a *week-day preacher,* who will be worthy of the name." A number of Hollingshead's contributions were deemed unsuitable by Macleod ("I am sorry to say," wrote Strahan concerning one such effort, "that 'Bread and Gin' don't go down here with that relish which you and I would wish"); but in time Hollingshead would manage to strike the required blend of secular and religious, prompting the *Bookseller* to remark that in the pages of *Good Words,* "John Hollingshead . . . appears in an entirely new character."[67]

Writers sufficiently well known to attract this kind of comment naturally commanded higher rates of payment than did Macleod's clerical friends. In his first letter to Ludlow (27 February 1860), Macleod wrote that "our ordinary pay is £1 a page . . . even to you I cannot offer more than £5 for each article, say of three or four printed pages."[68] Ludlow's rebuff came so promptly that two days later, Macleod wrote to revise his earlier offer: "*Your* terms are most reasonable. . . . My terms I acknowledge are very miserable." Although Macleod pleaded poverty ("the magazine at 30,000 *just pays*"), he agreed that Ludlow should have £2 a page.[69] Hollingshead drove an even harder bargain in the winter and spring of 1860–61, complaining that the £2 a page which Strahan offered was less than he was paid by the *Cornhill.* At one point in their negotiations, Strahan countered with the remark that "this is the rate at which we pay Miss Mulock," but Hollingshead remained dissatisfied until he and Strahan arrived at a curious compromise: Strahan promised that those pages of *Good Words* devoted to Hollingshead's contributions would be printed with more white space between each line, thus reducing the number of words on each page and increasing the rate of payment.[70]

Other letters provide evidence of the lax business habits that were to result in financial disasters for Strahan in later years. In June 1860, for example, Macleod wrote to Ludlow that he had hitherto "never enquired into my publishers' accounts with writers, as I never doubted that they would pay according to the 'rules of the trade.' But your note will make me more thoughtful on this point than I have been."[71] Macleod's letter was soon followed by a more curt one from Strahan, who enclosed payment for Ludlow's series of articles, remarking, "we find it more convenient to settle with our Contributors once a quarter, but we shall be glad to make any exception in your case that you may desire."[72] In March 1861, when Strahan wrote to Hollingshead enclosing a long overdue payment, he apologized for the delay by explaining that he had been away from the office for some time, and then asked, "is the amount of the cheque correct? I have got into a maze about the terms. You will see that we are very *un*fashionable publishers here."[73] But although Strahan might often find himself short of cash when it came time to make payment, his problems arose from a trait opposite to that of niggardliness. W. G. Blaikie, who had known Strahan at Johnstone and Hunter, and who became a contributor to *Good Words* in 1861, regarded Strahan's "generosity to authors" as "quite phenomenal";[74] Hollingshead would many years later recall Strahan as

> a liberal paymaster, a pleasant companion, and a sympathetic business editor. He had only one fault, which was common to both of us—we possessed the diseased activity of the parched pea in the frying-pan. We were bound to keep moving even if we moved in the wrong direction.... Dr. Macleod, with his generous views, practical but not obtrusive piety, and sound common-sense, was our salvation as a brake and our trust as a ballast. In this he was aided by Mr. Strahan's genial partner, Mr. Isbister.[75]

Meanwhile, the circulation of *Good Words* increased in leaps and bounds throughout 1861. The rapid ascent began with the first issue to contain signed contributions, that of January 1861, which featured, in addition to the work of Dr. Guthrie and Miss Mulock, articles signed by John Tulloch of the Church of Scotland; by Richard Whately, the Anglican archbishop of Dublin; by Archibald Geikie, who was professor of geology at Edinburgh; and by Dr. John Brown, author of *Rab and His Friends* (1859). The February issue offered Guthrie, Tulloch, and Whately once again, plus a series of devotional readings by A. P. Stanley, an article by Ludlow, and the first of Hollingshead's contributions. It was most remarkable, however, for including the first installment of Macleod's story of "Wee Davie," a child whose innocent example brings family and friends to true religion before his brief career as a "home missionary" is concluded by a classic Victorian deathbed scene. It was a tale so sentimental that when Macleod himself tried to read it aloud, he was more than once so choked by tears that he had to lay it aside;[76] and, in the opinion of one writer in the periodical press, it "by itself almost made the name of 'Good Words.' "[77] By March the magazine's circulation had increased to fifty thousand, and Strahan was bringing out new editions of the issues for January and February in order to meet the demand for them.[78]

It must have seemed that *Good Words* was well on its way to overtaking the *Cornhill*, which had settled down, by this time, to a circulation of between eighty and eighty-five thousand monthly.[79] But Macleod and Strahan were faced with a problem: Dinah Maria Mulock, whose serialized novel had been advertised as the main attraction of the 1861 volume, now sent word that illness prevented her from fulfilling her commitment. For a time Strahan toyed with the idea of substituting a serialized story or even a series of articles by Hollingshead. But too many of Hollingshead's contributions were proving unusable because, as Strahan put it, he failed to "keep the better nature in view."[80] Perhaps it was the popularity of "Wee Davie" which decided the matter. At any rate, the April issue included the first installment of *The Old Lieutenant and His Son,* Macleod's rambling story of Ned, a sailor boy who converts his rough companions to Christianity and then returns home to Scotland to undertake a tediously uneventful courtship which would be protracted through the issue for December.

In the spring of 1861, Strahan republished "Wee Davie" in volume form and sold twelve thousand copies within the first week.[81] But Macleod's delight turned to dismay when "'Wee Davie'—my dear wee mannie!" came under attack by Macleod's usual enemies, the extreme Evangelicals, who objected that in telling the story, Macleod had failed to refer to such specifically Calvinist dogmas as original sin, predestination, and eternal punishment for the unregenerate. Both the tract society of Edinburgh and the Pure Literature Society of London—a group headed by the famous philanthropist, the seventh earl of Shaftesbury—refused to recommend either "Wee Davie" or *Good Words.*[82] In August, Macleod was still brooding over the insult to "Wee Davie, poor little fellow!"; he wrote to Ludlow to complain that "my sermon (not story)" was "not sufficiently evangelical for them!"[83]

At much the same time, *The Old Lieutenant and His Son* was being pilloried, not by the tract societies, but by reviewers in the secular press, who dismissed Macleod's story as pious and unrealistic bosh. Macleod was relatively undisturbed by these criticisms. He explained to W. F. Stevenson that the novel had been written in order "to preach gospel to those who may hear for the sake of the story. . . . As a literary production Ned is a two-penny affair, but I am encouraged to write it as a medium of preaching Christ."[84] To Ludlow he boasted, "So long as I have *Good Words* there shall be 'preaching' in it, direct or indirect, and no shame, or sham, about it."[85] Events would prove that Strahan, intent as he was on increasing sales to those readers who were more impressed by the critics of the *Spectator* or the *London Review* than by the sour anathemas of the tract societies, was less complacent concerning the critical response to Macleod's "preaching." But Macleod's novel, although not the blockbuster which Strahan had hoped for when he made his arrangements with Mulock, does not seem to have depressed circulation: by September 1861, the *Bookseller* was proclaiming that "of religious magazines the only one that is progressing is *Good Words,* which appears to devour all others."[86] The success of the magazine seems to have encouraged Strahan to give free rein to his generous impulses: in December, Dr. John Brown, who had contributed a series of papers of medical advice entitled "Lay Sermons to Working People," was writing gleefully to his brother that he had been paid £105 "for my thinnest of Lay Sermons"—an effort that filled fewer than five pages in the December issue.[87] Certainly Strahan was in excellent spirits on 24 December, when he wrote to John Hollingshead to enclose a payment which he termed "a slight Christmas remembrance of the Northern barbarians."[88]

The volume for 1862 would already have been in the planning by this time. There would be contributions from the poet and essayist Alexander Smith, with whom Strahan had recently struck up a friendship,[89] and from "A.K.H.B." (Andrew Kennedy Hutchison Boyd), a minister of the Church of Scotland who had made his literary reputation by contributing to *Fraser's Magazine* the series of articles later republished as *The Recreations of a Country Parson* (1859). The Scottish scientist James David Forbes would contribute two articles on glaciers; Sir David Brewster would dissect "The Facts and Fancies of Mr. Darwin." Mulock's long-delayed novel, *Mistress and Maid,* would appear from January to December; a second serialized story, by "Sarah Tytler" (Henrietta Keddie), whose fiction had appeared in the *Cornhill* during 1861, would commence in the March issue. Holman Hunt and Arthur Boyd Houghton would supply illustrations; Mulock's novel would be illustrated by John Everett Millais, who had illustrated Trollope's *Framley Parsonage* in the *Cornhill.*

There was soon no room for doubt concerning the appeal of such names. Beginning with the issue for January 1862, *Good Words* achieved a monthly circulation of seventy thousand, putting it within striking distance of the *Cornhill.*[90] The next step in Strahan's campaign to make *Good Words* the most popular magazine of the day must have seemed obvious: early in April, Macleod wrote to Trollope to describe *Good Words* and to introduce "Mr. Strahan, as sensible a fellow as I know—truthful, honorable, generous—and with enterprise fit to cement again the American Union." Macleod promised that Strahan would pay handsomely for a novel to be serialized in *Good Words*. "I think," hinted Macleod in language which recalls Strahan's correspondence with Hollingshead, "you could let out the *best* side of your soul in *Good Words*—better far than even in *Cornhill*— Strahan is in London & is to call for you."[91] Strahan and Trollope had their meeting on 7 April, emerging with the understanding that Trollope would contribute a novel to be serialized between July and December 1863.[92]

Strahan was not in London merely to meet with Trollope. The "Northern barbarians" were about to move their business from the Scottish capital to the English one, and during much of the winter and spring of 1862 Strahan was arranging that move. By the end of June, the "*un*fashionable" publishers were established on Ludgate Hill in offices remarkable, according to the *Bookseller*, for their "elegance and completeness." It was from these headquarters that, as the *Bookseller* put it, Strahan and Company would henceforth "distribute their GOOD WORDS to all parts of the Kingdom."[93]

CHAPTER IV

Anchor of Hope: A Scottish Publisher in London, 1862–66

This great, cruel, splendid, gloomy capital drew him to it. . . . Year
after year he wandered in it as a traveller might explore a strange land.

—Alexander Strahan (1880)[1]

Ludgate Hill in the early 1860s was, according to one eyewitness, "a
steep, narrow, inconvenient causeway, with a double row of ugly
houses, tumbled or rather jammed together." By day, the street was
obstructed "with every conceivable form of horse drawn vehicle . . .
imperilling each other at every turn . . . all sorely in danger of being
pounded into one shapeless mass." Overhead on the newly con-
structed railway viaduct, foolhardy and impatient pedestrians unable
to cross at street level went "bobbing, at the risk of life or limb,
between the triple row of lumbering locomotives." Even by night the
area was congested, with laborers, or drunkards, or "others staggering under the load of age or poverty—half-naked children with no
home, miserable girls prematurely old, worn by vice and want." In
dry weather pedestrians were blinded by swirling dust; in wet or dirty
weather—that is, nine months out of the year—the mud and slush
were ankle-deep.[2] The printing and publishing firm of Cassell, Pet-
ter, and Galpin occupied Belle Sauvage Yard, just off Ludgate Hill;
Paternoster Row was a moment's walk away, up the hill and around
the north side of Saint Paul's Cathedral, which towered over all.

The newest residents of Ludgate Hill were given a warm welcome
in the August 1862 issue of the *Bookseller*, their nearby neighbor at
Warwick Lane: "Messrs. Strahan & Co. have opened their London
House with great spirit," proclaimed the trade journal. "Messrs.
Strahan, who are amongst the youngest of our publishers" were
praised for being better aware than most of their competitors "that a
new generation of readers has sprung up during the past ten years—

readers whose standpoint is very far in advance of men who look back upon fifty summers." These readers, who were, according to the *Bookseller,* regularly to be encountered in the commuter carriages departing from the London Bridge railway station, required worthwhile reading at low cost, and Strahan and Company was precisely the firm to supply it. The *Bookseller* was particularly impressed that the newly arrived company announced "twelve new books, and have taken the field with one, of which the *first edition* consists of ten thousand, seven thousand copies of which are already sold."[3] This was the "popular edition" of A. K. H. Boyd's *Recreations of a Country Parson,* which, as one of the volumes in "Strahan's Family Library of Books at Once Cheap, Valuable, and Instructive," sold for a mere 3s.6d. Boyd's work was a far cry from that of the newly popular "sensation novelists" such as Wilkie Collins, Mrs. Henry Wood, and Mary Elizabeth Braddon, who specialized in suspenseful tales of illegitimacy, bigamy, insanity, and murder. But Strahan managed to sell tens of thousands of copies of such works as *The Pathway to Promise; or, Words of Comfort to the Christian Pilgrim* and *The Higher Christian Life* by the Reverend W. E. Boardman; he also profited from the volume editions of works that had first appeared in *Good Words,* such as John Brown's *Health: Five Lay Sermons to Working People,* John Tulloch's *Beginning Life: Chapters for Young Men on Religion, Study and Business,* and "Sarah Tytler's" *Papers for Thoughtful Girls,* not to mention Macleod's own *Wee Davie.*[4]

All this was cause for rejoicing, and Strahan was surrounded by friends and relatives who felt a share in his success. He had been followed from Edinburgh by some of the artists who illustrated *Good Words;* three of these—John Pettie, W. Q. Orchardson, and Tom Graham—took lodgings together, and Pettie found it possible to live upon the £10 paid by Strahan for each of his drawings that appeared in the magazine.[5] A number of the writers who contributed to *Good Words* would also take up residence in London, or at least become regular visitors: "Sarah Tytler," for example, who was in real life Miss Henrietta Keddie, always stayed at the home of Strahan and his unmarried sister when she had business in the South. Keddie would one day recall that "we were all fellow-Scots, fellow-Church people, publishers and contributors, immensely proud of McLeod [sic] as our leader."[6] Strahan steadily swelled their ranks by bringing kinsmen or former neighbors all the way from Tain to London to serve as employees in the Ludgate Hill firm;[7] and he made strong new friendships among compatriots who had preceded him to the English capital. Dr. Johnson had remarked eighty years earlier that no Scotsman could publish a book in London or have a play brought upon the London stage but that there were five hundred other Scotsmen ready to applaud him.[8] Strahan, however, would become aware that such partisan advocacy might not always achieve its end: thirty-one years after his arrival in London he would remark, in a memoir of John Pettie, that

> the English are jealous of Scotch recommendations of Scotsmen; and it is well known that Sir David Wilkie was actually the means of keeping his friend William Duncan out of the Academy for many years, simply by his persistence in urging the claims of "Wullie Duncan," as he always called him, to the amusement of the southerners.[9]

Macleod, who of course continued to reside in his Glasgow parish, was no less sensitive than Strahan to the difficulties facing Scotsmen in England: although a firm believer in the principle of church establishment and a close friend of many Anglican divines, he was barred by law from Anglican pulpits; yet in 1863 he was rebuked by an English member of Parliament for preaching in Nonconformist chapels in the south, on the grounds that such visits demonstrated a lack of respect for the national church.[10] Strahan would one day write that *Good Words* met with "much bigotry" upon its arrival in London, and that "not a little of the prejudice . . . was owing to its being supposed to have about it a Nonconformist odour." Strahan was indignant that the periodical that he had intended to be "liberal" and "unpartizan" was, "because it was not church . . . set down as in some way chapel." His solution was to persuade "a conspicuous Churchman . . . to make himself prominent among the contributors," and to this end he arranged that Henry Alford, the dean of Canterbury, should become a regular writer beginning with the issue for January 1863.[11]

Meanwhile, the London press directed a new round of criticism against Macleod's fiction. Strahan had republished *The Old Lieutenant and His Son* in volume form, and on 18 October 1862, the *Spectator* opened fire, complaining, in a lengthy review, that Macleod's novel was "very like what a children's religious story would be if it were spun out into two volumes. It reads like elaborated tracts. . . . No one who knows what life is could possibly be impressed with moral stories like this."[12] The *London Review* of the same date entitled its critique, "A Scotch Minister's Novel," and asserted that "the story-telling is put in, as the treacle or jam into a medicine-spoon for docile but irresolute infants, to make the sermonising go more sweetly down." Yet "the unreality, the conventionality, the stale pea-slop of this novel" was deemed more tedious than any sermon: "It is a very feeble and frigid production, which no sensible reader, whether or not he sympathize with its religious tendency, can peruse without much carnal impatience." *Good Words* in its entirety was likened to a "wholesome and palatable milk diet."[13]

"I am pretty well convinced," wrote Macleod to the Reverend W. F. Stevenson on the day he read these reviews, "that I am not able to be of use in that line . . . although self-love makes me think that [*The Old Lieutenant*] cannot be so bad as they make it."[14] Macleod's fictional *Reminiscences of a Highland Parish* were to be serialized in the 1863 volume of *Good Words*. Nonetheless, Strahan seems to have decided at this juncture that the magazine might benefit from a bit of remodeling, or at least a new public image: Macleod wrote to J. M. Ludlow that the reviews had "done for my poor *Good Words*" and that "the old *Good Words* is dead and buried."[15] Strahan wrote to Trollope in November to offer £100 for a Christmas tale of ten pages or so;[16] within weeks, the two also arrived at a new understanding concerning the novel Trollope had already consented to submit for serialization from July through December 1863. Now, it was agreed that the novel should be double the length originally intended, and that Strahan should pay £1,000 solely for the right to publish it in *Good Words*.[17] Trollope's tale, "The Widow's Mite," duly appeared in the issue for January 1863; and Strahan stepped up his already massive advertising campaign to inform the reading public that serialization would soon commence of a new novel by "the author of *Framley Parsonage*," to be illustrated, as that novel had been in the *Cornhill*, by John Everett Millais. By 17 January, Strahan was advertising the "Second Edition, making 110th Thousand" of the current issue, which included, in addition to "The Widow's Mite," articles by such prominent Anglicans as Charles Kingsley and Henry Alford.[18] On 28 January, he outdid himself by taking a full-page advertisement in the *Times* to trumpet the glories of the February issue; marvelled the *Publishers' Circular*,

The advertisement of *Good Words* in the *Times* . . . constitutes a new feature in the advertising of our popular periodicals—copious specimens being given of each paper, extending in some cases to almost an entire article; the advertisement, which occupies an entire page in small type, costing about one hundred and thirty pounds.[19]

Strahan was also hard at work transforming his very first periodical, the monthly *News of the Churches and Journal of Missions*. Early in 1863 it was renamed *Christian Work Throughout the World,* and supplied with an epigraph by Tennyson:

> Fly happy, happy sails and bear the press,
> Fly happy with the mission of the Cross,
> Knit land to land, and blowing heavenward,
> Enrich the markets of the golden year.

Strahan made heavy use in his advertisements of a letter written from South Africa by the famous missionary Dr. David Livingstone, who had strong words of praise for the journal: "I feel inclined to write some papers for it, telling how much missionaries are needed." The same advertisements explained that henceforth *Christian Work* would, in addition to providing news of foreign missions, devote much space to a "catholic narrative of Home Missions—understanding the term to include not only peculiarly Christian and ecclesiastical movements, but also the social aspects of the large towns and rural districts, the condition of the labourer and the artisan," and other kindred topics.[20] Strahan's imprint was already associated with the literature of "Home Missions." W. F. Stevenson, in his first series of contributions to *Good Words,* had described the activities of the Innere Mission, an organization founded in Germany in 1848 by J. H. Wichern, who sought to join evangelical preaching with active social work and thus give practical expression to the Reformation principle of the priesthood of all believers; in order to include as many evangelical Protestants as possible, the Innere Mission avoided any commitment to narrow theological formulations.[21] In 1862 Strahan republished Stevenson's articles under the title *Praying and Working: Being Some Account of What Men Can Do When in Earnest;* the book would remain on his lists for eighteen years.

As the publisher of *Christian Work* and *Praying and Working,* Strahan came to know a number of evangelicals from various denominations who took an interest in social amelioration. One of these was Alexander Ewing (1814–73), a Scottish Episcopalian who became bishop of Argyll and the Isles in 1847. Ewing, a Highlander, was one of the few ministers of the Scottish Episcopalian Church born a Presbyterian rather than a member of the wealthy, Anglicized gentry; he left the established church prior to the Disruption because of his strong aversion to Calvinist theology. Ewing was so impressed when he read *Praying and Working* in 1862 that he wrote Strahan to suggest ways of increasing the book's circulation. Strahan would later write that when he received Ewing's letter, "I scarcely felt towards him as though he was really a stranger," for Ewing's first pastoral charge had been in Forres, Moray, "the district," as Strahan put it, to which the Strachans had "belonged" before moving to Tain; and for many years Strahan had followed the career of one who, as an Episcopalian known to be a friend of F. D. Maurice, attracted "a kind of phenomenal interest in those days and that latitude."[22] The result of their correspondence was that in 1863, when Ewing visited A. C. Tait, the bishop of London, who was himself a former Scottish Presbyterian, Strahan was invited to call at Fulham Palace, where Tait personally took him on a tour of the premises, and Strahan explained to the two bishops the editorial principles governing *Good Words:* "No clearly representative views, which had enough sanction of authority to give them actual weight when publicly uttered, were inadmissible to that magazine. . . . The truth must declare itself in the ultimate issue of the conflict."[23] In time both Tait and Ewing would become contributors to periodicals published by Strahan; other works by Ewing would appear on his general publishing list.

Another Scot who became Strahan's friend and, in the 1870s, a business associate, was John Brown Paton (1830–1911). Paton was born in Ayrshire into a family that took great pride in its descent from one of the most famous of the seventeenth-century Covenanters. But there were factors in Paton's youth that predisposed him to a milder form of what has been termed "the deep-rooted Calvinism of his Scottish ancestry."[24] The Patons lived near Loudon, where Norman Macleod arrived in 1838 to undertake his first pastoral charge; John Brown's father became a friend of Macleod's, while the boy attended school with Donald Macleod, who lived with his much-elder brother. So precocious was John Brown Paton that even in his childhood he was influenced by the "broad" views of John Macleod Campbell, the cousin of the Macleod brothers. At the age of ten, Paton was employed for a year as a reporter and subeditor in the office of the *Kilmarnock Herald,* then edited by Alexander Russel, who would later achieve fame as the editor of the *Scotsman.*

In time the Paton family moved to Glasgow, where they joined a Congregational chapel; John Brown Paton entered Spring Hill College, Birmingham, to study for the Congregationalist ministry. The teacher there who influenced him most was Henry Rogers, future author of *The Eclipse of Faith* (1856); one of his fellow students was R. W. Dale, who would become the most prominent Nonconformist in Birmingham, and a leader of English Congregationalists. In 1853, the same year in which Paton commenced his ministry in Sheffield, he introduced Alexander Smith to Sydney Dobell, thus inaugurating a famous literary friendship. From 1858 to 1861, Paton coedited the *Eclectic Review* along with Dale; one of the proprietors of the *Review* was Samuel Morley, a wealthy Congregationalist manufacturer from Nottingham. In the early 1860s Paton wrote leading articles for another Congregationalist periodical, the *Patriot.* In 1863 he became first chairman of the Nottingham Congregational Institute, which had been founded for the training of ministers, missionaries, lay preachers, and colporteurs, with money provided by Samuel Morley.

It was inevitable that Strahan and Paton should meet. The Macleods were common acquaintances, as was Alexander Smith; Henry Rogers became a contributor to *Good Words* in February 1863. Paton was also a friend of W. F. Stevenson's and, like Stevenson, an admirer of the work of J. H. Wichern; so keen was Paton's interest, in fact, that he traveled to Germany to study the Innere Mission and returned home determined to establish one day, with Stevenson's help, a British counterpart to it. Strahan would write in March 1877 that he and Paton had been close friends and companions for fourteen years— which may mean that Paton arrived on the scene just as, in the spring of 1863, Strahan's efforts to increase the circulation of *Good Words* brought the magazine to the attention of the *Record,* the newspaper of Calvinist Evangelicals within the Church of England.[25]

The *Record,* founded in 1828, had been for many years notorious for its bitter and abusive attacks on any person or institution deemed less sound theologically than itself. It was an enemy to Dr. Arnold in the 1830s; it waged against F. D. Maurice a lengthy campaign that resulted in 1853 in Maurice's dismissal from his chair at King's College, London. By 1860 the *Record*'s influence was on the wane, and it failed in its attempt to prevent Maurice's appointment to St. Peter's, Vere Street; but this setback did nothing to moderate the newspaper's Calvinist zeal.

The *Record* had strong ties to the seventh earl of Shaftesbury, who worked with Thomas Guthrie in establishing "Ragged Schools" for the poor and who headed the Pure Literature Society of London, among other activities. Nominally the *Record* was edited by Edward Garbett, the earl's personal chaplain. But just as *Good Words* owed much to Strahan's efforts, the *Record* was actually in large part conducted by its chief proprietor, the man who was perhaps Shaftesbury's closest friend in later life, Alexander Haldane. Haldane was an Anglican, but he wasn't English. He was, in fact, a Scot, the son and nephew of a pair of famous evangelists who left the Church of Scotland even prior to the Disruption to mount an aggressive missionary campaign among the Scottish people. One historian of the Evangelical party within the Church of England has described him as "a true son of that uncompromising land beyond the Tweed, where toleration is deemed to be the eighth of the deadly sins. . . . His dour tone and unceasing controversy were deeply distasteful to many."[26]

Considering Haldane's friendship with Shaftesbury, it is not surprising that when the *Record* opened fire on *Good Words*, in a series of six articles published between 1 April and 13 April 1863, its criticisms echoed those leveled against "Wee Davie" by the Pure Literature Society. The *Record* was not amused by Strahan's attempts to plaster every blank wall in London with handbills advertising *Good Words:* "The Magazine owes much, very much, to industrious puffing and the parading of the great and good names of some of its contributors constantly before the eye of the public."[27] And yet, although the ubiquitous advertisements lured unwary readers with the promise of articles by such revered Evangelicals as, for example, Thomas Guthrie, the *Record* claimed to perceive "a marked deterioration visible in the latest as compared with the earliest volume. The purely religious articles of a high tone get fewer, and the purely secular get to be more numerous."[28] But much as the *Record* objected to "the trashy tales, and the weak, watery, and sentimental 'poetry,' " it found even greater cause for alarm in the conjunction of ministers from various schools of thought: "We think that this has a direct tendency to the utter confounding of truth with error; and we are convinced that in all such compromises . . . all the gain is on the side of error."[29] The *Record* was outraged that "our own beloved Church," the Church of England, should be represented in *Good Words* by the likes of A. P. Stanley and Charles Kingsley. It chose, however, to devote the bulk of its space to discrediting the theology of such Church of Scotland divines as John Caird, Robert Lee, and John Tulloch, not to mention Macleod himself; for although, according to the Anglican paper, Stanley and Kingsley at least possessed "the English characteristic of manly outspokenness,"

> their Scotch coadjutors, in this conspiracy to undermine the ancient faith, are more "canny," careful, and cautious. . . . It is easy work criticising Stanley or Kingsley; it takes long and careful study to find out the whereabouts of a M'Leod, a Tulloch, a Lee, or a Caird.[30]

Thus Macleod was made the subject of two of the six articles, one of which charged that his fiction taught, not the truths of redemption, but "love, love, love . . . the sort of love that Mr. Maurice teaches,—a maudlin, mawkish love, akin to weakness." Blustered the *Record*, "there is not the least indication of a fall, of a sinful nature, of a need of a Saviour. . . . This is muscular Christianity with a vengeance!"[31] In the midst of all this hatred, the *Record* could spare no more than a few words for "this year's chief sensation-writer for *Good Words*. To think of the conjunction of names—Anthony Trollope and Dr. Guthrie!"[32]

According to the *Weekly Review,* the *Record* attacks on *Good Words* "made a great noise, agitating the religious world from Cornwall to Sutherland."[33] Strahan seems to have been more pleased than not by all the fuss: soon after it began, he wrote to Macleod that more copies of the magazine were being sold than ever before. But Macleod—who confided to his journal that he had been "threatened . . . that unless I gave up Stanley and Kingsley I should be 'crushed!' "—could not be as indifferent to the fact that Strahan's management of the "new" *Good Words* had brought on these latest manifestations of hostility toward himself;[34] and from Glasgow he wrote to Strahan, "Let us be very careful, not to admit through oversight one sentence which ought to pain a Christian, however weak he may be."[35]

Good Words and its editor were not, however, to be without a champion. In a series of three articles appearing on 23 April, 30 April, and 7 May, a rebuttal to the *Record* attacks was mounted by the *Patriot*, a periodical that, as an organ of dissenting evangelicals, had little patience with the Anglican arrogance of the *Record.* These articles were unsigned, and Macleod wrote in his journal that he had no idea who the author might be. But it is a matter of record that John Brown Paton was at this time a regular contributor of leading articles to the *Patriot;* that his friendship with Strahan commenced at about this time; and that the author of the articles in the *Patriot,* if he was not Paton, was one with equal insight into Scottish ecclesiastical politics.

The *Patriot* was not uncritical of *Good Words:* "The extraordinary success of the magazine," warned the anonymous writer, was "in danger of becoming a snare to its conductors, by leading them to adopt questionable expedients to keep up and extend its circulation." The *Patriot* was particularly concerned that by featuring the writings of "Mr. Trollope and others of his class," *Good Words* was "thus entering into competition with the 'sensation' magazine."[36] But these were venial sins compared with those of the *Record,* which was said to have attempted, by taking passages out of context and otherwise misrepresenting the theological bias of many articles that had appeared in *Good Words,* to malign the personal reputations of many clerical contributors. And then the Nonconformist paper raised an intriguing question: Who had actually written the articles in the *Record?* True enough, the *Record* was a vociferously Anglican paper, and the author had referred to himself, in more than one passage, as a devoted adherent to the established church. But the *Patriot* perceived in the articles "a personal bias so strong that it is impossible to overlook"; pondered the fact that the rage of the writer seemed greatest when he contemplated "the prominence given to divines of the old Scotch Kirk" who wrote for *Good Words;* noted that some of the expressions used were ones which would come more naturally to a Scotsman than to an Englishman; and concluded, "Dr. M'Leod has to thank a fellow-Scotchman for these bitter effusions."[37]

The suspicions of the *Patriot* were soon confirmed by Macleod himself, who circulated a public letter stating that the writer in the *Record* was, "we are ashamed to say," a Presbyterian minister.[38] He was, in fact, the Reverend Thomas Alexander (1812–72) of the Ranelagh Presbyterian Church, Chelsea, whose theology was, in the words of the *Weekly Review,* "of the old Puritan type," and who had adhered to the cause of the Free Church Evangelicals at the time of the Disruption.[39] In vain did the *Record* return to the attack to explain that it took a Scot to catch a Scot, and that "when we were about to review a Scotch periodical, chiefly prepared for the London market by Scotch Presbyterians, we deemed it lawful and right to call in the aid of a well-known Scotch minister, of sound Evangelical principles";[40] for, as the *Patriot* put it, gleeful to catch the *Record* in its own Anglican trap,

> the opinions of this Presbyterian minister as to *Good Words* and its editor are not of the slightest importance except to himself and the small circle who believe in him; it is only because they have been adopted and published by a journal which professes to represent the Evangelical party in the Establishment that they are entitled to the slightest notice.[41]

But Macleod, despite the bravado of his publicly circulated identification of Alexander, was as disturbed as ever by the enmity of his fellow Presbyterians; and in May, he was made to understand that Alexander was by no means alone in his opinions: at its annual meetings, the Free Church of Scotland passed a resolution condemning *Good Words* as one of a category of periodicals that undermined the Sabbath by encouraging readers "to occupy themselves with amusing tales or papers on mere worldly matters on the Lord's Day."[42] It was perhaps at this juncture that Macleod addressed to Strahan an undated letter, preserved in his brother's *Memoir*, which read, in part,

> I beseech you to let me see every MS. or proof before being printed off. I, as a minister, am more conversant than you can be with religious topics and the pulse of the religious world. Besides, as you also know, my chief delight in *Good Words* is its power of doing good. God knows this is more precious to me than all the gold and silver on earth could be.[43]

Soon Macleod was poring over the proofs of the long-heralded novel that he himself had solicited so eagerly one year to the month before the *Record* attacks: *Rachel Ray*, by "this year's chief sensation-writer for *Good Words*," Anthony Trollope.

Trollope had begun writing the novel on 3 March 1863; he would finish it in late June.[44] Serialization was to commence in the issue of *Good Words* for July 1863, and a number of early chapters, which apparently met with Strahan's approval in London, had already been set in type when Macleod intervened to rule that the novel was unfit reading for the public of *Good Words*. Trollope got the news in time to write on 4 June to J. E. Millais, the illustrator, that *Good Words* "has thrown me over. They write me word that I am too wicked. . . . They have tried to serve God and the devil together, and finding that goodness pays best, have thrown over me and the devil."[45] Trollope must have made similar remarks in his reply to Macleod, for on 11 June, Macleod wrote to deny that "merely because of your Name I have sacrificed you to the vile *Record*. . . . What you mean by my attempt to serve God & Mammon, I do not understand."[46]

In his *Autobiography*, Trollope would describe Macleod's letter as one "full of wailing and repentance," and would assert that Macleod's main objection was to the dancing which takes place in an early chapter of the novel.[47] But although his letter does refer to "a glory [cast] over balls till 4 in the morning," Macleod had a more grievous complaint than this. He protested that Trollope had failed to depict any aspects of the "truly Christian" life other than "the *canting* and humbug ones."

> The weaknesses—shams—hypocrisies—gloom of some species of professing Christians are all described & magnified, but what of the genuine human born Christian element? . . . I thought you would either bring out more fully the positive good side of the Christian life than you had hitherto done, or avoid at least saying anything to pinch, fret, annoy, or pain those Evangelicals who are *not* Recordites.

Macleod would, in fact, have sympathized heartily with Trollope's evident distaste for two of his creations: Mrs. Prime and Mr. Prong, those extremely unpleasant Calvinists who refer frequently to "the Elect" and "the Evil One," to "walking in darkness," "seeing the light," and "saving brands from the fire." Unfortunately, he would not have been as complacent as Trollope when it came to the foibles of the other clerical characters in *Rachel Ray*. There is, for example, the genial Mr. Comfort, rector of Cawson, who is said to have been a Calvinist in his youth and a more moderate believer in middle age; by the time the reader of *Rachel Ray* meets Comfort, he has become "lukewarm, but not absolutely stone cold." Then there is Dr. Harford, the rector of Baslehurst, who has "never been warm at all"—except, that is, in his hatred of dissenting ministers, a sentiment hardly calculated to endear him to the Presbyterian, Congregationalist, Wesleyan, and Baptist readers of *Good Words*. Comfort emerges as the most lovable of the clerics, but for a reason that should hardly have been admissible in a magazine that sought to "blend 'the religious' with 'the secular'": there is a happy "discrepancy" between Comfort's "doctrine and conduct," and although from force of habit he continues to preach Calvinist dogma every Sunday, he never troubles himself or his parishioners with any attempt to apply these teachings to their everyday lives. All in all, it was enough to make *Rachel Ray* a most unsuitable novel for any magazine conducted in accordance with the principles set forth in the original prospectus and advertisements for *Good Words*. Nor could Macleod, for all his vaunted indifference to the maledictions of the *Record*, have been entirely unshaken when he came across a passage in which Rachel Ray herself remarks that Mr. Prong drops his *h*'s when he speaks, and connects this fault with the fact that Prong has been educated "at Islington"—a clear reference to the Church Missionary Society at Islington, an institution founded by Recordites and operated by Lord Shaftesbury's Church Pastoral Aid Society.

For his part, Trollope maintained, in a letter to Strahan dated 10 June, that he had written "just such a story as you had a right to expect from me,—judging as you of course did judge by my former works."[48] Under the circumstances, author and publisher arrived at a more amicable financial settlement than might have been expected. Trollope had already arranged to sell to Chapman and Hall for £500 the right to publish fifteen hundred copies of *Rachel Ray* after its serialization in *Good Words*. Now that there was to be no prior magazine serialization, Chapman and Hall agreed to pay £1,000 for the right to publish three thousand copies; and Trollope, concerned only to make the same income that he had counted upon all along from the novel, was satisfied with £500 from Strahan, rather than the full £1,000 that was probably his legal due.[49]

Once again, as when in 1861 Miss Mulock failed to deliver the novel she had promised, Strahan was left at the last possible moment with many extra pages to fill, and once again, he turned to Macleod. For the rest of the year, readers of the magazine would be treated not only to regular installments of Macleod's *Reminiscences of a Highland Parish*, but to a second series "By the Editor" entitled "Good Words for Children." There would also be a four-part serial "By the Author of 'East Lynne,'" and although "Martyn Ware's Temptation" was not written in the same "sensational" vein as the novel which had made Mrs. Henry Wood's fame, it is curious that the explicit reference to *East Lynne* does not seem to have inspired any comment by the magazine's usual enemies. Perhaps they were disarmed by the insertion, in the same issue that was to have included the first installment of *Rachel Ray,* of "A Word of Remonstrance with Some Novelists," an essay that served to put on record the official opposition of *Good Words* to all forms of "sensational fiction."[50] Trollope was aware of the implications for his reputation: "You know that my novels are not sensational," he remarked to George Eliot when he wrote to say that a copy of *Rachel Ray* was being sent to her.[51]

Meanwhile, Strahan had reason to be gratified by the backlash against Evangelical indictments of *Good Words.* The revelation that the magazine's assailant was himself a Presbyterian Scot went some way, as the *Patriot* had known it would, toward undermining the authority of his opinions; and when word arrived that the Free Church presbytery of Strathbogie, far to the north in the Highlands, had gathered together all copies of *Good Words* to be found in the neighborhood and then solemnly burned them in the marketplace, the delight of the secular press knew no bounds.

On 13 June the *London Review,* once so severe a critic of the magazine, expressed its wonder, in an article entitled "The Twa Kirks," that Free Churchmen should regard the reading of *Good Words* on a Sunday as being "on the same level of iniquity as intemperance or profligacy."[52] In the months to come, the Edinburgh *Scotsman* publicized the exceptionally high rate of illegitimate births in Strathbogie.[53] The *London Review* returned to the subject to remark, "It is hopeless, indeed, for an Englishman to try to understand these Scotch Presbyterian ministers who can swallow so gross a camel and strain at so tiny a gnat. . . . The crusade against *Good Words* [was] a purely Presbyterian manifestation. . . . A Presbyterian clergyman raised the cry in the *Record.*"[54] The *Bookseller* got in on the fun by declaring that "some sour men are to be found who dislike" *Good Words,* and by reprinting from the *Scotsman* "The Reel of Bogie. A New Song," which ran, in part,

> There's cauld kail in Aberdeen,
>   But *het* stuff in Strathbogie,
> Where thro' the reek, they've lately gi'en
>   A luckless lad his cogie.

The Free Kirk o' Strathbogie, sirs,
  The Free Kirk o' Strathbogie,
For some bad blood and ancient feud,
  Hae gi'en Macleod, his cogie.

. . . .

"Wee Davie" seems a douce bit lad—
  But then the graceless dogie
Forgets his birth-state was sae bad,
  Which angers a' Strathbogie.
The clergy o' Strathbogie, sirs,
  Of orthodox Strathbogie,
Put brimstone in to cleanse the skin,
  Whene'er they mix a cogie.[55]

It was better publicity than a full-page advertisement in the *Times,* and the circulation of *Good Words* continued to rise steadily, even without benefit of a serialized novel by Trollope. Not that Trollope's name would be forever banned: the issue for December 1863 included his story of "The Two Generals." By then, the *London Review* was asserting that "the popularity of this magazine has become a great fact of the day," and the *Bookseller* was proclaiming that "the most remarkable literary success of recent times is that of 'Good Words.' "[56]

Strahan would later say that *Good Words* first became a profitable venture in 1863.[57] But unfortunately, many debts had been incurred in the course of moving to London, refurbishing the two periodicals, and conducting the massive advertising campaigns; and in February 1863, Strahan and Company found it necessary to turn to their stationers, the firm of Spalding and Hodge, for a loan of £4,000. It was agreed that the debt should be repaid in February 1866. Until then, Strahan and Company would pay 5 percent interest annually. Security for the loan was the copyright to *Good Words,* which probably meant that until the debt was discharged, Strahan and Company would not have access to the magazine's profits.[58]

The prosperous firm of Spalding and Hodge, founded in 1796 by two Scotsmen, was a prime example of what one historian has termed "the strongly personal nature" of the nineteenth-century business world, "with its family concerns and close personal ties."[59] During Strahan's time, the head of the firm was Thomas S. Spalding (1805–87), a strict Congregationalist who was a Sunday School superintendent and a deacon; Spalding contributed large sums toward the building of chapels, and entirely supported one City of London missionary.[60] The firm would survive into the twentieth century under the supervision of generations of Spaldings and Hodges. Many of these family connections served as apprentices in allied firms before taking up their places in the family business, and during the 1860s, Thomas Spalding was much preoccupied with making such arrangements for his younger kinsmen.

The bonds thus formed with allied companies were further reinforced by intercompany loans; other loans were made to shore up faltering concerns whose trade might eventually prove profitable to Spalding and Hodge. By 1872, for example, the stationers invested close to £16,000 in an attempt to bolster the American publishing firm of James R. Osgood and Company, which imported its paper from them.[61] Closer to home, Thomas Spalding's son Howard was apprenticed in the 1860s to the London publishing firm of (George) Bell and (Frederic Richard) Daldy, another pair of partners who were of Scottish origin or descent. Bell and Daldy naturally purchased their paper from Spalding and Hodge, and in 1864, the stationers lent the publishers part of the £35,000 necessary to purchase the famous "Bohn's Library."[62] The Bohn transaction proved to be a lucrative investment for all concerned. It would lead indirectly, however, to the less advantageous involvement of Bell and Daldy, through their connection with Spalding and Hodge, in the financial affairs of Strahan and Company.

The agreement of February 1863 between Spalding and Hodge and Strahan and Company was in fact destined to be the first of several such agreements leading eventually to financial disaster. But a debt of £4,000 was no great matter, and Strahan betrayed no particular anxiety as he went about soliciting contributions for the 1864 volume of *Good Words*, which would feature by far its most "sensational" offering to date: Mrs. Henry Wood's *Oswald Cray*, a suspenseful narrative of concealed motives, overheard conversations, and suspected murder, which would be serialized throughout the year. Macleod seems to have slipped back into the habit of allowing Strahan a free hand in such matters; and in the course of 1864, if Strahan's own advertisements are to be believed, *Good Words* achieved an average circulation of a staggering 160,000 monthly, outselling not only the *Cornhill* but every other monthly magazine in the English-speaking world.[63]

Meanwhile Strahan and Macleod, along with Macleod's younger

brother Donald, set off in February 1864 on a two-month tour of eastern missions which Macleod would describe in the volume of *Good Words* for 1865. Strahan, who would record in his own autobiographical essays that he had heard Macleod preach not only in Athens, Alexandria, Damascus, Jerusalem, and Constantinople, but also in Amsterdam, Paris, Berlin, Vienna, and Rome, recalled that on this trip, "in out-of-the-way nooks in Palestine," Macleod delighted his companions by gravely demanding of the indigenous Arabs, "as if everything was at stake on their opinion,"

> what *they* thought of the great organ question and of Dr. Begg. When no answer came, he would heighten their comical astonishment by blandly offering them the alternative of giving him their well-considered views on the Free Church as against the Established.

The three Highlanders had equipped themselves before setting out with a large store of fireworks, and one of their pastimes was to set off these devices nightly in the Syrian deserts.[64]

When they returned, Strahan set to work on a variety of new projects. He seems to have drawn from the *Record* attacks the lesson that although it was not possible, after all, that *Good Words* should be all things to all readers, it was probable that good was to be done, and money made as well, by catering to the various audiences which could not be served by a single magazine. There was, for example, the audience that would purchase a magazine only if it included far more "sensational" fiction than had ever been intended for *Good Words;* and there was the audience that most interested Strahan personally—an audience thirsting after differing opinions on questions of philosophy, theology, politics, history, and literature, all to be encompassed within a single monthly review.

In 1864, however, Strahan was primarily concerned with launching a new periodical, the third in his stable, that would appeal to those readers who adamantly refused to regard *Good Words* as suitable reading for the Sabbath. Strahan was well aware that such a magazine could succeed only under the "auspices" of an editor who commanded the respect of Calvinist Evangelicals; and so he managed to persuade Dr. Thomas Guthrie to take on the job. One of Guthrie's requirements was that Strahan should also enlist, as assistant editor, William Garden Blaikie, who in the 1850s edited the Edinburgh *Free*

Church Magazine for Johnstone and Hunter, and who in 1863 ended a three-year stint as editor of the *North British Review*. Both men were well qualified to assist Strahan in his goal of using the new *Sunday Magazine* "as a means of appealing in matters of social reform to the mighty class whose philanthropy, if rightly challenged, would be stimulated by the ardour of religious conviction":[65] Guthrie was the author of a number of books on urban social problems; Blaikie's *Better Days for Working People* had appeared under Strahan's imprint in 1863, to achieve a sale of eighty thousand copies.[66]

In July, Strahan launched another massive advertising campaign, this one to inform the public that the first issue of the *Sunday Magazine,* a sevenpenny monthly, would appear on 1 October 1864. Perhaps in order to lull the suspicions of wary Calvinists, these first advertisements did not name the magazine's publisher, although the address given was that of Strahan and Company. Guthrie's name was prominent in all the advertisements, and he signed the lengthy prospectus, which promised, in a direct reversal of the formula made famous in advertisements for *Good Words,* that the *Sunday Magazine* would provide reading intended specifically for the Sabbath, rather than for all the week. Other statements in the prospectus, however, indicated goals common to the two periodicals: the *Sunday Magazine,* it was said, would "bring the Bible into relation to common life," and serve as "a catholic serial" by including contributions not only by clergymen of various denominations, but even by laymen.[67]

In August, Strahan and Company borrowed another £6,000 from Spalding and Hodge, increasing their debt to £10,000, all still at 5 percent interest. To guarantee the loan, the copyright of the projected *Sunday Magazine* was assigned to the stationers, who continued to hold the copyright to *Good Words.* It was agreed that the £10,000 should be repaid in three installments, on 16 July 1865, 1866, and 1867.[68]

The first issue of the *Sunday Magazine,* which appeared on schedule dated October 1864, commenced with an article by Guthrie, "The Angel's Song," which outlined the standard evangelical doctrines of salvation. Other contributors included Blaikie, Macleod, Alford, and Stevenson. There were illustrations, poems, and the first installment of a serialized story, "Kate the Grandmother." In years to come, Guthrie would frequently be called upon to explain how a magazine that included fiction could be regarded as fit reading for the Sabbath;

his usual retort was that Christ did much of his teaching by means of parables.[69]

Guthrie and Blaikie had more difficulty countering allegations that the theological bias of the magazine was too "broad," for in point of fact, the two Free Church ministers secretly agreed with these charges. But Blaikie and Guthrie lived in Edinburgh, and time and time again, when the magazine issued forth from its London publishing house, it included articles that the coeditors would have rejected. In his autobiography, Blaikie would pin the blame squarely on Strahan, who personally served as the magazine's subeditor. Thus it came about that even while Blaikie was privately doing his best "to keep it on Puritan lines," he was publicly suspected of "loose and latitudinarian tendencies."[70] In 1873, when Strahan was no longer connected with the magazine, Blaikie would resign the editorship when an article was published that he had not first approved. But Blaikie and Guthrie seem to have tolerated Strahan's acts of editorial subversion with better humor, perhaps because both became deeply attached to their young publisher: Blaikie in particular would recall Strahan as one who "drew men by a fascination of his own." And even though Strahan's subediting may have offended some strict evangelicals, it must also have made the magazine's success, for as Blaikie put it, "the wooden and the leaden had no chance with him."[71] Sales of the first few numbers exceeded one hundred thousand before settling down to an average of ninety thousand or more monthly; by the end of 1865, ten thousand copies of each issue were being exported to the United States.[72]

Some of the sales were undoubtedly achieved at the expense of *Good Words*. Strahan himself would explain the slump in circulation of that magazine in 1865 as the result of the unpopularity of the serialized novel, Charles Kingsley's *Hereward the Wake*: "For some the story was at times too learned; for others there was too much fighting in it."[73] Other observers, including the *Bookseller*, were astonished that the proprietors of *Good Words* would be so bold as to set up a rival to their own publication.[74] Even while the *Sunday Magazine* remained a best-seller, however, sales of the elder magazine rebounded in years to come; and Strahan was consulted by publishers who wished to establish similar periodicals in Germany (*Daheim*) and America (*Scribner's*).[75]

In the mid-1860s, Strahan was also rapidly expanding his list of authors. One of the new names was that of Robert Buchanan (1841–1901), who has been termed "the most Scottish" of poets, "conscious of the Highland blood in his veins; he was a Clansman, a Celt; and it was this clan-feeling which hurried him into the Celtic Revival."[76] Although Buchanan had imbibed from his atheist father a hatred of all orthodox religion, he was an intense mystic and in some ways the purest of Puritans: by his own account he was horrified, when he came to London in 1860, to find himself surrounded on all sides by "fleshliness."[77] Buchanan's first volume of poems, *Undertones* (1863), appeared under the imprint of Moxon and Company, a firm which already counted Tennyson among its authors. When *Idyls and Legends of Inverburn* appeared in 1865, Strahan was so impressed with the volume that he bought Buchanan away from Moxon, taking over publication of the *Idyls* and of such works to come as *London Poems* (1866), which made Buchanan's name, and the mystical *Book of Orm* (1870). Buchanan and Strahan worked out an arrangement whereby Buchanan supplied Strahan's periodicals with a certain amount of copy each month; his contributions, which ranged from verse to fiction to weighty essays, were frequently unsigned or signed with pseudonymns. Strahan's generous payments enabled Buchanan to return to the Highlands to live.[78] They may also have given him the security to indulge to the full his notorious egotism and contentiousness: when Moxon brought out Swinburne's *Poems and Ballads,* Buchanan attacked the volume in an unsigned review in the *Athenaeum* of 4 August 1866. On 15 September, the *Spectator* published "The Session of the Poets," an anonymous lampoon of Swinburne that included among its secondary characters such other Moxon authors as Tennyson and even Buchanan, who was described as "moony, conceited and narrow." Despite this subterfuge, it soon became common knowledge that Buchanan had written both the review and the lampoon, publications which played no small part in frightening Moxon into withdrawing *Poems and Ballads,* and which marked the beginnings of Buchanan's long-running feud with Swinburne. Their quarrel was not entirely literary: according to one historian, Buchanan hated Swinburne as a member of the English aristocracy, while Swinburne reciprocated with a corresponding distaste for the Scots.[79]

Meanwhile, Strahan added yet another Scot to his list and to his circle of personal friends. George MacDonald (1824–1905) is remembered today for his children's stories, such as *At the Back of the North Wind* (Strahan, 1871) and *The Princess and the Goblin* (Strahan, 1872).[80] But in the 1860s, he wrote a series of novels for adults—*David Elginbrod* (1863), *Alec Forbes* (1865), and *Robert Falconer* (1868)—that depicted the narrowness and fanaticism of many Calvinists. MacDonald had gathered his material firsthand: the son of a farmer, he came to England to serve as the minister of a Congregationalist chapel in Sussex; but the deacons there, deeply suspicious of his theology, forced his resignation, and he moved on to London. *Phantastes, a Faerie Romance* was published by Smith, Elder in 1858, and MacDonald contributed to the first issue of Smith's *Cornhill Magazine*. For a few years he attended a Congregationalist chapel where he came to know the parents of Robert Browning. By the mid-1860s, however, in large part as a result of his admiration for F. D. Maurice, he joined the Church of England. Along the way he became a close friend of many literary figures, including John Ruskin; Derrick Leon writes, in *Ruskin the Great Victorian,* that MacDonald,

> with his passionate belief in a world of the spirit interpenetrating the world we know, and his scarlet cravats that gave him a strange look of "barbaric splendour," had soon surrounded himself with many of the most brilliant intellects of the day.[81]

In 1866, MacDonald's fictional *Annals of a Quiet Neighbourhood* were serialized in the *Sunday Magazine,* and he became something of a Strahan regular: in years to come, nearly all of his work would appear first in one or another of Strahan's periodicals. According to MacDonald's son and biographer, "his financial position was now easier, and remained easier—thanks largely to Alexander Strahan . . . a most generous publisher."[82]

At about this time, Strahan began to make occasional use of the publisher's device which identified many, although by no means all, of his books and periodicals. This was an anchor suspended by a hand which reached down out of a cloud. On the left side of the anchor appeared the word *Anchora,* and on the right, *Spei,* a reference to Hebrews 6:19 ("Which hope we have as an anchor of the soul, both sure and stedfast, and which entereth into that within the veil"). The first and last initials of Strahan's name were apparent in the capitalized letters of *Anchora Spei,* and soon the bindings of many of his books would be stamped with another trademark: the letter S super-imposed over the letter A.

But although in the late 1860s the *Anchora Spei* appeared on nearly every volume written by George MacDonald or Robert Buchanan, it did not appear on the title pages of two new periodicals commenced by Strahan late in 1865, two periodicals which would put great strains on his financial resources. One of these was the *Argosy,* a sixpenny monthly magazine. The other was a half-crown review which Strahan had been planning for years, and which he would always refer to as his "most important literary enterprise": a "Journal of Criticism—Theological, Literary, and Social," which he named the *Contemporary Review.*[83]

CHAPTER V

The Sea of Faith: The *Contemporary Review* and Its Mission, 1866–68

It is true, the *Saturday Review* maintains that our epoch of transformation is finished; that we have found our philosophy; that the British nation has searched all anchorages for the spirit, and has finally anchored itself, in the fulness of perfected knowledge, on Benthamism.

—Matthew Arnold, "Preface" to *Essays in Criticism* (1865)

Even though Strahan's personal allegiance to the "broad" party within the Church of Scotland brought his avowedly "unpartizan" periodicals under attack on the one hand by Scottish Calvinists and on the other hand by Anglicans eager to defend the English Establishment, there is no evidence that Strahan ever seriously considered changing his denominational affiliation. In remaining a Presbyterian, he differed from many other Scottish immigrants to England. It has been estimated that of the hundred thousand Scots in London in 1823, no more than five thousand attended Presbyterian services.[1] The Presbyterian *Weekly Review* lamented in 1872 "the sad want of loyalty to our Church" among the thousands of Presbyterians who crossed the border every year: "it is astonishing to find how few of these find their way to our places of worship."[2] Thus James Hannay, writing anonymously in the *Cornhill Magazine* in 1866, was undoubtedly correct in asserting that "in London . . . Presbyterianism has no influence commensurate with that of the masses of Scotsmen here. . . . Once out of his own country, [the Scot] finds his Presbyterianism sit lightly upon him."[3]

Those Scots who did remain Presbyterian seem to have done so at least in part for reasons of ethnicity: one of their ministers jested that his congregants "send regularly for their oatmeal to some remote region of the north that they may get it of pure grit,"[4] while the *Weekly Review* took exception to the widespread belief that "Presbyterianism is an institution more for the conservation of Scottish colonies in

England than for preaching the gospel to sinners." Other immigrant
Scots joined what the *Weekly Review* described as the "more fashionable Church of England."[5] The Establishment naturally held great
appeal for those who possessed the wealth, or the educational background, or the social aplomb to suppose that they would feel at home
there; it was of course also necessary that they should be willing or
even eager to see their children become English, as was true, for
example, in the case of William Ewart Gladstone's father. But the Scot
who became an Anglican through sheer ambition, although he undoubtedly existed, was probably not as common as cynics and Calvinists tended to suggest. Archibald Campbell Tait, for example,
traded Presbyterianism for Anglicanism when he arrived at Oxford,
according to one student of his career, "both through conviction and
as an avenue to usefulness and power"; like so many of his compatriots who took the same step, he had long been repelled by the
rigid Calvinism which was more prevalent in the Church of Scotland
prior to the Disruption of 1843 than after it.[6]

Those Scots who remained Presbyterian, then, could hope at the
very least to preserve their ethnicity; those who joined the Anglican
church, where they naturally constituted a minority, were more ready
to assimilate to English culture. Between these two alternatives lay all
the various dissenting denominations of predominantly English
membership. Unitarianism attracted barely a handful of Scots, hardly
more, in fact, than did Roman Catholicism. A fair number were attracted by the Baptists, who added to orthodox Calvinism a belief in
adult baptism which struck many logical Scots as eminently reasonable. But the Nonconformist denomination that counted the greatest
number of Scots among its members—so great a number, in fact, that
they came close to constituting an identifiable, unassimilable faction—
was Congregationalism; and their influence within what was by far
the largest, the wealthiest, and the most politically powerful of English dissenting communions made them a power in the land.[7]

Many of these Scots had become Congregationalists even before
leaving Scotland. Scottish Congregationalism, which maintained a denominational organization entirely separate from that of the Congregational Union of England and Wales, had grown rapidly from
the time of its emergence, in the first decade of the nineteenth century, as part of the general evangelical awakening that led also to the
Disruption of 1843. Scottish Congregationalism, which was Calvinist

in its theology, flourished prior to the Disruption by opening "Missionary Kirks" in those parishes staffed by "Moderate" ministers of the Church of Scotland. The gains thus made were not always permanent: Hugh Miller tells of one Highland parish where the local Congregationalist chapel lost its entire membership to the Free Church established after the Disruption.[8] Miller's story demonstrates that what had been an advantage prior to the Disruption—the specific form of church government practiced by the Congregationalists, who reserved to each individual chapel the right to call its own minister, determine its own forms of worship, and safeguard its own theological orthodoxy—might become a handicap afterward; for Scots tended to prefer the tighter discipline of Presbyterianism, which assigns to each presbytery extensive powers over all the congregations within its geographic boundaries, and makes the presbytery responsible in turn to its synod.

Many Scots remained Congregationalists, however; and when they moved south, they tended to retain more of their Calvinist heritage later into the century than did their English coreligionists. Within the Congregational Union of England and Wales, Scots such as Strahan's friend John Brown Paton were always among the first to complain at any deviation from orthodoxy. They were also capable of calling, at times, for stronger church discipline and even for mandatory adherence to credal formulations—guarantees of doctrinal conformity that would have been taken for granted in Presbyterian churches, but that struck at the basic principles of Congregationalism. The dogmatism of the Scots offended many of their English associates; as one of their historians has written,

> the Scottish brand of Congregational churchmanship, just because of its Presbyterian provenance, reveals some resemblances to Presbyterianism . . . much to the surprise and chagrin of our Congregational brethren of other traditions, whose historical provenance is different.[9]

In 1876, these tensions within the Congregational Union were to affect the management of Strahan's *Contemporary Review*.

Meanwhile, it was natural that evangelical Scots, who were scattered throughout various English denominations, would come together in the transdenominational associations fostered by the evangelical movement. They were prominent in the Evangelical Alliance from the time of its founding in 1846; they supported foreign missionary activities; and they took part in the various organizations—such as John Brown Paton's "Inner Mission"—established to promote evangelical Christianity as a panacea for social problems at home.

These "Home Missionaries" encountered formidable ideological opposition in their attempts to "Christianize" all classes of society. George Jacob Holyoake (1817–1906) and Charles Bradlaugh (1833–91), for example, were so zealous in preaching the virtues of rationalism, secularism, and, in the case of Bradlaugh, outright atheism, that one historian has termed them "apostles as self-sacrificing and implacable as any of their evangelical Christian contemporaries."[10] In the 1830s Holyoake was a "social missionary" for an organization ("The Universal Community Society of Rational Religionists") founded to propagate the ideas of Robert Owen. He published *Rationalism, a Treatise for the Times* in 1845; over the years he produced a string of antitheological pamphlets which pronounced science "the sole Providence of Man" and postulated a "secularist" morality which would be "independent of Christianity." "Secularism," explained Holyoake, "trusts reason, science, and experience only";[11] to spread this message he edited several periodicals with titles such as the *Oracle of Reason*, the *Herald of Progress*, the *National Reformer*, and the *Secularist*. Even Holyoake, however, was embarrassed by Bradlaugh's militant atheism, which prompted one writer to remark, "There is no God, and Bradlaugh is his prophet."[12] Bradlaugh, who regarded any trace of religious feeling as a dangerous barrier in the way of progress, founded in 1866 the National Secular Society, which at its peak in 1885 would have over a hundred branches throughout the country. For years he also edited and published a periodical called the *Freethinker*.

But however much Christian believers were angered by the activities of such notorious firebrands, the greater and more irresistible threat to faith came from the general intellectual currents of the age. The year 1859, which saw an outbreak of religious revivalism in parts of the British Isles, was also the year of publication of Mill's *On Liberty* and Darwin's *Origin of Species,* works that led, according to one historian, "to the outburst of anti-clerical books and articles in the 'seventies and to the secularization of intellectual life."[13] Along the way there appeared Herbert Spencer's *First Principles* (1862), which seemed to suggest that man can know nothing of the ultimate nature of the world; T. H. Huxley's *Man's Place in Nature* (1863), which asserted for the benefit of lay readers that man is descended from a lower animal form; Renan's *La Vie de Jésus* (1863), which depicted Jesus not as the son of God, but as merely a remarkable itinerant preacher; and Strauss's *New Life of Jesus* (1864), which, like the earlier *Life* (1835–36), sought naturalistic rather than supernatural or miraculous explanations for the events it described. W. E. H. Lecky's *History of the Rise and Influence of Rationalism* appeared in 1865, propounding a definition of *rationalism* which explains why this term—along with such others as *materialism, positivism, Benthamism, Hegelianism, scepticism,* and, of course, Holyoake's favorite, *secularism*—struck fear into the hearts of so many Christian believers. Rationalism, according to Lecky, is "a certain cast of mind" which "leads men on all occasions to subordinate dogmatic theology to the dictates of reason and conscience."

> It predisposes men, in history, to attribute all kinds of phenomena to natural rather than to miraculous causes; in theology, to esteem succeeding systems the expressions of the wants and aspirations of that religious sentiment which is planted in all men; and, in ethics, to regard as duties only those which conscience reveals to be such.[14]

Ideas such as these were treated with broad-minded tolerance in the famous *Fortnightly Review,* which appeared for the first time in May 1865. Advertisements promised that the new periodical would "endeavour to further the cause of Progress" by publishing signed articles reflecting the varied opinions of their authors, rather than the consistent line of a specific party.[15] But the first editor, G. H. Lewes, was known to be a disciple of Auguste Comte, the French "positivist" who looked forward to a time when the test of truth would be empirical rather than theological, and traditional belief would be replaced by a "religion of humanity"; and Lewes's reputation did not encourage public trust in the "catholic" intent of the *Fortnightly.* Anthony Trollope, one of the founders of the review, would explain in his autobiography that

> liberalism, free-thinking, and open inquiry will never object to appear in company with their opposites, because they have the conceit to think that they can quell those opposites; but the opposites will not appear in

conjunction with liberalism, free-thinking, and open inquiry. As a natural consequence, our new publication became an organ of liberalism, free-thinking, and open inquiry.[16]

Thus by February 1866, the *Spectator* was already complaining that

> the *Fortnightly* has usually, we notice, masterly papers on the sceptical side and very poor ones on the spiritual side of religious questions. Does the editor think it quite fair to trim his balance so that the contributors with a hearty Christian faith shall be ordinarily chosen from among the men of what we may call fluffy intellect, while those who avow "positive" (or negative) philosophy are ordinarily of the first rank of intellectual power?[17]

In January 1867, Lewes was succeeded as editor by John Morley, who was deeply inspired by John Stuart Mill's call, in *On Liberty*, for a conflict of opinions out of which would emerge new truths.[18] When Mill died in 1873, Morley praised him in the *Fortnightly* for having set an example of tolerance, patience, and the fair examination of hostile opinions.[19] But Morley himself was not so patient, and in his *Recollections* he would term literature "a weapon, an arm, not merely a literary art."[20] In "On Compromise," which appeared in the *Fortnightly* in 1874, Morley expressed his disappointment that Mill's posthumous *Essays on Religion* were so tolerant of the premises of Christian faith; for Morley, much like Charles Bradlaugh although on a higher intellectual level, believed that orthodox religion and "supernaturalism" were enemies to the "cause of Progress" no less than to the "diversity of opinion" that the *Fortnightly* had been established to foster. In "On Compromise," Morley charged the Church of England with being "fast moored by ancient formularies."[21] He had already, in the *Fortnightly* of September 1873, termed her "as inveterate a foe to new social hope as . . . to a new scientific truth";[22] and despite the occasional appearance of a clerical contributor, the *Fortnightly* was, throughout Morley's tenure, an enemy to the principle of church establishment. When he retired from the editorship in October 1882, Morley would claim that the *Fortnightly* had always "been open, so far as editorial good will was concerned, to opinions from many sides." Yet on the same page he boasted that "the clergy no longer have the pulpit to themselves, for the new Reviews became more powerful pulpits, in which heretics were at least as welcome as orthodox."[23]

And although these "new Reviews," which cost two shillings or half a crown each, were clearly intended for the prosperous and educated few, they had tremendous impact in an age when "doubt and theological uncertainty percolated downwards into the ranks of ordinary believers to an extent unprecedented."[24]

It was perhaps the appearance of the *Fortnightly* that galvanized Strahan into launching his own half-crown monthly review, the *Contemporary*. Strahan would later recall that since at least 1863 he had been planning a new form of "critical organ" that would differ as much from the expensive, anonymous, long-established quarterlies as *Good Words* differed from the typical religious magazine of the first half of the century. The new periodical was to include signed contributions in order that it might, like *Good Words,* open its pages to a variety of opinions, "trusting to truth to establish itself in the conflict." In these ways, of course, the *Fortnightly* anticipated the *Contemporary*. But while the bias of the *Fortnightly* was toward positivism and skepticism, Strahan's review was meant to counteract "the dissemination of a more or less materialist philosophy" founded on "the progress of physical science": "I believed," wrote Strahan, "that those who undertook to oppose the modern scepticism were . . . too fearful of scientific inquiry, and that a bolder, less narrow defence of faith would have its advantages."[25] Strahan did not intend that his new review should be handicapped in the accomplishment of this mission by that "Nonconformist odour" which had prevented *Good Words* from being accepted as "a perfectly liberal, unpartizan periodical." Three years earlier, he had attempted to make *Good Words* acceptable to Anglican readers by including regular contributions from Henry Alford, the dean of Canterbury. Now, he persuaded Alford to become editor of the *Contemporary*.

No name could have served better to attract the readers and the contributors Strahan sought. Alford (1810–71) came from a virtual tribe of evangelical Anglican vicars, including his great-grandfather, grandfather, father, uncle, and brother-in-law (he had married his cousin); he naturally had long-standing ties of friendship with many other evangelical families within the established church.[26] Alford's own zeal had been moderated during his undergraduate years at Cambridge, where he was, at the same time as Tennyson, a member of the famous "Apostles." After leaving Cambridge, Alford settled down in a vicarage near Nottingham. For a time he edited *Dearden's*

Miscellany, a Nottingham-based periodical that made "acknowledged Christian truths" the basis of all editorial decisions;[27] he also supported the establishment of a Mechanics' Institute, an effort on behalf of popular education that prompted a local paper to charge him with "Liberalism and Low Churchmanship."[28]

A turning point in Alford's career came in the summer of 1847, when he went to Bonn to study German so that he might keep abreast of textual studies of the Bible. There he became a friend of I. A. Dorner (1809–84), the Lutheran theologian who incorporated into traditional evangelicalism the philosophical insights of Schleiermacher, Hegel, and Kant. Alford's studies in Germany enabled him to undertake his life work, a revised text of the Greek New Testament; when the first volume appeared in 1849, he was barraged from all sides with charges of "rationalism." Wrote Alford to one critic,

> I have no sympathy whatever with rationalism; one of my great objects is to deal truthfully with the word of God, that I may, if it please Him, furnish to our students of Scripture fitting weapons for the coming struggle with infidelity.[29]

But the attacks continued; and over the years, many Anglicans concerned for the dignity of their church were offended, as well, by Alford's warm relations with Nonconformists. During a visit to Berlin in the late 1850s, Alford triggered a controversy by celebrating communion in his hotel room with a group of non-Anglicans; as the admiring Strahan later put it, Alford forgot "the technical restrictions of his position, in the impulses of religious sympathy." A similar offense was committed in 1868 when Alford, accompanied by Strahan, presided over the centennial celebrations of Cheshunt (Congregational) College, "somewhat to the displeasure of certain among his less courageous clerical brethren," according to Strahan.[30]

By this time, however, Alford—who became dean of Canterbury in 1857—was far gone in eminent respectability, and his views concerning the Greek Testament and other matters were being challenged as too conservative by many "Broad" Churchmen. The *Saturday Review,* intent on teasing, referred to him in 1866 as

> a gentleman of undoubted learning and ability [who] publishes a commentary on the Greek Testament; he exhibits a great deal of knowledge, and, after diving into the dangerous labyrinths of German commentators, comes safely back as orthodox as he started.[31]

More respect would be shown, in 1871, in his death notices. The *Spectator* would term him "one of the foremost men in the party of comprehension" and "a great popularizer . . . very few indeed of our dignitaries thought so much of the people, and worked so hard to teach them."[32] The Presbyterian *Weekly Review*, which rarely yielded a point in any discussion of the personal merits of individual Anglicans, would eulogize Alford with even greater warmth, remarking, "There was not another Churchman of position so catholic in his sympathies, while evangelical in his faith."[33]

Certainly Alford agreed readily with Strahan's ideas concerning the new *Review;* and it was he who wrote the widely advertised prospectus which promised, for months before the *Contemporary* made its debut on 1 January 1866, that the periodical would

number among its contributors those who, holding loyally to belief in the Articles of the Christian Faith, are not afraid of modern thought in its varied aspects and demands, and scorn to defend their faith by mere reticence, or by the artifices too commonly acquiesced in.[34]

To this end, Alford set about soliciting contributions from, in his words, nearly fifty of "the best men in the country"[35]—who, with the exception of a few longtime cronies of Strahan's, and despite the dean's latitudinarian proclivities, turned out to be members of the Anglican church almost to a man. Alford's own name was not mentioned in the advertisements, nor was it ever to appear on the title page of the *Contemporary*. But, as the *Weekly Review* would soon be remarking, "The name of Dean Alford is connected with it in common rumour;"[36] and so it is not surprising that the first issue of the *Contemporary* commenced by taking up the cudgels against an ecclesiastical movement that was of great concern to evangelical Anglicans generally, and to Dean Alford in particular: "ritualism," or the revival by some "High Church" clergymen of medieval church practices such as genuflection, reservation and adoration of the eucharistic sacrament, auricular confession, and the use of altar lights, vestments, wafer bread, the mixed chalice, and incense—practices that were supposed by many evangelicals to symbolize Roman Catholic doctrines.

"It may be worth mentioning," wrote Strahan in his account of the founding of the *Contemporary*, "for [Alford] himself never forgot it, that the first MS. which reached him for the Review, was an article by Mr. B. Shaw, on the subject of 'Ritualism.' "[37] Benjamin Shaw (1819–

77), a personal friend of Alford's, was the barrister most often retained to combat the Ritualists in cases before the ecclesiastical courts. In his *Contemporary* article, Shaw argued that the customs of the medieval church had no standing in English law, and that the only permissible practices were those prescribed by the Act of Uniformity, the prayer book that it authorized, and other post-Reformation English statutes and precedents. Within weeks, an opponent of the Ritualists would argue in the Convocation of Canterbury that Shaw's guidelines, as explained in the *Contemporary*, should be adopted as a basis for "solving many of our rubrical difficulties."[38] For the next few years Alford would take active part in the ongoing dispute; he would also ensure that dozens of articles and scores of book reviews expressing opposition to ritualism, several of them written by himself, would be published in the *Contemporary*.

Not that the battle against skepticism and "rationalism" was to be neglected. Shaw's article in the inaugural issue of the *Contemporary* was immediately followed by the first installment of a two-part paper on "The Philosophy of the Conditioned: Sir William Hamilton and John Stuart Mill," an unsigned article that many astute readers would have recognized immediately as the work of Henry Longueville Mansel (1820–71), professor of moral and metaphysical philosophy at Oxford, and the preeminent authority on the thought of Hamilton, a leading member of the "Scottish School of Common Sense." Mansel, who has been described as "the new defender of the faith" against the inroads of skepticism, had made his position clear in his celebrated Bampton Lectures of 1858.[39] Like Hamilton, Mansel maintained that although we have intuitive certitude of the existence of God, our human reason, limited as it is to the finite or "conditioned," is unable to afford us any knowledge of God's infinite, "unconditioned" nature. Human reason is competent, however, to teach us, on the basis of historical and other evidence, that the Christian Bible is a supernatural revelation; and once this has been decided, the teachings of the Bible must be accepted without question, lest further analysis cut the "most precious truths" of theology "from the anchor which held them firm, and cast [them] upon the waters of philosophical speculation, to float hither and thither with the ever-shifting waves of thought."[40] Mill, who regarded Hamilton's "intuitional philosophy" as "one of the chief hindrances to the rational treatment of great social questions, and one of the greatest stumbling blocks to human improvement,"[41] attacked its bases in the *Examination of Sir William Hamilton's Philosophy* (1865) by arguing that man's knowledge and beliefs originate, not in any intuitive consciousness of an "unconditioned," but in inferences from experience, as explained by the psychological theories of David Hartley. Mansel's *Contemporary* articles, which perpetuated the quarrel without adding anything new to the debate, had no effect on the eventual outcome: according to one twentieth-century philosopher, the "Scottish School" never fully recovered from Mill's critique, "although it lingered on for some time in Scotland and the United States, where it became a sort of 'official philosophy' in the less adventurous Colleges."[42] Mansel's performance was gratifying to many readers of the *Contemporary*, however: the *Weekly Review,* for example, praised the author of the *Contemporary* articles for "maintaining the noble, healthful, reverent doctrine of the Edinburgh metaphysician against the now too popular Positivism of John Stuart Mill."[43]

In addition to taking up a position on the battle lines drawn against the evils of ritualism and rationalism, the first issue of the *Contemporary* addressed a third highly controversial topic, "Sunday"—a title that in January 1866, would have been immediately understood to refer to the theological storm currently raging about the person of none other than Norman Macleod.

The immediate background to Macleod's problems was that in 1865, when the North British Railway Company began running Sunday trains between Edinburgh and Glasgow, the (Established) presbytery of Glasgow protested against this desecration of the Sabbath in a "Pastoral Letter" to be read from every pulpit. Macleod, however, could not agree with the premises of the letter. In November, in a three-and-a-half-hour speech before the presbytery, he argued that the Decalogue was a covenant made only with Israel, and that Christian observance of the Sabbath need not be as strict as the Jewish observances based on the Fourth Commandment. Macleod's views were not particularly original: nine years earlier, Dean Alford had taken much the same position in *A Letter to J. Sperling, Esquire.*[44] But Macleod's usual enemies took full advantage of his apparent transgression against orthodoxy. He was snubbed and even hissed at in the streets of Glasgow by Calvinist ministers, and a Free Church mission house was opened next door to his own pulpit, the Barony Church. Within the Church of Scotland, Macleod was charged with having departed from the Westminster Confession of Faith, and the assembly convened a hearing on whether or not to depose him.[45]

At this point Principal John Tulloch rushed into the fray to deliver an address upon the "Study of the Confession of Faith." Tulloch contended that formulas such as the Westminster Confession were products of specific times and circumstances, "historical monuments, marking the tide of religious thought."[46] Framed by man, they were subject to error, and it was thus unreasonable to expect that those who signed them should give more than general assent to their contents. Tulloch's address "shook all Scotland," according to his biographer;[47] and his and Macleod's opinions were caricatured in a ballad, "Norman's Blast," which referred in several stanzas to the Disruption of the Church of Scotland, more than twenty years earlier.[48]

> Your fair 'Good Words' had cleared the way
> To rid us o' the Sabbath Day,
> Besides commandments twa or three mae
>   I needna name.
> I fear this haste may spoil the play
>   And lose our game.
>
> . . . .
>
> Thae dour auld carles, they were sae blind
> As to believe the creeds they signed,
> And when the State would force or bind
>   What they ca'd conscience,
> They'd cast their stipends to the wind—
>   And sic like nonsense!
>
> . . . .
>
> Let nae weak scruples haunt your min'
> That ye sud place or pay resign,—
> The *Scotsman*, Hope, the *Superfine*,
>   And Holyoake,
> All hail this anti-Sabbath shine
>   Your master-stroke.[49]
>
> . . . .
>
> But troth, he's little cause to fear
> Wha's hand in glove wi' the Premier,
> And at the Palace mony a year
>   Has cringed and bowed—
> The Queen's ain chaplain! wha daur steer
>   Norman Macleod?

In January, Macleod was defended in the *Fortnightly Review* by Anthony Trollope, who appealed to the wording of the Fourth Commandment to argue that strict Sabbatarianism was itself incompatible with true religion.[50] Macleod's champion in the *Contemporary* was Edward Hayes Plumptre (1821–91), professor of divinity at King's College, London, and a brother-in-law of F. D. Maurice. Plumptre contributed regularly to the *Sunday Magazine* and to *Good Words*, and in his *Contemporary* article on "Sunday" he recalled the fanaticism that had prompted the Calvinist campaign against *Good Words* in 1863. Plumptre agreed with Macleod that although the Decalogue commands the obedience of Christians insofar as it contains elements of genuine moral truth, it is not to be applied by them in the same legalistic sense in which it is binding on the Jews. The most eloquent passages of "Sunday," however, evince the keen social consciousness that was to characterize so many articles published in the *Contemporary*. Plumptre builds up to the conclusion that

> the wisest course . . . for those who think, as I do, that the Sundays of most of our large towns in England are a scandal and a reproach, is . . . to welcome any Government action which really relieves labour and improves the condition of the labouring poor; to take away the false rigour which makes the Lord's day wearisome and unattractive; to abstain from imputing a fictitious criminality to acts which are themselves indifferent; to adapt our worship and our preaching, more than we have done, to the wants of our time. . . . In the name of the Lord of the Lord's day, we may protest against the tyranny of one class over another, of the class who can pay for pleasure over the class that must work for bread; and so the day may yet become, as the Sabbath was meant to be, "a delight, holy to the Lord, honourable."[51]

In the months to come, Macleod would be required to explain his views at length to the other members of his presbytery; he would acknowledge that he had been perhaps just a bit extreme in his public utterances. But it was no small matter to be exculpated in print by such scholarly divines as Tulloch and Plumptre, and by the conclusion of the annual May meetings of the Church of Scotland, Macleod knew that he had escaped with no more serious consequence than an official admonishment. The bitterness of the "Sabbatarians" who opposed him throughout this episode inspired his story of "The Starling," serialized in *Good Words* in 1867, in which a minister is so angered by the cheerful singing of a pet bird on the Lord's day that he attempts unsuccessfully to have the offending creature strangled.

Meanwhile, the *Contemporary Review* was garnering its first notices in the press. The warmest welcome came from the *Weekly Review,* which clearly took a greater interest in the Scottish Presbyterian publisher of the *Contemporary* than in its Anglican editor.

> The tendencies of thought in our day have become so marked, so self-conscious, so exclusive of each other, that a new publication, professing to bring us fresh applications of the truth of God to human problems, immediately provokes inquiry as to it[s] special *whereabouts.* The name of the publisher is an indication of this, so far at least. He has gathered round him a school of thinkers and writers, as a whole substantially orthodox and evangelical. . . . Of this school and class of writing it can be said that, thanks, no doubt, in large measure to Mr. Strahan, it has at once gained the public ear, and attained a wide influence and popularity.[52]

Other critics greeted the *Contemporary* kindly, but calmly. The *Guardian* remarked of the inaugural issue that "the patient search after any form of truth seldom leads at first to any startling consequences" and suggested that the *Review*'s chances of success would be improved by an "admixture of lighter matter."[53] The *Spectator* commented after two numbers that "the theological element preponderates at present, almost to the exclusion of other matters; this gives the list of contents an appearance of heaviness, which will not be found really to exist by those who have the courage to plunge *in medias res.*"[54] In March the *Spectator* commended "this ably conducted Review," which continued "to display . . . the moderation and discrimination that attracted our sympathies in the opening numbers";[55] in May the *Contemporary* was said still to be pursuing "its grave course, to the satisfaction, we believe, of serious mankind."[56] The *London Review* was more brusque: it pronounced in November that the tone of the *Contemporary* was "too theological to make it widely popular," and suggested that the rival *Fortnightly* was more likely to attract an extensive readership.[57] Connop Thirlwall, the bishop of St. David's, held much the same opinion: he jested, in a letter to A. P. Stanley, that although he had to read the *Fortnightly* every month to keep abreast of new intellectual developments, he never neglected to read the *Contemporary* as a "corrective."[58] The correspondence of Edward Dowden, who wrote on literature for the *Contemporary,* suggests the constraints on those contributors who did deal in nontheological subject areas: Dowden wrote to his brother John, the bishop of Edinburgh, that when he submitted his first article, on "French Aesthetics," Alford asked him to change the word *nude* to *unclothed*.[59] Dowden wanted to write on the poetry of Whitman, but feared that the article would be "out of place in such an English clerical company." He was right: after the article was already set in type, "Strahan and Dean Alford had a talk over it and decided it was too 'dangerous' to appear. . . . Poor Dean Alford . . . he always loved the safe and mediocre."[60]

By the autumn of 1866, there were rumors that the young *Review* would not survive its first year. Alford responded in November to a query from Henry Allon, the Congregationalist editor of the *British Quarterly Review*, by writing that he himself knew "nothing of the C.R. coming to an end."

> I have made my arrangements for the Jany number, and saw Strahan about it yesterday. And I have good promises from distinguished writers, quite enough for 3 months issue. . . . Our prospects are very good—sales moderate but good (about 2,000) and [we] are certainly doing a good work in & beyond the Ch. of England.[61]

Alford seems not to have realized that once again, Strahan was involved in more publishing ventures than Strahan and Company had resources to sustain.

One of these was the *Argosy*, a sixpenny monthly magazine that began publication in December 1865. Strahan always claimed to have projected the *Argosy:* "Not a few of the writers with whom I had formed connections," he wrote in his autobiographical essays, "wished for a publication in which topics could be treated with a freer literary manner than was quite practicable in *The Sunday Magazine* or even *Good Words*."[62] There is some mystery, then, in the fact that the *Argosy* was first advertised in October 1865 by Sampson Low, Son, and Marston, a firm that was a neighbor to Strahan and Company on Ludgate Hill. In addition to publishing a list of its own, this house served as a wholesale distributor for many other publishers, and had distributed *Good Words* for a time before Strahan and Company moved to London. The novelist Charles Reade, who was a contributor to the first volume of the *Argosy*, referred to Sampson Low, in a letter to his American publishers dated 13 October 1865, as Strahan's "agent on the matter."[63] This may mean that Sampson Low invested some capital in the venture and was granted in return the right to distribute the magazine and collect a commission. It is also possible that, as in the case of the *Sunday Magazine*, Strahan wished the *Argosy* to be well established before his connection with it was publicly proclaimed. For this was not the magazine that readers might anticipate from the publishers of *Good Words*, the *Sunday Magazine*, and *Christian Work Throughout the World*.

The first editor of the *Argosy* was Isa Craig (1831–1903), an Edinburgh-born poet who had already published under Strahan's imprint. Craig secured three contributions from her close friend, Christina Rossetti.[64] But her connection with the magazine seems to have been short-lived; and it was Strahan who enlisted the majority of contributors to what the earliest advertisements described as a "light Magazine Craft" and a "New Literary Adventure," under the epigraph, from Ben Jonson's *Leges Convivales,*

> Welcome, Learned, Urbane, Hilarious,
> Welcome, all the honest crew!
> And, to make our bliss more various,
> Welcome, choicest Ladies, too![65]

None of the contributors were ministers, although many—such as Alexander Smith, Sydney Dobell, Robert Buchanan, Jean Ingelow, Amelia B. Edwards, George MacDonald, and "Matthew Browne" (William Brighty Rands)—appeared regularly in Strahan's other periodicals. Anthony Trollope would contribute short stories to the issues for May, July, and September 1866. The main attraction, however, was the serialized novel: Reade's *Griffith Gaunt, or, Jealousy*, a tale of bigamy and suspected murder firmly in the tradition of "sensational" fiction. Three years earlier, Reade had been paid £300 when his novel *Hard Cash* was serialized in *All the Year Round*. For the right to serialize *Griffith Gaunt*, Reade was paid £1,500, a sum that enabled him to pay off his debts and achieve financial security for the first time in his career.[66] Small wonder, then, that in late 1865 he termed Strahan "the most honorable and liberal man" in the publishing trade.[67]

In April 1866, Strahan and Company publicly took over the helm of the *Argosy*, supplying the magazine with a new epigraph said to be from an "Old Play."

> An Argosy doth ride our roaring Strand,
> Spicing the wind, and freighted with the spoils
> Of all the Orient.

In a letter to Anthony Trollope, Strahan explained,

> I was the projector of it and I have now become the publisher and proprietor. Hitherto it has not done well, but it must do well yet for it is very good and very cheap. I mean to make a cabinet question of it, as they say in the House of Commons, and stand or fall by its success.[68]

In the same letter, Strahan summoned up the courage to suggest that Trollope might be willing to propose him for membership in the famous Garrick Club, which at various times included among its members Dickens, Thackeray, Wilkie Collins, George Meredith, D. G. Rossetti, J. E. Millais, and three figures who, according to Strahan, would be willing to second his nomination: Norman Macleod, Charles Reade, and Eneas Sweetland Dallas, the *Times* journalist.[69] Perhaps Strahan was aware that Trollope had successfully nominated George Smith to the Garrick in 1865.[70] "But if you don't think I would be a desirable member (as very likely I would not be)," added Strahan, "please let the matter drop and forgive me for suggesting it." Strahan never was to become a member of the Garrick.[71]

He was less diffident when it came to advertising the books and periodicals appearing under his imprint. In the same month that he acquired the *Argosy,* Strahan took out a hefty sixteen pages in advertisements in a single issue of the *Bookseller,* prompting that trade journal to rhapsodize that

> We have had many lengthy announcements in our pages, but the most extraordinary list put forward for many a day is that of Mr. Strahan's in our present number. The fertility of this publisher is marvellous. . . . Indeed, it appears to have been Mr. Strahan's ambition to give a book as well printed, on as good paper, and as neatly bound for six shillings as others give at fifteen, and this may partially account for his success.[72]

One book on this list—E. H. Plumptre's two-volume translation of the *Tragedies of Sophocles*—had already won glowing words of praise from G. H. Lewes, who wrote in the *Fortnightly* that it was "quite a pleasure to take up such an elegant volume," and referred to Strahan as "not only a publisher of great enterprise but of taste" who was, by publishing an English version of Sophocles, "venturing on what must be a considerable risk."[73]

However heady such praise may have been to Strahan, it could not have been so very reassuring to his growing list of creditors, which by the summer of 1866 included J. S. Virtue and Company, the printers of the *Fortnightly*. The manager and major proprietor of this firm, James Sprent Virtue (1829–92), represented, as did Thomas Spalding, the second generation of a family concern. His father George Virtue (1794–1868) had come from Scotland to establish himself as a bookseller on Ivy Lane, Paternoster Row, in the early 1820s. There was scant demarcation in those days between the trades of bookselling, printing, and publishing, and soon George Virtue was making a lucrative living from the publication of popular fiction and Nonconformist devotional literature, in both parts and volumes. He is best remembered, however, as a publisher of illustrated art and travel books and of the *Art Journal*, which he purchased in 1849. For the production of these works he installed expensive machinery in a business on City Road; there he served also as a printer to other publishers. In 1851 he established his eldest son, George Henry, as a partner in the publishing firm of Arthur Hall, Virtue, and Company; in 1855 he retired in favor of his second son, James Sprent, from the family businesses on Ivy Lane and City Road, which became known as J. S. Virtue and Company. In 1862, the partnership of Arthur Hall and George Henry Virtue was dissolved, and James Sprent and George Henry together established yet another publishing firm, Virtue Brothers and Company.[74]

J. S. Virtue was also concerned in the mid-1860s with the expansion of the printing business on City Road, an expansion that seems to have led to his involvement in the affairs of Strahan and Company in 1866. By then, Strahan and Company was in such dire straits that it required a more massive infusion of ready cash than Spalding and Hodge were willing to undertake alone. The earlier agreements of February 1863 and August 1864 were merged into a new one, dated 12 July 1866, whereby Spalding and Hodge agreed to lend £15,000; J. S. Virtue and Company was named as creditor for an additional £10,000.

All was secured by the copyrights to *Good Words*, the *Sunday Magazine*, the *Contemporary Review*, and the *Argosy;* the entire £25,000 was to be repaid by March 1870. Until then, Strahan and Company were to pay 8 percent interest annually, a rate 3 percent higher than that specified in the earlier agreements. Spalding and Hodge were to supply paper for all periodicals published by Strahan and Company; J. S. Virtue and Company were to print and bind them.[75]

James Virtue would soon have reason to fear that he had taken on more business than he could manage. Nine days after this agreement was signed, George Henry Virtue, his partner in Virtue Brothers and Company, died at the age of thirty-nine. James Virtue made plans to sell the publishing business to Edward Tinsley, a partner in Tinsley Brothers and Company. But once again, Virtue's luck was bad in the extreme. On the very day in September 1866 that the papers of sale were to be signed, Tinsley, who was only thirty-one, died of an attack of apoplexy, and Virtue was left once again with the problem of how to dispose of the book list of the now-defunct firm of Virtue Brothers and Company.[76] His burdens were not lightened when in October 1866 Strahan and Company proved unable to pay certain bills that had come due. It was arranged that Strahan and Company would be granted an additional six months in which to discharge these debts; meanwhile, Virtue was pressed into service as one of four "Inspectors" whose job it was to oversee the operations of the defaulting firm. The other inspectors were Thomas Spalding; his nephew Samuel Spalding, who was a partner in Spalding and Hodge; and Frederick Evans of the printing firm of Bradbury and Evans, who were also among Strahan's creditors.[77]

It may have been these difficulties with Strahan and Company that led indirectly to Virtue's decision, despite the catastrophes which had overtaken him during the autumn, to establish his own monthly magazine. The initial idea seems to have been that Virtue should take over the *Argosy* in exchange for releasing Strahan from a certain portion of his indebtedness to J. S. Virtue and Company. Virtue may well have reasoned that since he already printed the *Argosy,* he might as well print for himself as for a company that could not pay its bills. Practical considerations such as these, however, were overwhelmed by enthusiasm for the project itself when Virtue succeeded in persuading Anthony Trollope to take on the editorship.[78]

Virtue and Trollope were already well acquainted. It will be remembered that Trollope was one of the founders of the *Fortnightly Review,* which Virtue printed, and the two met regularly throughout 1866 at meetings of the editorial board of that periodical.[79] Virtue was in no doubt concerning Trollope's editorial expertise. But soon he was having second thoughts about the *Argosy,* which was encountering unexpectedly stormy weather on its maiden voyage.

The problem was with *Griffith Gaunt,* which was being serialized simultaneously in the *Argosy* and, in the United States, in the *Atlantic Monthly*. On 11 August 1866, the *London Review* reported that Reade's novel was being "condemned in the strongest possible manner" in the United States, and quoted at length the remarks of a New York paper, the *Round Table*.

> It is not too much to say that "Griffith Gaunt" is one of the worst novels that has appeared during this generation. . . . The novels of the day have been tending more and more toward the delineation of adultery, and bigamy, and seduction, and nameless social crimes; but most of them have preserved at least the appearance of reprehending vice. . . . The publishers have no right to use their Magazine to insult young girls and virtuous women by thrusting upon them what no modest woman can read without a blush. It is an unpardonable insult to public morality for publishers of long standing to promulgate a novel which we understand was declined by some of the lowest sensational weekly papers of New York on the grounds that they did not dare undertake its production.[80]

The squall might have been weathered, had not Charles Reade been, in the words of a contemporary, a "naturally irritable and disputatious" man, whose "self-conceit . . . seemed to amount to something like mania," and whose "impatience of criticism . . . occasionally rendered him all but a laughing-stock to the general public."[81] Reade noisily announced his intention of suing both the *Round Table* and the *London Review* for slander; to the *New York Times* he addressed an attack on his critics, "The Prurient Prude," which was published on 6 October 1866. Reade insisted that in *Griffith Gaunt* he depicted the misery resulting from the crime of bigamy "in my double character of moralist and artist."[82] The *Times* was unimpressed, and riposted with a review of *Griffith Gaunt* that charged that Reade had forsaken the "pure tone" of his earlier novel, *The Cloister and the Hearth,* in order to enter "the shallow and muddy channels in which Mrs. Braddon and her precious colleagues are wont to revel."[83]

Reade had better treatment from his own countrymen, who seem to have rallied to his defense against the impudent Yankees. The *Spectator* asserted that "there is not throughout the book one scene the most pure-minded woman might hesitate to read."[84] Edwin Arnold, the poet, praised *Griffith Gaunt* in the *Daily Telegraph* and then wrote to Reade that although "in morals they call me a Puritan . . . I lent the book to my sister when I had read it."[85] The *Saturday Review* addressed itself to the American critics, demanding, "Why should a novelist be limited in his work to the decorous passions of a thriving shopkeeper?" and then went on to make the startling assertion that "there is no more indecency in two wives than in one."[86] A gracious notice in the *London Review* apparently dissuaded Reade from suing that periodical.[87] But he pressed on in his suit against the *Round Table,* even after Charles Dickens declined to testify on his behalf: Dickens explained, in a letter to Wilkie Collins, that as the editor of a mass circulation magazine himself, he would have objected to such "coarse and disagreeable" situations as those depicted in *Griffith Gaunt.*[88] Reade would eventually win his suit against the *Round Table.* His recompense, however, would be not the £25,000 he sought, but a mere six cents American.[89]

Given Strahan's equanimity in the face of the *Record* attacks on *Good Words,* it might have been expected that he would welcome the publicity generated by Reade's altercations. But this particular roaring on the Strand seems to have been less to his taste. He would never again have dealings with Charles Reade, or attempt another foray into the lucrative field of "sensational" fiction. Far from seeking to capitalize on the reputation now attaching to the *Argosy,* Strahan filled the place of *Griffith Gaunt,* when that novel was concluded in the issue of November 1866, with the more placid story of *Robert Falconer,* by George MacDonald. By May, the *Illustrated London News* was complaining that *Robert Falconer* was "too Scotch and too theological for general appreciation";[90] a month later, the *News* returned to the subject to comment that many English readers would be "repelled" by the novel's "uncouth Scotch and endless homilies on theological topics."[91] The abrupt change in tone does not seem to have increased sales of the *Argosy,* which at the low price of sixpence would not have earned a profit until tens of thousands of copies had been sold. Already James Virtue had made his decision: in November 1866 he wrote to Trollope that "perhaps it would be better to start an entirely new Magazine."[92] In October 1867, a year and a half after vowing to "stand or fall by its success," Strahan sold the *Argosy* to Mrs. Henry Wood, who would raise the price of the magazine to one shilling, fill it with her own "sensational" fiction, and make it a highly profitable venture for many years to come.[93] In the same month, Virtue published the first issue of *Saint Pauls Magazine,* a shilling magazine "edited by Anthony Trollope," as all the advertisements proclaimed. Virtue hoped that

Saint Pauls might achieve a circulation in excess of twenty-five thousand;[94] before too many months had passed, he would be forced to recognize the folly of these calculations.

In the meantime, yet another firm was becoming entangled in the financial affairs of Strahan and Company. This was the publishing house of Bell and Daldy, founded in 1848 by George Bell (1814–90), a "zealous Churchman" who in 1855 took into partnership Frederic Richard Daldy. They published the *Mission Field*, which was the organ of the Society for the Propagation of the Gospel in Foreign Parts (SPGFP), as well as the *Gospel Missionary,* a periodical intended to interest children in the activities of the SPGFP. The average child probably preferred, however, their famous *Aunt Judy's Magazine,* which first appeared in 1866.[95]

It has already been mentioned that Bell and Daldy were closely connected with their stationers, Spalding and Hodge, and that Spalding and Hodge lent Bell and Daldy much of the money that they used to purchase Bohn's Library. In the late 1860s, Bell and Daldy were still discharging this debt. At the same time, the acquisition of the library, which included hundreds of volumes, so enlarged their publishing business that they found it necessary to dispose of their retail outlets. This left them in need of a distributing agency, and perhaps as a result of intervention on the part of Samuel Spalding, who would have been glad of any opportunity to improve the precarious financial situation of Strahan and Company, Bell and Daldy signed on 27 March 1867 an agreement whereby Strahan and Company undertook exclusive distribution of their books.[96] Bell and Daldy remained responsible for advertising their own publications; but the books were sold to Strahan and Company for resale—an arrangement sure to result, as the years passed, in Strahan and Company's growing indebtedness to Bell and Daldy, as Strahan took Bell and Daldy stock "on account," and then failed to pass on the proceeds of sale. Bell and Daldy would then be in a highly unenviable situation: if they were to refuse to supply any more books for distribution, their own imprint would suffer. But if they undertook any action that might undermine the delicate stability of Strahan and Company, Samuel Spalding, who was their own major creditor as well as the major creditor of Strahan and Company, would be sure to object.

Strahan was not the man to worry unduly about matters such as these. The one subject that did preoccupy him from 1867 on was the

Contemporary Review. He would later recall that "success did not come until there had been sunk in the venture more thousands of pounds than it is pleasant to think of. I believe that on the whole I kept my own hopes pretty intact but I think Dean Alford's now and then drooped a little."[97] In fact, Strahan seems to have displayed more deference toward Alford than toward Macleod, Guthrie, or Blaikie. But as he himself was not so great a lover as was Alford of "the safe and mediocre," it could not have pleased him that critics complained of the "preachy-preachiness" of the *Contemporary*, and circulation hovered at two thousand or less.[98]

By November 1867, Strahan had convinced Alford that there was cause for anxiety, and the good dean wrote to a friend that "a real effort will be wanted to carry on the 'Contemporary Review'; effort to catch the public interest worthily."[99] Strahan also arranged that Alford should be assisted by a joint editor, E. H. Plumptre, who may well have been responsible for securing from his brother-in-law, F. D. Maurice, two articles advocating the disestablishment of the Irish church (January and April, 1868). Plumptre sent off a virtual flurry of letters requesting contributions from W. E. Gladstone, leader of the Liberal opposition in Parliament and soon-to-be prime minister (as of December 1868); Gladstone was not to become a contributor to the *Contemporary*, however, until February 1874, when his first government would be near its end.[100] Plumptre was also disappointed in the case of the Anglican scholar F. J. A. Hort, who replied to Plumptre's request for contributions by hinting that his ideas would be too daring for Plumptre's readers: "Middle ways have less attraction for me than the attempt to combine extremes."[101]

Although Plumptre would resign his editorial position within half a year, there was nonetheless a steady widening of the *Contemporary's* tone and range dating from the autumn of 1867. Dean Alford, for all his latitudinarian sympathies, had failed to enlist more than a handful of contributors who were other than English-born Anglicans. Now there appeared a host of new contributors, including numerous Scots, whose opinions tended to be "Broader" than those of Alford's friends; a few of them had even written in the *Fortnightly Review*. The Reverend John Hunt, for example, was a Scot who had departed Presbyterianism to become one of the "Broadest" of Anglicans. From December 1867, he wrote so regularly for the *Contemporary* that he became in effect its primary spokesman on all matters theological; his books were also published by Strahan.[102] Another new contributor was Peter Bayne, the Ross-shire native and Free Church minister who had been Hugh Miller's assistant on the *Witness* while Strahan was an apprentice at Johnstone and Hunter. In the early 1860s Bayne came to London, where he edited the *Weekly Review* until the proprietors of that paper discovered him to be "unsound on inspiration" and "tainted with rationalism." Bayne then became a contributor to the *Fortnightly*, where he praised such controversial works as Strauss's second life of Jesus. Bayne's combination of broad-minded liberalism and earnest evangelicalism was typical of many other clerics in Strahan's immediate circle; and from November 1867, he abandoned the *Fortnightly* to become a regular in the *Contemporary*.[103] In 1871, Strahan would publish Bayne's *Life and Letters of Hugh Miller*. Then there was the eccentric William Brighty Rands, one of Strahan's few close personal friends who was a native of England. Rands, the son of a candlemaker, had been raised a Calvinist dissenter, and had educated himself by peripatetic reading in secondhand bookshops. A sometime Congregationalist minister in Brixton, Rands was probably, in terms of sheer number of pages, the most prolific of all contributors to Strahan's various periodicals, although he usually wrote under pseudonyms such as "Matthew Browne." The bulk of his contributions to the *Contemporary* appeared after 1867.[104]

Strahan was in pursuit of greater names than these for his general publishing list, however. Sometime in 1867 he sent George MacDonald as his emissary, authorized to offer "fabulous terms" to Robert Browning for *The Ring and the Book*. But, as Browning explained it all years later to a friend, he rejected Strahan's overtures, partly out of distrust for "such 'monts et merveilles'—or as the Italians phrase it, 'promises of Roma e Toma.'"[105]

Thanks to the influence of Norman Macleod, there were few such rebuffs in the case of *Good Words*. On 1 November 1867, there was a dinner in London in honor of Macleod, who was about to depart on a seven-month tour of the Church of Scotland's Missions to the Heathen in India, and who was anxious that *Good Words* should not lack for illustrious contributors in his absence. Dean Alford was in the chair; E. H. Plumptre and George MacDonald were among the speakers. Strahan was present, of course, as were his major creditors, Thomas Spalding and J. S. Virtue. Anthony Trollope sent a letter expressing his regret at being unable to attend. So, too, did George

Douglas Campbell, the eighth duke of Argyll, who at about this time was assisting Macleod in his search for contributors.[106]

Argyll (1823–1900) was that rare creature, a lord who was none-theless a devout communicant of the Church of Scotland. He was also, in the tradition of his family, an active politician: he served in the cabinets of Aberdeen and Palmerston (1852–55, 1859–66) alongside Gladstone and was closely allied with Gladstone throughout the 1860s, a decade that saw the birth and coming of age of the Liberal party. Argyll's son would marry a daughter of Victoria, and in court circles he regularly encountered his fellow Highlander, Macleod. In what spare time was left to him, Argyll wrote treatises intended to reconcile the findings of science with the teachings of Revelation, a hobby which involved him in many a bitter dispute with scientists such as T. H. Huxley. One of these works—*The Reign of Law*—was se-rialized in *Good Words* in 1865 before being published by Strahan in volume form in 1867; Strahan would continue to accord it a place of honor on his lists through the sixteenth edition (1884). The 1868 volume of *Good Words* would include Argyll's *Recent Speculations on Primeval Man*, a challenge to Darwinian theories. The issues for Janu-ary, February, and April would include, as well, a three-part serial essay by Gladstone, apparently secured by Argyll.[107]

Gladstone chose to begin what would be a lengthy connection with Strahan's periodicals by mounting a defense of *Ecce Homo* (1865), an anonymous life of Christ (actually written by John Robert Seeley, the historian) that angered orthodox and atheistic thinkers alike by its emphasis on the humanity of Jesus and on the ethical rather than the supernatural teachings of the New Testament. The earl of Shaftes-bury denounced *Ecce Homo* as the "most pestilential book . . . ever vomited from the jaws of hell."[108] But Gladstone, whose well-known personal piety was one of his greatest political assets, argued that the Gospels themselves taught Revelation by presenting Christ in his human aspect, and that "such a mode of treatment" was "eminently suited to the exigencies of the present time."[109] Soon Connop Thirl-wall was writing to A. P. Stanley to express his satisfaction that "Glad-stone has taken up the pen in defense of 'Ecce Homo'"; Thirlwall was particularly pleased that "the defense appears in a very orthodox Presbyterian magazine."[110]

Meanwhile, on 21 December 1867, Strahan wrote to his new con-tributor to express his "honour" at being called to a personal interview: "It will be difficult for me to summon up courage enough to present myself at Carlton House Terrace."[111] Apparently the two men discussed common acquaintances as well as financial arrangements: when Strahan wrote again, on 18 January, he referred to the possibility that Gladstone might write future articles for *Good Words* on "the subject suggested by Dr. Macleod to the Duchess of Argyll." Strahan also mentioned the sum of £1,000 to be paid for the series on *Ecce Homo* and for the right to republish it in volume form.[112]

Soon Strahan's advertisements would be proclaiming that the January issue of *Good Words* had run through three very large editions.[113] These sales were not, however, to be explained entirely by the excitement generated by Gladstone's article. For there was a second great name in this issue, that of Alfred Tennyson, the poet laureate, who was, like Gladstone, a friend of both Macleod and Argyll. In his discussion of *The Reign of Law*, Argyll had included a number of quotations from Tennyson's poetry, so it is not surprising that in June 1867, according to Mrs. Tennyson's journal, she was deeply engrossed in reading Argyll's book, which had just been published in volume form by Strahan and Company.[114] In October, the Tennysons together were reading yet another volume that had been serialized in *Good Words* before being published separately under Strahan's imprint: Macleod's *Reminiscences of a Highland Parish*.[115]

It was at about this time that Argyll and Macleod were working together to secure contributions for the 1868 volume, and on 5 December, Mrs. Tennyson recorded in her journal that "By A's desire I send 'The Victim' off to *Good Words*."[116] Its appearance in the January issue marked the first stage in a process that would lead to Tennyson's becoming, within a year's time, the brightest star on Strahan's publishing list. The Tennyson contract was not a prize to be won easily or cheaply, and there is reason to believe that Strahan lost money on it. But it did carry with it one incidental benefit: through Tennyson, Strahan would come to know James Thomas Knowles, an architect from Clapham who had recently become a trusted family friend of the Tennysons; and in time, Knowles would take on more and more of the responsibility for attracting famous contributors to the *Contemporary Review*.

CHAPTER VI

All the Best Men: The Fortunes of Strahan and Company, 1868–72

All we want is, a fair field, and no favour.
—Alexander Strahan, January 1866[1]

James Thomas Knowles (1831–1908), Victorian architect and editor, was also a social climber of genius; dozens of memoirs and letters testify to the fact.[2] In the early 1870s, Laura Forster, sharp-tongued aunt of E. M. Forster and a neighbor of Knowles's at Clapham, wrote to Miss Henrietta Darwin that the "wonderfully good natured" Knowles, although "a snob," was the perfect dinner guest: "I am more and more struck with what good talk he draws out; he doesn't shine himself but there is sure to be light in his neighbourhood." Not that Knowles was reluctant to speak on his own account. Forster records that he

> liked talking nonsense about great people every bit as [much as] we did hearing him. So he went on assuring us that [Henry Edward] Manning was a really good fellow to whom he, Knowles could speak his mind, and that he should insist on Gladstone doing this that and the other.[3]

John Stuart Blackie was a witness to Knowles's friendship with the prime minister: in 1872, Blackie wrote to his wife that at Gladstone's home he had encountered "Knowles, an architect, who is always there when I am there, which made me mistake him for Gladstone's secretary."[4] The mistake was understandable, if credence be given to the witty, waspish description of Knowles provided by T. H. S. Escott who, writing anonymously in 1885, attributed to Knowles "the same craze for social omniscience which I have repeatedly observed among the private secretaries of Ministers or the more aspiring of Foreign Office clerks." According to Escott, Knowles brought to his editorial work a keen sense of "the order of social precedence": "Dukes and

marquises first, then peers of inferior degree, then bishops and phi-
losophers, the procession being wound up by any poor devils who
have contrived to puff themselves into momentary novelty."[5] When
Knowles died in 1908, the *Times* would remark that he had been "seen
everywhere,"

> and though some people resented this ubiquity on the part of a mere
> editor, and some failed to understand how a man who was an authority
> neither in literature nor in politics could wield such literary and political
> influence, the influence was undoubtedly there.[6]

But Knowles had not been born to hobnob with dukes and prime
ministers any more than Strahan had been. His father James Thomas
Knowles, Sr. (1806–84), the descendant of six straight generations of
glaziers, had risen in the world to become the wealthy proprietor of a
building and architectural firm; still, Knowles Senior was not of the
social class to send his son to university, and James Knowles became
an apprentice in the family firm at the age of fifteen. He was already
aware of the social implications, in those days before architecture had
become a respected profession distinct from building work, and in
later life he would recall feeling

> more and more that my abominably neglected schooling must be re-
> paired or supplemented by something, as I was not to go to Oxford or
> Cambridge. . . . I was ashamed wherever I went, finding I had no foun-
> dation, as it were, to stand upon, had done nothing and had seen
> nothing.[7]

As it turned out, Knowles was to make his building and architectural
practice a springboard to better things. But when in 1877 he and
Strahan fell to bitter quarreling over the conduct of the *Contemporary
Review*, Strahan knew how to draw blood: he wrote to Knowles that at
the time Knowles began to work on the *Contemporary*, "you had no
more experience of Magazine Editing or of editing of any kind, than I
had of brick-laying."[8]

If Strahan meant to suggest that Knowles had no such experience
whatsoever, he was mistaken. For during the 1850s—the same decade
in which Strahan was working his way up in the Edinburgh publishing
world—Knowles, thoroughly bored with his apprenticeship, was in
his spare time developing the talent for promoting intellectual debate

which was to serve him so well in years to come. Knowles was founder and joint editor, along with a friend, of the short-lived *Clapham Magazine*, which appeared in November 1850 proclaiming a desire to forward "the mutual instruction of its contributors and readers" and promising a "fair field" for the expression of *"diverse or opposite opinions."*[9] When the magazine ceased publication after only three issues, Knowles, nothing daunted, founded a group that met regularly to discuss "music, art, philosophy—in fact, everything."[10]

Knowles was also attempting to educate himself in literature. His greatest living hero was the poet laureate, to whom he referred as the "divine Alfred"; and when the first *Idylls of the King* appeared in 1859, Knowles was inspired to compile from Malory a volume for boys entitled *The Story of King Arthur and His Knights of the Round Table*. It appeared in 1861, dedicated by permission to Tennyson. In the course of the next few years, Knowles did his best to reinforce this slight connection, dispatching letters and even presents until, in January 1866, Tennyson wrote to request that Knowles refrain at least from gift giving: "You are laying a heap of obligations upon me which I cannot return & as I am not your enemy 'the coals of fire' can be of no object to you."[11] Someone less determined might have given up these attempts to force a friendship. Knowles managed, within the year, to pay his first personal visit to the Tennysons.

The meeting was facilitated by the fact that Knowles and Tennyson had a friend in common: Dr. Charles Pritchard, a pioneer in stellar photography who was to become in 1870 Savilian Professor of Astronomy at Oxford. From 1834 to 1862 Pritchard was headmaster of the Clapham Grammar School, and although Knowles did not attend the school, he knew Pritchard in the community. Pritchard was also neighbor to the Tennysons: in the 1860s he maintained a home on the Isle of Wight, not far from the Tennysons' home, "Farringford"; and since Pritchard, who had been ordained in the Anglican church, shared with Tennyson an interest in the harmonization of science and religion, the two came to be frequent companions.[12]

Knowles arrived on the Isle of Wight, ostensibly to visit Pritchard, in October 1866. By his own account, Knowles determined to call on Tennyson in order "to thank him personally for what he had written to me" in the preceding years.[13] Whatever exasperation Tennyson may have felt when Knowles was announced, he must have found the younger man to be excellent company, as they sat together in the poet's attic study discussing "King Arthur . . . a subject of common interest and sympathy";[14] or perhaps Tennyson was merely beginning to see the futility of resisting his amiable but persistent admirer. The Tennysons had purchased land to build a second home on Blackdown, Sussex; and Emily Tennyson's journal entry for 16 June 1867 summarizes with comic brusqueness the next stage in their relationship with Knowles, whom Tennyson encountered accidentally while on a visit to inspect his new property.

> A. met Mr. Knowles at the [railway] Station. When he was at Farringford A. had said to him as he does to most strangers, "I am so shortsighted that I shall not know you if I meet you unless you speak to me." Mr. Knowles accordingly spoke to him, reminding him of this. Having then been told A's errand [he] said I am an architect. A. replied, you had better build me a house, & Mr. Knowles said "On one condition that you take my services freely only paying the journeys." Afterwards this was agreed upon.[15]

The foundation stone for "Aldworth" was laid on 23 April 1868, a date chosen because it was Shakespeare's birthday; the Tennysons moved into their new home in July 1869. By then Knowles had become general factotum to Tennyson and host to the poet whenever he had business in London, an arrangement that immensely improved Knowles's prospects: according to the most recent biography of Tennyson, the poet's friends, having been Knowles's guests in Clapham while Tennyson was in residence, had no choice but to grant Knowles access to their own tables, even though "many disliked having him constantly riding on Tennyson's coat-tails"; Francis Turner Palgrave, for example, referred to Knowles as Tennyson's "keeper."[16]

Meanwhile, Tennyson was annoyed by a series of disagreements with Moxon and Company, who had published his work since 1832. Tennyson had been on terms of friendship with that firm's founder, Edward Moxon, who also maintained close personal connections with his stationers, Spalding and Hodge, and with his printers, Bradbury and Evans.[17] When Moxon died in 1858 and the management of the firm was taken over by Bradbury and Evans, Tennyson considered a change of publishers. His discussions with Alexander Macmillan, who published the work of Tennyson's close friend F. D. Maurice, led to the appearance of "Sea Dreams: An Idyll" in *Macmillan's Magazine* for January 1860.[18] But when Frederick Evans, pleading the financial

interests of Moxon's widow and son, protested that if Tennyson were
to abandon the firm of Moxon it would collapse, Tennyson decided to
remain where he was for the time being.[19]

The real trouble began when J. Bertrand Payne replaced Bradbury
and Evans as the manager of Moxon and Company in 1864. In the
same year, publication of *Enoch Arden and Other Poems* prompted some
reviewers to hail Tennyson as a "Poet of the People," and Tennyson,
greatly flattered, arranged for Moxon and Company to issue a selection of his poems in eight sixpenny parts dedicated to the working
men of England. When Payne insisted that *A Selection from the Works of
Alfred Tennyson* should also be published in a five-shilling volume, the
poet gave his reluctant consent. But when the volume appeared, Tennyson was disgusted by what he regarded as its too highly ornamental
style.[20] In 1867, Tennyson was annoyed to find inaccuracies to his
own detriment in the Moxon accounts. Further angered by gossip
that the firm might be in financial difficulties, he addressed to Payne
an ominous letter, dated 26 September 1867.

> I did not choose to bother you but when it came to a rumour that your
> house had actually failed I considered that my best and handsomest
> course was to apply directly to yourself—Seeing that I have stuck to the
> house of Moxon from the beginning thro' evil report & good report, &
> REALLY HAVE BEEN & AM THE MAIN PILLAR OF IT, it seems to
> me—that I should be fully informed of the state of affairs.[21]

In the first few months of 1868 Tennyson allowed five of his poems
to appear in periodicals: "The Victim" and "1865–66" in *Good Words*
(January, March); "The Spiteful Letter" in *Once a Week*, a periodical
owned and published by Bradbury and Evans (January); and "Wages"
and "Lucretius" in *Macmillan's*, which by this time was being edited by
George Grove (February, May). An exasperated Mrs. Tennyson, who
objected to the publication of her husband's poems in the periodical
press prior to their appearance in volume form, was soon fielding
correspondence from other importunate editors; to one of these she
explained that Tennyson had

> yielded to the entreaties of friends that he would do what he could to
> relieve Dr. Norman Macleod's mind of anxiety during his Indian mis-
> sion, then his friend Mr. Grove would be hurt if he refused, then his
> printers must have something.[22]

It seems likely, however, that Tennyson was motivated by more than mere friendship. Once again he was considering a change of publishers, and once again, Payne gave cause for offense. For some time Payne had been urging Tennyson to allow publication of a four-volume standard edition of his works, and although Tennyson doubted that the poems could be stretched out sufficiently to fill four honest volumes, he might have been persuaded to agree to some sort of collected edition had not Payne begun advertising the four-volume edition he intended even before the Tennysons made up their minds. Mrs. Tennyson's journal entries for March 1868 record that they were distressed partly because the advertisements seemed dishonestly to suggest that some new poems would be included, partly by the general tone of the publicity. She was particularly anxious that Payne's "love of excitement" should not "mislead the public" into supposing that Tennyson was concerned above all with "enriching" himself; to one close friend, the sculptor Thomas Woolner, she wrote, "What I do really care for is that my Ally should stand before the world in his own childlike simplicity and by this he would be made to appear a mere low, cunning tradesman and it shall not be if I can help it."[23] Payne may not have realized it yet, but by his premature advertising he had ensured that the standard edition of Tennyson's poems that he envisioned would never appear under Moxon's imprint.

Yet for all her bitter complaints against Payne, even Mrs. Tennyson must have realized that he was not entirely to blame for the public ridicule that came Tennyson's way in 1868. Indeed, Payne's advertising may have been prompted by the fact that new poems by Tennyson were appearing in the periodical press at this time; and while Alexander Strahan boasted to all and sundry of the huge amounts he had paid to secure his prizes (£700 for "The Victim" alone),[24] readers were remarking their poor quality. Browning expressed his dismay to William Rossetti; Swinburne wrote to R. Monckton Milnes, the first Lord Houghton, to ask whether Houghton, a friend of Tennyson's, could not prevent the laureate from "making such a hideous exhibition of himself. . . . *I* blush, and avert my eyes with disgust and pity."[25] The Tennysons themselves were distressed by the appearance of a number of parodies of the poems, including one that made fun of the advertising campaigns mounted by Strahan and by Bradbury and Evans.

1867–1868

I sat in a 'bus in the wet,
"Good Words" I had happened to get,
  With Tennyson's last bestowing;
And I said, "O bard! who works so hard,
  Have ye aught that is worth the knowing?"

Verses enough and so boring,
  Twaddle quite overflowing,
Rubbish enough for deploring;
  But aught that is worth the knowing?
Placards on walls were glowing,
  Puffs in the paper pouring,
"Good Words" roaring and blowing,
  "Once a Week" blowing and roaring!

Another parody suggested that "the Editor knows ere now, I suppose / That *he* is the victim."[26] In fact, Strahan was in no way displeased, either by the poetry or by the publicity; and when he learned from F. D. Maurice, who in the spring of 1868 was a contributor to the *Contemporary Review,* that Tennyson was in search of a new publisher, Strahan seems to have determined to pay whatever price was necessary to add the poet laureate to his list.[27] Thomas Spalding and Frederick Evans, who had long supplied the paper and done the printing for the volumes by Tennyson that appeared under Moxon's imprint, would probably have used on Strahan's behalf whatever influence they had with the poet; for it will be remembered that both men were among Strahan's creditors in the late 1860s.

Yet Strahan was not the clear front-runner in the competition to win the Tennyson contract. One of the correspondents to whom Tennyson complained concerning Payne's "tremendous style" of advertising was Alexander Macmillan, and in June, while on a visit to Knowles's home, Tennyson met with Macmillan.[28] The conjunction of people and events led Tennyson to discover that his architect had talents in addition to house building: Knowles, who naturally handled most of the business connected with Aldworth, now proved more than willing to undertake much of the drudgery and legwork involved in Tennyson's publishing negotiations. Macmillan's offer, when it came, was £3,000 per annum for the right to publish works that had already appeared; presumably he was also prepared to give Tennyson at least as generous a share of the profits on new works as Moxon and Company had always done.[29] But Strahan was not to be outbid so easily. At some point he hurried to the Isle of Wight where, closeted with Tennyson in the attic study until four in the morning, he made his proposals amid clouds of tobacco smoke. For the right to publish old works Strahan offered £5,000 per annum for five years to come. As for new works, Tennyson was, in effect, to be his own publisher, paying all expenses of production and pocketing all earnings; Strahan was content that his imprint should appear on the volumes, which he proposed to produce and distribute to retailers without even deducting a commission from the proceeds of sale. Tennyson, "staggered" by these terms, attempted to persuade Strahan that he could not afford to be so generous, and that a commission on new works would be entirely reasonable.[30] Unlike Browning before him, Tennyson was not ready to reject his eager suitor out of hand. But he did take his time deciding; and as the summer dragged on without a contract being signed, it is likely that Strahan had many occasions to discuss the negotiations with Tennyson's agent, James Knowles.

In the meantime, Strahan did his best to keep up the Gladstone connection. In late June, he sent Gladstone the July issue of the *Contemporary*, "containing an article which has special reference to yourself."[31] This was "Mr. Gladstone's Position," by Bernard Cracroft, a barrister who praised Gladstone's public statements on behalf of the lower classes. "I know you set no great store on newspaper or review criticisms," wrote Strahan in the covering letter, "but perhaps this article, expressing as it does the deep convictions of Writer, Editor, and Publisher alike, may have the fortune to be in some degree exceptional."

Perhaps it seemed to Norman Macleod—who returned from India, greatly fatigued, in the same month that this letter was written— that a publisher who could directly approach a Tennyson or a Gladstone would have far less need than before for the influence of a queen's chaplain. Strahan would later recall that at about this time he and Macleod were debating which of them should solicit a contribution for *Good Words* from the then bishop of Oxford, Samuel Wilberforce. Macleod, "choosing for the moment to ignore the fact of his own connection with court circles," said, in his drollest manner, " 'No, no, a plain Scotch parson mustn't pretend to rub shoulders with these English Church dignitaries. Try your own hand at it. In fact, regarded as possible contributors, I make you a present of the whole bench of bishops!'"[32] Strahan made good use of his "present." Wilberforce became a regular contributor; and by October 1868, a speaker at the annual congress of the Church of England was remarking that *Good Words*

> gives for sixpence the original thoughts, not only of men who are foremost in the republic of letters, but [also of] those who are highest in rank in both Church and State. . . . The staple of the religious teaching . . . is given by bishops and deans, doctors and divines, of the Established Church.[33]

Never mind that this same speaker went on to comment that both *Good Words* and the *Sunday Magazine* were edited by Presbyterians, and to express his apprehension, "looking at it from a clerical standpoint," that in these periodicals differences between the systems and beliefs of Presbyterians and Anglicans might be "glossed over" to an extent unacceptable to the Establishment. For years to come, Strahan would cite the first portion of his remarks in advertisements for *Good Words*. Times had changed since 1865, when Margaret Oliphant wrote to her regular publisher, John Blackwood, proprietor of *Blackwood's Magazine,* to report that she had been offered £1,000 for a story to be serialized in *Good Words:* "Of course it is a little tempting . . . but . . . if you have any dislike to seeing the name of your contributor in Dr. Macleod's somewhat ragged regiment, I will not think of it further."[34] Now, in 1868, Henry Kingsley wrote to his publisher, Macmillan, to plead,

> Will you let me write one little article for *Good Words?* It will scarcely interfere with what I have to do for you, but it gives me prestige. They are whipping in all the best men, and they have sent to me (observe the modesty of this, will you).[35]

Strahan could still find the occasional use for Macleod's name. In mid-October, for example, he was advertising a new sixpenny monthly for children, *Good Words for the Young,* which was to appear with the November magazines, and which was said to be "Edited by Norman Macleod." In fact, the ailing Macleod probably had little to do with this venture. Most of the featured contributors already wrote for *Good Words* or for the *Sunday Magazine,* and the main serial attraction was, not another of Macleod's pious fictions for children, but rather George MacDonald's "faerie-allegory," *At the Back of the North Wind.* During the same weeks, Strahan's other advertisements gave evidence of an important new alliance: Knowles's book for boys, retitled *The Legends of King Arthur,* was about to be republished under Strahan's imprint. Perhaps Knowles carried messages from Strahan when, on 24 October, he and his wife crossed over to the Isle of Wight for a two-day visit to Farringford.[36] At any rate, Strahan soon received the signal he had been awaiting: on 1 November, Mrs. Tennyson confided to her journal that she was sending off "a letter to Mr. Strahan in answer to his liberal offers." On 11 November, Tennyson was off to Clapham, where he would remain for several weeks "on publishing business."[37]

It was a very busy time. On 13 November Strahan came to dinner and boasted so vociferously that Tennyson, who feared Strahan might not be able to live up to his generous promises, recorded the publisher's remarks in his letter diary: Strahan, wrote Tennyson, "quite laughs at all [our] warnings. . . . Strahan asserts that he makes a clear profit of £7,000 a year by *Good Words* alone, and that my business would bring no end of grist to his mill."[38] After dinner Tennyson read aloud "The Holy Grail," and Strahan took away a copy of the new poem in order to have it printed. On the morning of the fourteenth, Tennyson read "The Holy Grail" to another visitor, Robert Browning, who returned in the evening along with Alexander Macmillan. Browning read aloud from *The Ring and the Book,* which Tennyson found to be so "full of strange vigour and remarkable in many ways" that he doubted "whether it can ever be popular."[39] Browning was asked but declined to join a dinner-cum-debating club that Knowles was planning, and that was clearly intended to be a major league version of the group he had conducted in the early 1850s. Knowles would later recall that it was Tennyson who provided the impetus for the new group during his visit of November 1868.

> While King Arthur was being so much and so frequently discussed between us the mystical meanings of the Poem led to almost endless talk on speculative metaphysical subjects—God—the Soul—free will—Necessity—Matter & spirit—& all the circle of Metaphysical enquiry.

Tennyson expressed the wish that these subjects could be "debated by capable men in the manner & with the machinery of the learned

Societies"; and the obliging Knowles replied that if Tennyson would join such a group, he himself would endeavor to get it up.[40]

On 23 November, Tennyson recorded in his letter diary that the agreement with Strahan was ready for signature.[41] Apparently Strahan had been prevailed upon to curb his generous impulses, for the final agreement specified that Strahan should pay for the right to publish old works, not £5,000 but £4,000 per annum, and that Strahan and Company should deduct a commission of 5 percent on the proceeds from new works. Another clause granted Tennyson a veto over "distasteful" advertisements.[42] Meanwhile Mrs. Tennyson was writing from Farringford to insist that her husband refuse to contribute any more poems to *Good Words:* "Make a stand at once; it may save future trouble."[43] It must have been at about this time that Strahan rushed into the office of his fellow publisher, William Tinsley, "all excitement because he had signed an agreement with Tennyson to publish his books for a certain number of years, and boasted that he had gained the blue ribbon of the publishing trade."[44] Soon Strahan had still more cause for celebration: on 1 December, following the Liberal victories in the parliamentary elections, Gladstone was requested by the queen to form his first government. Within days the advertisements of Strahan and Company were proclaiming that "on and after January 15th, 1869, all of Mr. TENNYSON'S WORKS will ISSUE FROM THEIR HOUSE," and that the second edition of the new prime minister's essays "On 'Ecce Homo'" was to be obtained from the same source.

Even as these momentous events were unfolding, Strahan did not neglect his developing relationship with James Knowles. When the *Contemporary Review* for February 1869 appeared, it included an article on the "Alternation of Science and Art in History," signed "J.T.K." Knowles's biographer suggests that the article "has perhaps been too much dignified in retrospect as 'neo-Hegelian'";[45] in fact, it consists of little more than a naive tabulation of alternating periods of analysis (science) and synthesis (art), which Knowles purports to trace throughout both the history of the individual and the history of mankind. Knowles concludes his panoramic saga of "the human mind," its "wanderings, its progress" with the hope that if his "view have any truth in it," "the fashionable materialism of the hour" will be only the prelude to an opening of "the golden gates of the twentieth century of Art and Poetry and Faith."[46] Strahan also allowed himself to be drawn into the planning for an introductory reading book for children, to be prepared by Knowles's Clapham neighbors, Henrietta Synnot and her aunt Marianne Thornton. According to a letter written by Miss Thornton, Knowles declared that Strahan "would take twice as much interest" in the book if only the ladies would invite him to dinner; but the project came to nothing when Henrietta, who had met Strahan at Knowles's home, "declared he was too dirty a little bookseller to sit by a clean table cloth."[47]

Certainly there was no idea of including Strahan in Knowles's new discussion group, which by this time had been christened the "Metaphysical Society."[48] With Tennyson's help, Knowles enlisted an impressive array of well-known figures, including A. P. Stanley, dean of Westminster; Henry Alford, dean of Canterbury and editor of the *Contemporary*; J. R. Seeley, professor of Modern History at Cambridge from 1869 and author of *Ecce Homo;* George Grove, editor of *Macmillan's;* James Martineau, the leading Unitarian theologian of the day; R. H. Hutton, the Unitarian coeditor of the *Spectator;* Walter Bagehot, editor of the *Economist,* who was perhaps Hutton's closest friend; James Hinton, a mystic Unitarian philosopher whose ideas were greatly admired by Tennyson; Henry Edward Manning, the Catholic archbishop of Westminster; W. G. Ward, Manning's close friend and editor of the *Dublin Review;* T. H. Huxley and John Tyndall, scientists well known for their hostility to Christian belief; and Prime Minister W. E. Gladstone. The society held its first meeting at the Westminster Deanery on 2 June 1869. Tennyson was not present; but he did send "The Higher Pantheism," rewritten for the occasion, to be read aloud by Knowles.

Sir James Fitzjames Stephen, who became a member of the Metaphysical Society in 1873, always maintained that Knowles formed the group for the sole purpose of answering Tennyson's doubts concerning immortality.[49] Knowles, a lifelong Anglican whose first wife was the daughter of a vicar, seems not to have been troubled by such questions: in 1876, in a letter to Gladstone, he would assert that he himself "should be more than satisfied with theism."[50] Wilfrid Ward, son of W. G. Ward, thought that "the philosophy of religious belief had no special interest" for Knowles. "But accident led him to discover that the subject had at that moment very special interest for a large number of exceedingly eminent and representative men."[51] Sir Frederick Pollock, the jurist, who became a member of the society in 1879, assumed that Knowles started the group with half an eye to business; but

Knowles was also motivated, according to Pollock, by the belief that if men of differing opinions could only be brought together on neutral ground to discuss their ideas, "the ultimate truth, or a sure clue to it would somehow emerge." Commented Pollock, "Such an expectation is of course . . . exceedingly simple-minded in the eyes of anyone who has attempted a serious study of philosophical questions, which Knowles had not."[52] It was a simpleminded expectation shared, however, by the publisher of the *Contemporary Review;* and given Strahan's usual practice of attaching himself to individuals with entrée to social circles closed to himself, it is likely that he followed with interest the progress of Knowles's society.

Strahan was also concerned, in the spring of 1869, with the sudden expansion of Strahan and Company as a result of James Virtue's determination to diminish his own publishing activities. Virtue had still not succeeded in selling the stock and copyrights of Virtue Brothers and Company, a firm defunct since the death of George Henry Virtue in 1866. Early in 1869 he was also attempting to sell, to the firm of Chapman and Hall, *Saint Pauls Magazine,* which he had launched with so much enthusiasm in 1867 under his own imprint (Virtue and Company of Ivy Lane), and which had been losing money ever since.[53] By May, however, Chapman and Hall had decided against the purchase. Virtue's solution—to transfer to Strahan and Company, not only the magazine, but also all the other titles published either under his own imprint, or, in the past, under the imprint of Virtue Brothers—could not have been a financially remunerative one: Strahan already owed Virtue many thousands of pounds, and all that Virtue seems to have gained from this latest transaction, aside from the relief of supposing that the magazine and the two book lists would now be managed by someone else, was a greater financial interest than ever before in Strahan's business.[54]

Nor is it likely that Anthony Trollope, the editor of *Saint Pauls,* was particularly well pleased with these arrangements. Since the *Rachel Ray* episode six years earlier, Trollope had had occasional dealings with Strahan, and in 1867, Strahan undertook publication of a number of stories by Trollope, including some that had appeared in *Good Words* or the *Argosy.* But Strahan misjudged his man when he neglected to tell Trollope until after the stories were set in type that he had decided to issue them in two volumes rather than in the single volume that had been agreed upon—a tactic that would nearly double the retail price.

"This will enable me," explained Strahan, "to spend a good deal more in advertising it and making it more widely known. And if I make a little more profit to myself I am sure you will not object." Trollope's reply took the form of a vigorous scolding in which he asserted that he had always "endeavored to give good measure to the public";[55] and when *Lotta Schmidt, and Other Stories* appeared in August 1867, it was in a single volume. This had been the only title by Trollope on Strahan's list. But in May 1869, as soon as he acquired the Trollope copyrights that had been among Virtue's stock, Strahan proudly began advertising the fact that henceforth *Phineas Finn* and *He Knew He Was Right* would appear under the *Anchora Spei*.

While Strahan was thus increasing his indebtedness to Virtue, his other major creditors, the papermaking and stationery firm of Spalding and Hodge, were deciding it was high time that some of the £15,000 and more owing them should be repaid. As usual, it seems to have been out of the question that Strahan should accomplish this feat on his own; and so Spalding and Hodge turned for assistance to the firm of Bell and Daldy, which was itself heavily in debt to Spalding and Hodge, and which had already, in 1867, entered into the agreement whereby Strahan and Company served as the distributor of volumes published under the Bell and Daldy imprint. Now, in the absence of George Bell, who was away from the business for some time in 1869 due to illness, a representative of Spalding and Hodge persuaded F. R. Daldy that it would be a profitable venture to take over some of the "management" of Strahan and Company, while at the same time guaranteeing payment of £10,000 of the amount due Spalding and Hodge by Strahan and Company.[56] Surviving documents show how it was probably arranged. By early September, it had been agreed that Bell and Daldy should "purchase" from Strahan and Company £8,000 worth of copyrights and stock; for another £6,000, they were to have the right to issue what would be the first collected edition of the works of Tennyson. The £4,000 over and above the £10,000 intended for Spalding and Hodge would probably have gone to liquidate some of the debt that Strahan and Company had built up to Bell and Daldy by their practice of taking Bell and Daldy books on credit for distribution, and then neglecting to pass on to Bell and Daldy the proceeds of sales. The new arrangements were effected, not by cash payments, but by promises all around to pay at some later date. There was, however, one immediate problem: according to a memo from Strahan and Company to Bell and Daldy, Tennyson had "insuperable objections to another change of publisher, or what would appear as such to the public."[57] The solution which emerged, after some discussion with Tennyson, was that although Bell and Daldy would issue and collect the profits from what is now known as the ten-volume "Pocket" or "Miniature" edition, which appeared in 1870 and sold for £2 5s., the edition was to be published under the imprint of Strahan and Company.[58]

In December 1869, just in time for the Christmas trade, two other volumes by Tennyson appeared under Strahan's imprint. *The Holy Grail and Other Poems* (with a title page date of 1870) continued the series of Idylls, begun in 1859; *Idylls of the King* (1869) brought together the eight Idylls written to date. Both volumes were printed by Bradbury and Evans; each sold for 7s. By early November, some thirty-one thousand copies of the collected *Idylls* and twenty-six thousand copies of *The Holy Grail* had been ordered in advance.[59] Orders for *The Holy Grail* may have totaled as many as forty thousand just prior to publication, and Tennyson would receive over £6,000 during 1870 from the proceeds of this volume alone.[60] Despite such high sales figures—or perhaps because of the high rate of payment to Tennyson—later developments would indicate that Strahan and Company were losing rather than making money as a result of the Tennyson contract.

Tennyson, meanwhile, was gratified by two laudatory reviews of the Idylls. The first of these, signed by Dean Alford, appeared in the *Contemporary* of January 1870, which Strahan would have been distributing to retailers, in the days just before Christmas 1869, along with the two new Tennyson volumes. A few days later, there appeared in the *Spectator* of 1 January an anonymous article, "Tennyson's Arthurian Poem," which was actually written, as all his many friends and acquaintances knew very well, by James Knowles. It is not surprising that Tennyson was pleased by Knowles's article, for Knowles based his interpretation of the Idylls on discussions conducted in the presence of the poet himself. What did raise some eyebrows was that so many of the ideas in the *Spectator* seemed to have been repeated from Alford's signed review in the *Contemporary*. In fact, as an embarrassed Knowles explained in a letter to Gladstone, "*I* have not plagiarized from *him*"; and Knowles was able to enclose a copy of a letter from Alford to himself, dated 16 December, in which Alford had requested that Knowles "write me a letter expounding a little more of what you began last night—the exposition of A T's design in the Idylls."[61] In his reference to "last night," Alford alluded to a meeting of the Meta-physical Society, at which he had been present along with R. H. Hut-ton, coeditor of the *Spectator*.[62]

On the same day that Knowles's review appeared, the *Athenaeum* was reporting, in some awe, that nearly five hundred people were employed in connection with *Good Words, Good Words for the Young*, and the *Sunday Magazine*, and that 336 tons of paper per year were required for their production—figures which explain why Spalding and Hodge, who supplied that paper, were so eager to keep Strahan and Company afloat.[63] But not all of the periodicals were turning a profit; and in the autumn and winter of 1869–70—perhaps as a result of Bell and Daldy's involvement in the "management" of Strahan and Company—a number of editorial changes were made.

There was no idea of altering *Good Words*, which in June 1869 achieved the accolade of a typically sardonic critique, "Magazine Writ-ing and Dignitaries," in the *Saturday Review*. So familiar was *Good Words* that although this piece alluded to articles that had appeared in the magazine in the course of 1867 and 1868, it was not considered necessary to refer to the quarry by name. The *Saturday Review* com-mented upon the poor quality of the articles; suggested that they had been published merely because they were signed by famous names; and regretted that as a result of widespread speculation on the part of the "foolish vulgar" concerning the high rates of payment made in each case, these "bishops and deans . . . a great Minister and a great duke" experienced some loss of dignity.[64] There could have been no better publicity for *Good Words*, which continued on its way under the nominal editorship of Norman Macleod and the "working" edi-torship, as he himself would describe it in a letter to Gladstone, of Alexander Strahan.[65]

Macleod did not remain even nominal editor of *Good Words for the Young*. The October 1869 issue of that magazine concluded with an announcement that henceforth George MacDonald would serve as editor; readers were assured that "like a splendid racing yacht, *Good Words for the Young* will beat all competitors, having such a fine 'Old Boy' at the helm, and a steady 'North Wind' at his back." MacDonald was promised £600 a year for editing the magazine.[66] He was lucky, for by January it had been decided that neither *Saint Pauls Magazine* nor the *Contemporary Review* could any longer bear the expense of their editors' salaries.

Anthony Trollope, who had earned £750 a year for editing *Saint Pauls* while it was the property of James Virtue, got the news in separate letters, both dated 25 January 1870, from the past and present publishers of the magazine. "I hear from Messrs. Strahan today," wrote Virtue, "that they intend . . . to beg the Editorship for themselves by way of economy." Virtue, who regretted "that any change should have become necessary," explained that he could not intervene, "as although I am largely interested in Strahan's business—I have always declined and intend to decline—any active share in its management." Added Virtue, "I know that all this will seem a little curious to you, and that I have the power of 'control'— if I choose to exercise it."[67] Strahan's letter to Trollope explained that it had been decided "that perhaps 'Saint Pauls' might be allowed to follow the example of 'Blackwood' and 'edit itself,' that is put up with such editing as publishers can give."[68] Before his actual departure in the summer of 1870, Trollope expressed his opinion in a letter to John Blackwood: "I cannot answer for what the magazine may see fit to do when it edits itself,—as does another periodical we know of," wrote Trollope. "I fear to leave Mss to Strahan's tender mercies, knowing that he has already on hand many tons of contributions which, if not accepted, are not rejected."[69]

In the case of the *Contemporary,* Strahan may have hoped, not merely to save money as a result of Alford's departure, but also to increase circulation. Already, during Alford's tenure, there had been a remarkable "broadening" of the tone and content of the *Review.* In the issue for October 1868, for example, the good dean himself gave offense to those readers quick to take fright at any possible manifestation of the dread German disease "Hegelianism," by explaining, in support of his contention that the era of church establishment was fast drawing to a close, that

> history, to those who read it aright, is the God of truth working out truth. As the ages pass on, one great principle after another . . . finds its way to the front, struggles for a time, is borne down and repressed, but breaks out again, and ultimately gains the day. . . . At each such conquest, mankind passes into a higher phase of thought and action.[70]

In the experience of Alford's clerical audience, such language and such notions had usually been employed in the service of causes that found their champions among contributors to the *Fortnightly*. Nor was Alford's the only article to give notice that the *Contemporary* would no longer serve as a "corrective" to the rival periodical. There was, for example, the single contribution in the late 1860s by Frederic William Farrar, a master at Harrow who would become dean of Canterbury in 1895. Farrar was conspicuous among the clergy for his sympathy with the work of Darwin and other scientists; and in the *Fortnightly* of November 1868 he sternly chastised his fellow Anglican ministers for resisting the findings of science. One month later, Farrar turned up in the *Contemporary* to explain further his opinions concerning "The Attitude of the Clergy Towards Science."[71] Even more alarming was the newly evident capacity on the part of some regular contributors to the *Contemporary* to discern praiseworthy elements in the writings of such a scourge to orthodox religious belief as T. H. Huxley. In his famous essay on "The Physical Basis of Life," which appeared in the *Fortnightly* of February 1869, Huxley dismissed "spiritualistic terminology" to insist that the property of "life," whether it appear in the lowliest plant or in the highest animal, man, is to be located in the chemical properties of "protoplasm," an organic substance common to all living creatures. So much excitement was generated by Huxley's evident disbelief in a soul independent of the body that this issue of the *Fortnightly* went through seven editions.[72] Opinions far less heretical than these had been soundly rebuked in the *Contemporary* of earlier years. But in the issue for June 1869, John Young, a Scottish mathematician and fervent anti-Calvinist who had already published one volume of theological speculation under Strahan's imprint, devoted twenty-three pages to extolling what he took to be the mystical virtues of "protoplasm": "It makes the whole world kin. Men, animals, plants, earth, air, seas, and skies, are allied mysteriously but really and essentially." In short, asserted Young, Huxley had actually demonstrated that "science is emphatically the record of Divine physical providence."[73]

Dean Alford seems to have raised no objection to the publication of such articles, even though one Scottish Calvinist in London, perhaps responding to Young's piece, assailed Alford "for permitting to appear unchallenged in the *Contemporary Review* an article which avowed opinions of a not very orthodox character,"[74] and the *Literary Churchman*, an organ of Ritualists and "High Church" Anglicans, referred with scorn to "our *Broad-Church* CONTEMPORARY" before going on to explain that "in good truth *Broad-Churchism* is only the English outcome of German Hegelianism."[75] But Alford, who would die in January 1871, was in failing health; even more to the point, he seems, whether or not he understood it, to have been in the way: in 1877, when Strahan and Knowles were quarreling so bitterly that their differences landed them in a court of law, an Anglican newspaper would remark, in its account of the legal proceedings, that Alford had retired as a result of the *Contemporary*'s "being not so successful as was anticipated."[76] Naturally there was no hint of this in the announcement of Alford's retirement that appeared in the *Contemporary* for March 1870.

On 1 March, Alford wrote to his friend Henry Allon, editor of the *British Quarterly Review,* to exclaim, "The C. R. is to have no editor! Strahan means to work it himself. He has admirable judgment in literature, but is sadly deficient in punctuality; & I doubt the arrangement answering."[77] In fact, Strahan did not intend to manage the *Contemporary* entirely on his own. As he told the story in 1877, he had been approached at some unspecified date in late 1869 or early 1870 by Tennyson, who asked if he might not find some occupation for Knowles that would bring the architect "into connection with literary people." Strahan claimed that in order to oblige Tennyson, he had allowed Knowles to become assistant to himself in editing the *Contemporary.*[78]

Knowles, who had no professional experience as a writer or an editor, and who continued to earn his living as an architect, would not have been paid on the same scale as a MacDonald or a Trollope. In the early years at least, his duties seem to have been light: like Plumptre before him, Knowles was probably expected to expend most of his energy in attracting new contributors; and from the spring of 1870 there was a steady increase in the number of contributions signed by members of the Metaphysical Society.[79] R. H. Hutton appeared for the first time in the issue for June; James Martineau and T. H. Huxley became contributors in July; A. P. Stanley discussed "The Athanasian Creed" in August. Secular periodicals were quick to voice their appreciation. On 9 July the *Illustrated London News* referred to the "improvement recently remarked" in the *Contemporary;*[80] on 2 August the *Bookseller,* a periodical well versed in publishing world gossip, slyly "supposed" that the *Review* must be under "new and more vigorous editorship": "The number for August is not only readable, but positively interesting."[81] It would be a mistake, however, to overlook Strahan's part in the continuing transformation of the *Contemporary*. Many of the more controversial articles were signed by such longtime friends and associates of his own as Peter Bayne, John Hunt, Alexander Taylor Innes, John Tulloch, and the duke of Argyll. He seems also to have been responsible for securing five articles by Giuseppe Mazzini, the Italian Republican, which attracted great attention when they appeared between April 1871 and September 1872.[82] Above all, Strahan knew how to make the most of Knowles's acquisitions. In September 1871, for example, Knowles wrote to T. H. Huxley, who in the early 1870s employed Knowles as his architect and became a more regular contributor to the *Contemporary* than to the *Fortnightly,* to report that Strahan was "fully as much in love" as himself with Huxley's controversial defense of evolutionary theory entitled "Darwin and His Critics." Knowles went on to explain that although the article had been intended for the October issue, Strahan wished to delay its appearance until November in order to have all the more time "to blow the trumpet about our prize"; Knowles hoped that Huxley would "understand this serpentine wisdom."[83]

What the October 1871 issue did include was an article destined to become one of the most notorious literary attacks of the century. Although "The Fleshly School of Poetry" was signed "Thomas Maitland," the actual author was Strahan's friend Robert Buchanan, who in this irresponsibly virulent piece perpetuated his ongoing feud with Swinburne and the pre-Raphaelite poets. The uproar that followed showed Strahan, Knowles, and Buchanan all working at cross-purposes.[84] Strahan had supplied the pseudonym, as routinely if not as innocently as he supplied pseudonyms for many other articles contributed by Buchanan to his various periodicals. But Knowles, who was already referring to himself, during his forays into society, as the editor of the *Contemporary Review,* told more than one person that the author was Buchanan; Knowles also expressed his disagreement with Buchanan's opinions.[85] "Just think what a fool and sneak [Knowles] must be," wrote D. G. Rossetti when the news reached him. "Fancy editor, publisher, and critic leaguing together for a shabby trick like this and then going about afterwards calling each other cowards to outsiders."[86] Worse bungling was to follow. On 2 December, the *Athenaeum* identified Buchanan as the author of the *Contemporary* article.[87] Two weeks later, the *Athenaeum* published a letter from

"Strahan and Co." denying that there was any basis for the attribution; this remonstrance was immediately followed, in the same column, by a letter from Buchanan, who wrote from Scotland that the pseudonym had been supplied in London by the publishers of the *Contemporary*. The same issue of the *Athenaeum* included D. G. Rossetti's riposte, "The Stealthy School of Criticism."[88] It was not enough to silence Buchanan, whose article, revised, expanded, and as ill-tempered as ever, reappeared in 1872, under Strahan's imprint, as *The Fleshly School of Poetry, and Other Phenomena of the Day*, prompting the *Saturday Review*'s whimsical comparison of Buchanan to "a knight of tremendous prowess and overpowering reputation, who found it necessary, in order not to alarm antagonists too much, to enter the lists with closed vizor and borrowed shield."[89] In July 1872, Swinburne would publish *Under the Microscope*, his reply to Buchanan's volume; Buchanan's return volley, a doggerel entitled "The Monkey and the Microscope," would appear in *Saint Pauls Magazine* for August 1872.

Alexander Strahan had greater problems than this to contend with in the course of 1871 and 1872, however. Although his publishing lists during this period included at least one runaway best-seller—*Ginx's Baby* by Edward Jenkins, which went through thirty-seven editions between 1870 and 1877[90]—neither *Saint Pauls* nor *Good Words for the Young*, the only unmortgaged periodicals in his stable, were doing well; and his creditors—who, it will be remembered, held in mortgage the copyrights to the *Contemporary*, the *Sunday Magazine*, and *Good Words*—were becoming increasingly alarmed, as Strahan's debts to them continued to outstrip the proceeds of the magazines. In the early months of 1871, the creditors seem to have decided upon a course of action: the intrusion of James Virtue as a "partner" in the Ludgate Hill firm. It may have been Thomas Spalding who overcame Virtue's extreme reluctance, so recently expressed to Trollope, to become involved: for at some point in 1871, Spalding's nephew Samuel became a partner in Virtue's printing business on City Road; and as Samuel had been a partner in his uncle's firm since 1864, it is reasonable to assume that he brought with him a sizable infusion of Spalding capital.[91] It is equally likely that Virtue's mission, when he arrived on Ludgate Hill, was to inspect the books and report any irregularities to the Spaldings and to Strahan's other major creditors, Bell and Daldy.[92]

The list of irregularities would have been a long one. Isabella Fyvie

Mayo, a regular contributor to Strahan's magazines during this period, would in her autobiography profess herself unwilling "to go into the mess of bewilderment and contradiction in which his connection with his partners ended."[93] Nonetheless, Mayo provides the fullest catalog of Strahan's more venial sins, recalling, for example, that he "showed an awkward facility in postponing for a whole year engagements already made"; that "he never wished to make definite or written agreements"; and that "his verbal ones were not always to be relied on." Mayo describes Strahan's clannishness, which led him to dismiss an established employee in order "to make a place for a connection of his own who had been in not too successful business in Glasgow"—an apparent reference to Strahan's brother-in-law, Alexander Pollock Watt, who joined Strahan's firm as a clerk in 1871.[94] "Nor was it fortunate," adds Mayo,

> for Mr. Strahan to be surrounded by relatives who found themselves at that time ready to uphold all he did, wise or otherwise. Absolutely dependent on him themselves, some of them were too much inclined to regard Mr. Strahan's literary staff as also mere dependents, who had no right to see any side of aught save that which he presented.

Above all, Mayo names that trait of Strahan's which was universally remarked upon—"his general lavishness"; and W. G. Blaikie, also, would one day write that it was Strahan's "phenomenal" generosity to authors, "joined to a lack of financial insight, that led him into difficulty."[95]

Strahan would cite in his autobiographical essays a lengthy letter to himself from Macleod, dated 15 May 1871, and prompted by what Strahan vaguely referred to as "partnership matters." "As businessmen," wrote Macleod, "our ways have been such as are not common upon 'Change or in Paternoster Row, for we never had a bargain. . . . I don't believe I ever gave you even a receipt for money received, but we had unhesitating confidence in each other's honour and friendship." Macleod expressed his eagerness to do whatever he could to help Strahan through the current crisis, "and all for '*free gratis and for nothing*,' yet joyfully, if that is required by thee, my friend."[96] Soon George MacDonald proved equally loyal, offering to forgo his salary for editing *Good Words for the Young*;[97] and in the September 1871 issue of the *Sunday Magazine*, MacDonald paid Strahan a touching tribute: in the first chapter of his serialized novel,

The Vicar's Daughter, he depicted a genial publisher, "Mr. S.," who is "not like any other publisher,"

> for he is so fond of good work that he never grumbles at any alterations writers choose to make—at least he never says anything, although it costs a great deal to shift the types again, after they are once set up.[98]

Their sacrifices would not be enough to save Strahan from disaster. Perhaps it was inevitable, from the time of James Virtue's arrival, that Strahan would sooner or later depart in circumstances of disgrace. But he managed to hang on for a time, and to uninformed readers of the periodicals, it must have seemed that Strahan and Company was a flourishing concern. The *Contemporary* for December 1871 commenced with "The Last Tournament," a new Idyll of the King, 756 lines in length, for which Strahan paid Tennyson £500; and by 23 December, Strahan was able to advertise the third edition (tenth thousand) of that month's issue.[99] Meanwhile R. W. Dale, one of the leaders of English Nonconformity, was referring, in the current issue of the *Christian Witness and Congregational Magazine,* to those unenlightened days before "Mr. Strahan, who by his sagacity and boldness has created a new species of religious periodical literature," had "come to Ludgate Hill."[100]

In fact, George Bell was about to take the step that would trigger the collapse of the delicately balanced business arrangements of 1863 through 1869, and incidentally bring Strahan's term on Ludgate Hill to an end: on 24 December he gave F. R. Daldy six months' notice of his intention to end their partnership.[101] Immediately the two men faced a problem. Unless they could find a way either to collect the money owing them by Strahan and Company, or to circumvent their agreement to pay £10,000 of Strahan's debt to Spalding and Hodge, they would have precious few assets to divide. The parties involved would be many months settling their financial disputes. But Spalding, Bell, and Daldy were all agreed that Strahan was to blame for the mess they were in, and that no satisfactory redistribution of assets could be made until he was out of the way. Apparently Spalding's ally on Ludgate Hill, James Virtue, was able to persuade even William Isbister, who had been Strahan's partner for close to fifteen years, to join their cause; and on 5 March 1872, Strahan wrote to Bell and Daldy to convey the information that he had retired from Strahan and Company "in compliance with a proposal made to me by [Virtue and Isbister] . . . undertaking to hold me free from all liabilities in connection with the business."[102] One of the terms of the separation was that the Ludgate Hill firm should have the right to use Strahan's name until September 1874.[103] "Bother all publishers!" seems to have been the dark opinion of Tennyson, whose contract bound him to Strahan and Company until January 1874.[104]

In May 1872, J. S. Blackie wrote to his wife that "Isbister, a frank, sensible fellow . . . now sits in the chair of Strahan";[105] but Isbister seems to have had little say in the arrangements effected by Spalding and Virtue. In the spring and summer of 1872, Virtue somehow squeezed out of the Ludgate Hill firm £11,000 which was transferred to Bell and Daldy in payment of their claims; Bell and Daldy used this money to pay off their own debts to Spalding and Hodge.[106] In the end, however, they were not held to the agreement of September 1869, which had bound them to pay much of Strahan's debt to Spalding and Hodge. According to Edward Bell, George Bell's son, Thomas Spalding "realized that his firm had simply transferred a threatened loss on to our shoulders"; and as Spalding now wished to place his son Howard in business, he agreed to take over the stock of Strahan and Company that had been assigned to Bell and Daldy by the 1869 agreement, along with the liability attached to that stock, and transfer all, plus Howard, and, it is to be assumed, a fair amount of Spalding capital, to yet another publishing house—J. S. Virtue and Company of Ivy Lane.[107] A few months later F. R. Daldy arrived at Ivy Lane, bringing with him his share of the assets of the now-defunct firm of Bell and Daldy; and as of July 1873, the business became known as Virtue, Spalding and Daldy.[108]

There were soon to be changes of name at Ludgate Hill as well. By late 1873 that firm, preparing for the day when it could no longer legally use Strahan's name, began to call itself W. Isbister and Company. But this, too, was temporary. In 1874 Daldy, who remained a partner in Virtue, Spalding and Daldy, became a partner as well in the Ludgate Hill firm, which became Daldy, Isbister and Company. All of these businesses were interconnected; and in 1875 Virtue and Company Limited was incorporated to own and manage them. James Virtue was the largest shareholder in the limited company, followed by the Spaldings and Daldy. Isbister did not own any shares, although he seems to have served as manager of the Ludgate Hill firm. In 1878 he would purchase that business from Virtue and Company Limited; and as Daldy would choose to remain with Virtue and the Spaldings, the Ludgate Hill business would once again become Isbister and Company.[109]

Meanwhile, in March 1872, Strahan left more than his name behind. His very first periodical, *Christian Work Throughout the World*, became the property of the Evangelical Alliance, which merged it with the Alliance's monthly newsletter, *Evangelical Christendom*. *Good Words* and the *Sunday Magazine*, which had both been mortgaged since 1864, remained with Strahan and Company of Ludgate Hill, a fact that did not go unremarked by the strict Scottish Calvinists who had long been Strahan's enemies. The Edinburgh *Presbyterian*, a Free Church periodical, was particularly pleased that Strahan was no longer connected with the *Sunday Magazine:* "There is more, even in the 'stories,' of that distinctly Christian tone and sentiment of which many Christian people felt the want before."[110]

But for Strahan's friends, there could be anguish in the revelations of slipshod and perhaps even criminally liable business practices that attended his resignation. Norman Macleod took it the hardest. According to Mayo, many of Strahan's contributors and even some of his office staff "followed him out into the wilderness,"

and I would have done so also, but for the express mandate of Dr. Guthrie, who, in his turn, would have done so too, but for the warnings of Dr. Macleod . . . who loved [Strahan] so deeply that it was thought by some that the final severance . . . contributed greatly to his breakdown in health.[111]

Strahan did manage to hold on to a few copyrights, and to a few old friends. Neither *Saint Pauls Magazine* nor *Good Words for the Young* had been mortgaged, and these went with him. George MacDonald stayed on, still without pay, to edit the children's magazine, which was now, following its separation from *Good Words*, rechristened *Good Things for the Young*. MacDonald would resign the editorship in 1873; but he continued to sell his fiction to Strahan even though, according to Greville MacDonald, "Strahan, having separated from his partners, was unable to offer such prices as he used to give for a new book."[112]

Strahan's most urgent problem during this period, however, was the need to find some source of funding for the *Contemporary*, which had been mortgaged, but which went with him nonetheless. Perhaps the *Contemporary*, which despite its increasing circulation was not yet the money-maker it was to become, was of little interest to Virtue and the Spaldings; or perhaps it was the promise that the *Contemporary* would be left to him that made Strahan decide to give up *Good Words* and the *Sunday Magazine* and go as quietly as he did from the publishing house he had founded.

In 1877 Strahan would recall, in a letter to James Knowles, "a dark time in the Review's history," when "I had to find all the funds . . . had to sell everything I possessed to keep it going,—and then when this was not sufficient had to borrow more until the whole amounted to close upon £12,000." Strahan would recall that he had asked Knowles "to purchase a quarter share for a mere trifle to enable me to meet an urgent claim in connection with it. You declined to aid me."[113] There is evidence, however, that Knowles carefully considered Strahan's proposal, which was probably made not long after Strahan's departure from Ludgate Hill. As Knowles reminded Tennyson in a letter written in 1877, the two of them had discussed the matter, and Tennyson had suggested that he and Knowles together might purchase the *Contemporary*. But Knowles held back, and Strahan was forced to turn elsewhere.[114]

Strahan ended up with Henry S. King, a former partner in Smith, Elder, and Company who had opened his own publishing house in 1871. For the sake of having his imprint appear on so prestigious a review as the *Contemporary*, King seems to have been willing to invest heavily in Strahan's homeless periodicals. His imprint replaced that of the Ludgate Hill firm on the *Contemporary* for June 1872; in time he would become Strahan's associate in other ventures as well.

Before these arrangements could be worked out, however, there came news of the death of Norman Macleod, in Glasgow, on 16 June. Strahan attended the funeral and then returned to London to write the tribute to Macleod that appeared in the *Contemporary* for July. "Besides *Good Words*," wrote Strahan,

> The Contemporary Review, The Sunday Magazine, and Good Words for the Young can call him father, for without his generous aid and encouragement at the beginning and all through, I could never have projected or established any of them.

Strahan denied that "any cloud, even of the size of a man's hand" had ever appeared "to darken our horizons,"[115] and those who might have contradicted him held their tongues, at least publicly. But Donald Macleod, who succeeded his elder brother as editor of *Good Words*, set the record straight in a letter to John Malcolm Ludlow, who had expressed some sympathy for Strahan. "I assure you," wrote Donald Macleod, "I am the last man that would say a harsh word about Strahan—but it is only fair to state that I consider him by far the least aggrieved party in the unfortunate separation." In the opinion of Macleod, "there were very decided knaves on the one side as well as on the other."[116]

CHAPTER VII

The Blank Shield: On Paternoster Row, 1872–76

Hereafter ye shall know me—and the shield—
I pray you lend me one, if such you have,
Blank, or at least with some device not mine.

—Tennyson, "Lancelot and Elaine" (1859)

In March 1872, just as Strahan was leaving the Ludgate Hill firm, there appeared in the *Contemporary Review* an article by his childhood friend from Tain, Alexander Taylor Innes, who unlike Strahan had remained a faithful congregant of the Free Church of Scotland. "Dean Stanley at Edinburgh" was a response to four lectures delivered by A. P. Stanley in January 1872 on the history of the Scottish Establishment. Stanley's theme had been the increase of latitudinarianism, and in one passage singled out by many evangelical critics he praised the Establishment for bearing "a blank shield, with no device of sect or party." Innes, outraged by the suggestion that "the Church with the majestic Puritan creed" had done right to reject its theological heritage, quoted Hugh Miller to buttress his argument that the essence of Scottish Presbyterianism survived only in the Free Church.[1] By the time Innes was answered, in the *Contemporary* of October 1872, by another of Strahan's friends, Principal John Tulloch, the review would be appearing under the imprint of Henry S. King and Company, and "Broader" readers than Innes would have far more to complain of than Tulloch's denigration of "Scottish religion, here dark with the shadow of the Covenant, and tinged with the red, fierce light of fanaticism."[2] Strahan was inclined toward Tulloch's way of thinking: "What a big thaw is going on all over Scotland," he wrote in October 1872. "It is good to be living just now."[3] In years to come, however, Strahan would have more and more reason to temper his liberalism with evangelical piety—a development that would adversely affect his relations with James Knowles and with Henry S. King.

King (1817–78) was from the start an unlikely associate for Strahan: an old-fashioned Tory in politics, he staunchly supported the Anglican Establishment despite the fact that his own religious views were as liberal as his politics were conservative.[4] Born the grandson of a wealthy banker, he might have led a life of leisure had not his father lost the family fortune while King was still young. King supported himself as a bookseller in Brighton until his first marriage, to a sister of George Smith's wife, led to his becoming in 1853 a one-quarter partner in Smith, Elder, which was at the time a strange amalgam of publishing house and East India banking agency.

King's first wife died in 1860. In 1863, he married Harriet Eleanor Hamilton, a niece of Lord Aberdeen and of the duke of Abercorn. Mrs. Hamilton King, as she always called herself, was so great an admirer of Giuseppe Mazzini, the Italian nationalist, that prior to her marriage she wrote to Mazzini, begging to be allowed to come to Italy and join the *Risorgimento*. But Mazzini refused her request, and within the year she wrote to announce her engagement to King, whom she met when Smith, Elder published her poem on "The Execution of Felice Orsini": "His political views are not on all points identical to yours; but in those feelings and truths which meet above the range of temporary questions, he is one with all noble souls."[5] In fact, King's political conservatism seems to have been reinforced by his keen awareness of his wife's family connections. But when Mazzini visited England in 1864 King accompanied his wife to her only personal meeting with her hero; he also arranged that Smith, Elder should publish the English edition of Mazzini's works that appeared in six volumes between 1864 and 1870. Mrs. Hamilton King became an intimate friend of Mazzini's English translator, Emilie Ashurst Venturi, and remained a correspondent of Mazzini's until his death in 1872.

During the same years, political differences added to what seems to have been temperamental incompatibility prevented King from getting along well with George Smith. In 1865, when Smith launched the *Pall Mall Gazette*, King consented to the venture only after it was agreed that the periodical should be completely under Smith's management, and that King should have the option at any time to require that Smith either discontinue the paper or buy out King's interest in it. The first number fulfilled King's apprehensions: he wrote to Smith that the *Pall Mall's* support of the Liberal government was awkward for him, given his family connections and political affiliations.[6] The *Pall Mall Gazette* survived, but the former brothers-in-law ended their uneasy partnership in 1868. Under the terms of their separation, Smith took the publishing branch of the business, while King retained the India agency under his own name at the famous address, 65 Cornhill. It was agreed that King should not engage in publishing for three years following the separation.[7]

When King did resume publishing in 1871, the first book to appear under his imprint was *Freedom in the Church of England* by Stopford Augustus Brooke, a notably freethinking Anglican; another author on his list was James Hinton, the Unitarian thinker whose mystic philosophy so impressed Tennyson. King soon became the London publisher of the "International Scientific Series," which had been founded in the United States by E. L. Youmans, and which consisted of volumes on scientific subjects written for a lay audience. In London, the nominal editors of the series were Herbert Spencer, T. H. Huxley, and John Tyndall, whose wife Louisa was a first cousin of Mrs. Hamilton King. Contributors to the series included such well-known figures as Walter Bagehot, William Benjamin Carpenter, John Lubbock, and William Kingdon Clifford.[8] King was not content, however, merely to publish works of theology and science. He aimed also to become a publisher of poets, and in the autumn of 1871 he sent Emilie Ashurst Venturi to seek a contribution from Swinburne for an anthology he was preparing. Swinburne was happy to oblige because, as he explained in a personal letter, King "applied to me through a friend as being himself on terms of friendship with Mazzini," the figure whom, as Swinburne would explain when Mazzini died, "I most loved and honoured of all men on earth."[9] The episode seems to have encouraged King to make several attempts to become Swinburne's regular publisher—attempts that came to nothing as a direct result of the appearance of King's imprint, in 1872 and 1873, on one after another of Strahan's periodicals.

King and Strahan had a number of acquaintances in common. George MacDonald knew King from the days when his work was published by Smith, Elder. In 1870, 1871, and 1872, Emilie Ashurst Venturi sent two articles of her own and five articles by Mazzini to the *Contemporary*. Of the contributors to King's International Scientific Series (ISS), Huxley, Carpenter, and Bagehot wrote for the *Contemporary;* Herbert Spencer's *Study of Sociology*, which was to become a volume in the ISS, began serialization in the *Contemporary* for April 1872. Huxley, Carpenter, and Bagehot were also, of course, along with Hinton, Lubbock, and Tyndall, members of Knowles's Metaphysical Society, and it is entirely possible that Knowles, concerned for the survival of the review, took some part in bringing Strahan and King together. Few documents survive to explain their exact relationship, which varied over the few years in which they were connected. Strahan, as we have seen, was in dire need of cash; he also required a distributor for the periodicals. King probably lent Strahan money; and although Strahan retained the copyright to the *Contemporary* and continued to edit it with Knowles, King became the "publisher" (i.e., distributor) of the review, on a commission basis, beginning with the issue for June 1872.

In the very next issue, John Tyndall appeared for the first time, as author of the "Introductory Note" to an anonymous article: "The 'Prayer for the Sick': Hints toward a Serious Attempt to Estimate Its Value." This article, the work of Henry Thompson, an eminent London surgeon, proposed that patients in certain hospital wards be designated objects of prayer while patients in other wards were left unprayed for, with an eye toward eventually tabulating the results in terms of deaths or recoveries. At least one observer believed that it was Tyndall's reputation as an outspoken atheist, "and not any intrinsic novelty or merit in the thing itself," that "gave significance and notoriety" to the article.[10] But the *Sunday Magazine,* from which Strahan had been parted so recently, and which rarely commented on such controversies, felt that "the very statement of the proposal caused a shudder of pain";[11] and John Brown Paton was spurred on in his "Home Missionary" activities by the knowledge that "science, in the person of Professor Tyndall, was defying the Church to prove by scientific tests that prayer had any real value for the sufficing of human wants."[12] Men of science other than Tyndall, however, proved eager to join in the fun. Sir Francis Galton, remembered today as the father of eugenics, wrote an article on "Statistical Inquiries into the Efficacy of Prayer" in which he advanced such negative evidence as the fact that those Evangelicals accorded obituary notices in the *Record,* whom he assumed to have been the objects of extraordinary amounts of prayer, died on the average at no more advanced an age than did those figures commemorated by obituaries in the *Times.* Galton submitted his article to *Macmillan's Magazine,* edited at this time by George Grove, a member of the Metaphysical Society; Grove, who apparently found the topic too controversial for *Macmillan's,* passed the article on to Knowles. Even Knowles proved leery: he wrote to Galton that "our constituents (who are largely clergymen) must not be tried much further just now by proposals following Tyndall's friend's on prayer."[13] After Galton's article appeared in the *Fortnightly* of August 1872, however, Tyndall and Thompson were allowed to defend the "Prayer Gauge" proposal against its critics in the *Contemporary* of October 1872.[14]

At the end of October, Tennyson remarked in his letter diary that "Strahan has joined himself to King."[15] But the partnership, if such it can be called, was a limited one. Strahan seems not to have taken any part in King's business at 65 Cornhill, although King's imprint began to appear on the works of several authors, including Edward Jenkins and Robert Buchanan, whose books had in the past been published by Strahan and Company of Ludgate Hill. It is unclear whether King purchased these copyrights, either from Strahan and Company, from Alexander Strahan, or from the authors; whether he owned these copyrights jointly with Strahan; or whether he merely served as the distributor of volumes whose copyrights were retained by Strahan. At any rate, by November 1872, Strahan and the periodicals were established in an office at 12 Paternoster Row that was listed under both his name and King's in the London Post Office Directory.

King's imprint began to appear on *Saint Pauls Magazine* in November and on *Good Things for the Young* in December. His name was also, of course, at the bottom of an advertisement for the *Contemporary* that appeared throughout December, which must have proved confusing to those readers who objected to the opinions of John Tyndall and friends. The advertisement commenced by reiterating Dean Alford's intention that the *Contemporary* should "represent those who, holding loyally to belief in the Articles of the Christian Faith, are not afraid of Modern Thought in its various aspects and demands, and who scorn to defend their faith by mere reticence, or by the artifices commonly acquiesced in." The list of contributors that followed, however, included not merely such "Broad" theologians as Martineau, Stanley, Tulloch, and Maurice, but even such avowed nonbelievers as Huxley, Tyndall, and Spencer.[16]

At the same time, King was advertising a new periodical that, although edited by Strahan and reflecting his religious and political views far more accurately than King's, was to be owned by them jointly. In the page-length prospectus to the *Day of Rest*, a penny weekly that appeared in time for Christmas 1872, Strahan promised, in part, that "the poor and lowly will have provision made for them in Narrative, and Homily, and Story, and Song, and Parable, and Picture."

> All classes will be kept in view, so that, as far as the "DAY OF REST" is concerned, a general truce may be called to the schemes which fill up the hopes, and fears, and wishes of everyday life; and the tide of worldliness be so stemmed that the soul may have time and opportunity to meditate on the things which are above the world, and beyond the boundaries of space.[17]

As the *Publishers' Circular* would eventually remark, "pious intention is manifest";[18] but the Edinburgh *Presbyterian* lost no time in charging that the *Day of Rest* was "evidently meant to be the organ of 'Broad Church' views on the subject of Sabbath observance . . . the 'Sunday Magazine' not being 'broad' enough for the taste of its late publisher, Mr. Strahan."[19]

Meanwhile, King's advertisements were attracting comment in far different quarters than these. On 6 December, four months after the appearance in *Saint Pauls Magazine* of "The Monkey and the Microscope" by Robert Buchanan, Swinburne wrote to a friend that he would have been glad to come to terms with King, for "any name connected [with Mazzini's] has a direct claim on my respect and good will." But, continued Swinburne, he had been surprised and disgusted to see King's name appear on "the very sweepings of Messrs. Strahan's refuse stock . . . periodicals which have for some time been persistently and consistently devoted to the defamation of Rossetti and myself."[20] The matter was settled once and for all when Swinburne saw that King was advertising a collected edition of Buchanan's poetry: "Faugh—it will be impossible for men of honour and character to publish with him afterwards."[21] In 1874, when Swinburne went to Chatto and Windus, he would specify that the *Gentleman's Magazine,* while published by that firm, was "never . . . to contain any line from the dung-dropping pen of the bitch-born Buchanan."[22]

King had better luck with Tennyson. In March 1873, at a meeting of the editorial staff of the *Contemporary Review,* Strahan asked Knowles whether King might make an offer to the poet laureate, whose contract with Strahan and Company of Ludgate Hill was due to expire in January 1874.[23] Five years earlier, Strahan had negotiated directly with Tennyson; but now Knowles, working with Tennyson's solicitor, served as a middleman, sorting out the various offers. Those from the Ludgate Hill firm were highly unsatisfactory: Virtue, who described the 1868 agreement as "disastrous," went so far as to suggest that Tennyson might make amends by allowing Strahan and Company to sell collected editions of the poetry without making any royalty payments whatsoever; he proposed to publish Tennyson's other works, old and new alike, on a straight 5 percent commission basis—terms that struck the laureate as "little short of an impertinence."[24] But King, who may have been thinking more of prestige than of profit, was willing to outbid even the 1868 contract: his terms were £5,000 per year for five years for the right to publish previous works, and a commission for himself of 5 percent on the proceeds of new works.[25] On 3 April, Knowles wrote Mrs. Tennyson to report on the negotiations, and to recommend that Tennyson move to King.[26] The new contract would be signed in December.

It is probably no coincidence that shortly after Knowles made his recommendation, he managed to secure for himself a contract that defined his connection with the *Contemporary*. Whatever the precise terms of his own arrangements with Strahan, King had reason to be concerned with the welfare of the review, and he may well have played a part in overcoming Strahan's habitual disinclination to sign any form of written agreement with his editors. At any rate, in April 1873 Knowles was officially designated "Joint Editor" of the *Contemporary* with Strahan, at an annual salary of £500. Knowles responded to Strahan's "kind and very liberal note" to this effect by referring to a prior, unwritten, "one-articled constitution, providing that we shall both agree about every paper before its insertion"; and he remarked that he was "quite content" with the new arrangement: "I can see no sort of reason why we should not go on working together as pleasantly as we have hitherto done."[27] Certainly Knowles, as secretary of the Metaphysical Society, was in a position to do great things for the review. The issue for March 1873, for example, included an article by John Ruskin on "The Nature and Authority of Miracle" that had already been read before the society; Ruskin contributed a second article, "Home, and its Economies," to the issue for May. The same issue included an anonymous article on "The Meaning of Mr. Tennyson's 'King Arthur'" that seems to have been written by Knowles himself.[28] Other articles in the months that followed were signed by such old and new members of Knowles's society as T. H. Huxley, John Tyndall, W. R. Greg, William Benjamin Carpenter, A. P. Stanley, and M. E. Grant Duff. Beginning in September 1873 there was a second series, in addition to Spencer's *Study of Sociology,* that would end up as a book on King's list: *Contemporary Evolution,* a challenge to the theories of Darwin and Huxley by a rival evolutionist, St. George Mivart, a convert to Catholicism who would be elected to the Metaphysical Society in 1874.

Perhaps because Knowles, as a result of the April 1873 agreement, was now taking a greater role in editing the review, Strahan seems to have devoted more and more time to his long-standing interest in evangelical social reform. He was involved in John Brown Paton's schemes to establish an English equivalent to Wichern's Innere Mission in Germany,[29] and he would probably have been on hand in September 1873 when Paton convened, in Nottingham, the first Conference of the Inner Mission "to consider the practical relations of Christianity to the social wants of our time." For the occasion, Paton drew up a circular explaining that Christianity was the true Social Science; James Stuart, a mutual friend of Paton's and Strahan's who was a fellow of Trinity College, Cambridge, urged, in a paper on "Christianity and the Higher Education of the People," "the sale and diffusion of good popular books and journals, which have on them the glow of a bright and healthy Christian spirit."[30] Such sentiments could not have been entirely novel to a publisher who had learned his trade in an atmosphere permeated by schemes for the Christian amelioration of social problems. But their articulation at Paton's conference may have influenced Strahan's immediate plans concerning the *Day of Rest.*

Already, in August 1873, King had written Strahan to complain that the magazine, which they owned jointly, was losing money and to suggest that Strahan buy out his half share. In October, King asserted that he had spent £8,000 more on the *Day of Rest* than he had received in revenue. Strahan replied that he would be willing to purchase King's half share by paying one-half of whatever sum King had lost by the time the ownership was transferred. It was agreed that payment would be made in annual installments of £1,000 a year, and that until the debt was discharged, King would hold in mortgage the copyrights to the *Day of Rest,* the *Contemporary, Good Things for the Young,* and *Saint*

Pauls Magazine, as well as to a new magazine that Strahan was to launch in about six months' time. King was also to have the right, throughout the period of indebtedness, to distribute the periodicals and to earn a commission of 5 percent on sales.[31]

When the *Day of Rest* completed its first year of publication, Strahan inserted in the first bound volume of the magazine a "Preface," dated 18 December 1873, in which he explained once again the ideals that guided him as editor and publisher. He began by referring to an article on "Our Very Cheap Literature" that he had contributed to the *Contemporary Review* of June 1870; there, he had called for cheap yet "good and useful" literature to counteract the "worthless and hurtful literature" that circulated so widely among poorer readers. He went on to assert, in terms that would have gratified his Nottingham friends, his "deep conviction" that "the age requires to be recalled by a living Christian faith."

> The attempt to reform the world by political economies, and such like, has failed, and always will fail, repeat the experiment as often as we may. Christianity . . . works out for us the highest social good here, as well as secures us the blessedness of Heaven hereafter. Christianity . . . once . . . changed the face of the world; and it can and will do so again.[32]

Strahan would later claim that in the first few months of 1874 he spent £2,000 on improving the *Day of Rest,* and that circulation increased by twenty-two thousand as a result. He needed the income: in April 1874 he heard again from King, who now claimed to have lost on the magazine not £8,000 but closer to £14,000. As Strahan later told the story, he accepted King's new figures without question, and signed an indenture of mortgage against the periodicals that committed him to pay King £1,000 a year until his own half share of the losses, plus interest, would be paid off in 1880.[33]

Despite these new ties to King, Strahan's name was beginning to reappear on the periodicals and on a handful of volumes written, for the most part, by contributors to the periodicals. According to the terms of his 1872 retirement, the Ludgate Hill firm was legally entitled to style itself Strahan and Company until September 1874; but the managers of that firm, preparing for the day when Strahan's name would revert to him, were gradually replacing it, in their advertisements and on their various publications, with the new imprint of W. Isbister and Company. Angered that his name, "a valuable business property," was falling into disuse, and undeterred by threats of lawsuits to be brought by his former partners, Strahan began in late 1873 to use the imprint, "Alexander Strahan, Publisher, 12 Paternoster Row."[34]

This was the imprint that appeared, in December 1873, on the first issue of the *Contemporary* to feature W. E. Gladstone's signature. His contribution consisted of nothing more than a letter objecting to Herbert Spencer's characterization of himself, in the last installment of *The Study of Sociology* (October 1873), as "the exponent of the anti-scientific view" in regard to evolution; but it served as a sign to Knowles and Strahan that their earlier attempts to secure contributions from the prime minister might now be about to pay off, and they worked together in pursuit of more substantial pieces.[35] In January Strahan begged permission to publish Gladstone's translation of Homer's "Shield of Achilles" in the *Contemporary,* "where Mr. Tennyson's last long poem ["The Last Tournament"] first appeared."[36] "The Shield of Achilles" would open the *Contemporary* for February 1874. On 14 January, even before the issue appeared, Strahan, with uncharacteristic promptitude, sent Gladstone's payment; in the covering letter Strahan referred to the prime minister's political problems, which would lead within weeks to a Liberal defeat at the polls: "Please allow me as a whole-hearted Liberal," wrote Strahan, "to express my deep regret at the political backsliding of the people. I feel that we, as a party, have failed in our duty."[37] Knowles wrote on the same day to request that he be allowed to keep Gladstone's manuscript of the translation from Homer, citing as precedent the fact that Tennyson had allowed him to keep the manuscript of "The Last Tournament": "I certainly should *greatly* like to be able to set this autograph of yours in the same cabinet."[38] Gladstone would send three more articles, all on the subject of Homer, for the issues for May, June, and July 1874.

Strahan was busy throughout 1874 planning new periodicals and making an important new business alliance. In March, *Saint Pauls Magazine,* the shilling monthly founded six and a half years earlier by another publisher (Virtue) and another editor (Trollope), was allowed to limp to its ignominious end in midvolume.[39] Strahan, who in the 1870s was interested in more pious and less costly magazines, was advertising a new penny weekly, the *Saturday Journal: A Miscellany of Pleasure and Instruction.* "For many years," explained Strahan, "I have entertained the wish to furnish the people liberally with literature not written for any class, but for all classes alike." Now he promised a magazine of essays and fiction "equipped for a wide and popular mission" and pervaded by "that spirit of human improvement which is the soul of all good Politics, and that spirit of Divine obligation which is the soul of Religion."[40]

The *Saturday Journal,* when it appeared in May, was one of the periodicals mortgaged to Henry S. King. In September 1874, Strahan informed King that he wished to discharge his entire debt plus the prospective interest to 1880, and thus redeem the copyrights. It was a surprising development, considering Strahan's track record as a chronic debtor. But King, also, behaved unexpectedly: he refused to accept the money, insisting that Strahan had no right to anticipate payments that were scheduled to continue for six years to come; and he pointed to a clause in the indenture of mortgage that made Strahan liable to a penalty of £5,000 for any breach of contract. King apparently refused payment because he wished to retain the right to distribute the periodicals; according to Strahan, King's commission of 5 percent amounted to £1,200 a year.[41] Strahan would make several more attempts in the years to come to persuade King to take the money and "relieve the magazines of the burden of his commission"—attempts that indicate that he had found a new source of funding for his publishing activities.

The most likely source was McCorquodale and Company, a printing and stationery firm founded by George McCorquodale (1817–95), who in the 1870s was in partnership with his son-in-law, Charles Edward (later Sir Charles) Hamilton (1845–1928). In 1874 McCorquodale and Company became Strahan's stationers and printers; they seem also to have invested in two periodicals published by Strahan beginning in 1874 or early 1875.[42]

The *Peep-show: A Thoroughly Amusing and Instructive Book for the Young* appeared on 26 October. A half-penny weekly intended for a younger audience than that of *Good Things,* the *Peep-show* was edited, as was *Good Things* also by this time, by Strahan; its contributors included such Strahan regulars as George MacDonald, Robert Buchanan, Jean Ingelow, Dora Greenwell, and William Allingham. As the *Congregationalist* would say of the 1876 volume, "A magazine like this makes one wish that one were six years old again."

> We have not counted the pictures, but the title page tells us that there are three hundred. There are some mild doses of science, scraps of history and legend, a few very simple essays on elementary moral questions, and pages upon pages of amusing, fanciful stories.[43]

Evening Hours, a sixpenny monthly, was not an entirely new periodical. It first appeared in March 1871 under the imprint of William Hunt and Company, billed as a "Church of England Family Magazine" edited by E. H. Bickersteth, an Anglican minister. In 1874 Bickersteth was replaced by Lady Barker (Mary Anne Stewart Broome, 1831–1911), a writer of children's stories and travel essays, who stayed on as a nominal editor after *Evening Hours* was purchased by Strahan in late 1874 or early 1875.[44] But although Strahan continued to describe *Evening Hours* as an "English Family Magazine," it was no longer "A Church of England Magazine," and in time it inevitably became, along with the *Day of Rest,* a source of offense to the *Church Quarterly Review.*

> The *Day of Rest* has some excellent contributors . . . but there is a tone of semi-Dissent about some of its papers that prevents us from committing ignorant readers to it. The like is the case of *Evening Hours.* . . . There is at this moment no perfectly satisfactory Magazine, that we know of, to send into the servants' hall after the first novelty, and then to pass on to the lending library.[45]

On 1 January 1875, Strahan signed with McCorquodale and Company an agreement that divided the ownership of all the periodicals—both those mortgaged to King (the *Contemporary, Good Things,* the *Day of Rest,* and the *Saturday Journal*), and those initiated or acquired since the mortgage (the *Peep-show, Evening Hours*)—into four equal shares. Two of the shares were assigned to McCorquodale and Company, two to Strahan. Attached to one of Strahan's quarter shares was a clause reserving to him personally the right to manage the periodicals entirely and to select any editors or publishers for them; this same share was encumbered with the debt secured by the mortgage to King.[46] The right of the Ludgate Hill firm to use the name "Strahan and Company" had expired in September 1874, and now, apparently as a result of his new partnership with McCorquodale and Company, Strahan began to use the imprint, "Strahan and Company, Paternoster Row." Their stable of periodicals was reduced by one when in April 1875, the *Saturday Journal* ceased publication at the conclusion of its first volume.

Meanwhile, the *Contemporary* remained a great success. The issue for April 1874 opened with an article by Henry Edward, Cardinal Manning, one of a few Roman Catholic members of the Metaphysical

Society who were becoming regular contributors to the review; it also included "The Metaphysical Basis of Toleration" by Walter Bagehot, who had already read his paper before the society, and who remarked that

> one of the most marked peculiarities of recent times in England is the increased liberty in the expression of opinion. . . . But already I think there are signs of a reaction. In many quarters of orthodox opinion I observe a disposition to say, "Surely this is going too far; really we cannot allow such things to be said."[47]

As if to illustrate Bagehot's observations, the Presbyterian *Weekly Review* of 18 April expressed bitter regret that Manning, "a Papal Legate in this country," should be allowed to use the *Contemporary* as "the vehicle of his elaborate exposition of Ultramontanism."[48] By September the *Weekly Review* was complaining of another contributor, also a member of Knowles's society, but one whose religious opinions were very different from Manning's: Bagehot's brother-in-law and close friend Walter Rathbone Greg, the extremely rationalistic Unitarian. In an article entitled "Mr. Gregg [*sic*] in the *Contemporary Review*," the Presbyterian weekly sounded the warning that

> a set of scientific and literary men who congregate in London have taken on themselves airs of superiority which demand some attention. They call themselves the representatives of modern thought, and claim the deference due to the utmost refinement of intellect.

The article named Tyndall, Huxley, and Spencer as prime offenders; Greg was singled out for his series in the *Contemporary* entitled "Rocks Ahead" (May, June, August), in which, according to the *Weekly Review*, he was "pleased to affirm that the higher intellect of the country has conclusively rejected the creeds of all the Churches, and is eternally divorced from Christian 'orthodoxy.'" But, retorted the *Weekly Review*, Greg spoke only for "a class of 'cultured' literary men to which he belongs, and which would arrogate to itself a priesthood of its own."[49]

If Strahan were disturbed by such harsh criticisms from a periodical that had once been eager to applaud his every publishing project, he could take some comfort in the praise of the *Publishers' Circular*, which proclaimed on 2 October, "Mr. Strahan is doing his utmost to raise the *Contemporary* to the highest rank. . . . Mr. John Morley [of the *Fortnightly*] has not so actively beat up recruits as Mr. Strahan."[50] It was probably James Knowles, however, who did most of the "beating up" for the remarkable October issue of the review, which included within its pages a name or an article certain to offend just about anybody.

One contributor, for example, was G. H. Lewes, former editor of the *Fortnightly* and a well-known critic of orthodox religion; "Lagrange and Hegel" was to be his single appearance in the *Contemporary*. Then there was a first-time contribution from W. K. Clifford, the mathematician, who wrote on "The Philosophy of the Pure Sciences"; Clifford, who contributed to King's International Scientific Series and had recently been elected to the Metaphysical Society, was fast becoming notorious as a near-fanatical crusader against Christianity.[51] A few believers—at least, those who did not distrust Roman Catholics more than they did Darwinians—might have been encouraged to see the fifth in St. George Mivart's long series of attacks on "Contemporary Evolution." But those to whom the very word *culture* had become a synonym for aggressive heterodoxy would have been alarmed by the first install-ment of a new series: Matthew Arnold's "Review of Objections to 'Literature and Dogma' " (later published as *God and the Bible*); Arnold, who appeared in the *Contemporary* at Knowles's invitation, announced that the "outcry" of those who attacked his earlier work as anti-Chris-tian and antireligious "does not make us go back one inch . . . it is they who in our judgment owe an apology to Christianity and to religion, not we."[52] Soon he would be writing to Knowles that the October installment had "made many people very angry."[53]

Pride of place, however, was reserved for Gladstone, who opened the October issue with his first article on a subject other than Homer: "Ritualism and Ritual," which in its initial draft had been a muted defense of ritualistic practices. But after the article was set in type, Gladstone inserted into the proofs a highly controversial passage in which he attacked the dogma of papal infallibility, promulgated in 1870. Rome, said Gladstone, had "substituted for the proud boast of *semper eadem* a policy of violence and change in faith"; furthermore, "no one can become her convert without renouncing his moral and mental freedom, and placing his civil loyalty and duty at the mercy of another."[54]

It was an article that would have boosted the circulation of any periodical, but Strahan knew better than most how to capitalize on it. Arnold was "amused," according to a letter to his sister, "to see Strahan's handbill stuck in all the magazines and book-stalls, announcing Gladstone and me as his two attractions this month."[55] Strahan went further than this: he sent early proofs of "Ritualism and Ritual" to the newspapers, which published long extracts; the *Times* devoted two leaders to discussing the article. Then Strahan inserted, in the *Publishers' Circular* of 2 October, a full-page advertisement quoting from the *Times* and other papers.[56] On 3 October, Knowles wrote to Gladstone that

> The rush has been so great that nobody but "the trade" has been able to get any—and "the trade" has almost literally taken them by force— There have been *seven* editions of the Review in *three* days—and "the cry is still 'they come'"![57]

The *Bookseller* of 5 October commented, "Not for many years past has there been any excitement over a magazine to be compared with that which we have witnessed during the last few days over the *Contemporary*."[58] A tenth edition was announced on 16 October, and on 2 November the *Publishers' Circular* was still marveling: "It is not often that a high-class and somewhat solid review is borne into the high heaven of a tenth or twelfth edition."[59] Strahan published several thousand reprints of the article; Knowles set to work barraging Gladstone with requests for a "sequel."[60] It was a difficult act to follow. But Knowles did his best with the November and December issues, including articles by Tyndall, by Greg, and by James Fitzjames Stephen, another outspoken enemy of Christianity who was elected to the Metaphysical Society in 1873, and who contributed to the *Contemporary* a paper on "Necessary Truth" that had already been read before the society. There was also a second installment of Arnold's "Review of Objections to 'Literature and Dogma.'"

Knowles and Strahan were still making some attempt to balance heterodoxy with orthodoxy, however, and the December 1874 issue included the first installment of a long-running series that would destroy the credibility of an anonymous, recently published work entitled *Supernatural Religion: An Inquiry into the Reality of Divine Revelation*. The author of this book, W. R. Cassels, was a self-taught amateur whose opinions were based on a specious use of the new techniques of

Biblical criticism. His book sold so many copies when it appeared that the publisher had difficulty keeping up with the demand; it also garnered high praise from John Morley, writing in the *Fortnightly* of October 1874.[61] The day was saved for believers, however, when Strahan's friend John Brown Paton persuaded Joseph Barber Lightfoot, a Cambridge scholar who in 1879 would become bishop of Durham, to demonstrate in a series of nine articles, also entitled "Supernatural Religion," that Cassels's book was far from being as learned as it appeared.[62] One month after Lightfoot's series commenced in the *Contemporary*, Cassels, writing in the *Fortnightly* as "the author of *Supernatural Religion*," attempted to defend his work against Lightfoot's careful and thorough exposure of its many errors. But Lightfoot went right on pulverizing Cassels's arguments in the *Contemporary* series, which appeared intermittently through May 1877. The articles were considered to have given new strength to the defense of the New Testament canon.

What the *Contemporary* didn't publish in 1875 was almost as significant as what it did. There were more articles by W. K. Clifford and by W. R. Greg; but the signatures of T. H. Huxley and John Tyndall—mainstays not only of Knowles's society but also of King's International Scientific Series—disappeared almost entirely, perhaps because, at the meeting of the British Association at Belfast in August 1874, both delivered highly controversial papers advancing the claims of Darwinian theories against those of orthodox Christianity. Herbert Spencer wrote to Edward Livingstone Youmans, the American projector of the ISS, that Tyndall's address "called forth many sermons"; even more alarming was Huxley's paper "On the Hypothesis that Animals are Automata, and its History," which was a revision of a paper read before the Metaphysical Society in 1871 under the more jaunty title, "Has a Frog a Soul?" "The occurrence of the two [papers] together," commented Spencer, "is regarded as a throwing down the gauntlet."[63] Huxley's paper appeared in the *Fortnightly* of November 1874; on 15 November he wrote to John Morley,

> I am always glad to have anything of mine in the *Fortnightly*, as it is sure to be in good company. . . . However, as far as the *Fortnightly* which is my old love, and the *Contemporary* which is my new, are concerned, I hope to remain as constant as a persistent bigamist can be said to be.[64]

In fact, Huxley was to publish only one more article in the *Contemporary* ("On Some Results of the Expedition of H.M.S. Challenger," March 1875); Tyndall would not appear again in those pages until 1882. Their disappearance may have had something to do with the fact that friends of Strahan's were among those who took up the gauntlet they threw down: in the *Congregationalist* of February 1875, for example, in an article entitled "The Twofold Alternative: Materialism or Religion," John Brown Paton deplored the scientific materialism that suggested, as Huxley had done in his paper, that men act, feel, and think only according to necessary physical processes.[65] Even more to the point, the *Contemporary* published, in the course of 1875, several articles that took issue with Huxley's and Tyndall's theories, including a two-part series "On the Doctrine of Human Automatism" by W. B. Carpenter (February, May); "On Animal Instinct in its Relation to the Mind of Man" by the duke of Argyll (July); and "Professor Huxley's Hypothesis that Animals are Automata" by Frederic Rogers (September). Eventually the *Contemporary* would publish the most famous of the responses to Tyndall's address: "Modern Materialism: Its Attitude Towards Theology," by James Martineau (February and March 1876). It would not be enough to still rumors that Huxley and Tyndall, behind the scenes, exerted over James Knowles an influence that was detrimental to the orthodoxy of the review.

Meanwhile, in the summer of 1875, Knowles's persistence in soliciting contributions from Gladstone was again rewarded. For the June issue, Gladstone sent a paper on the "Life and Speeches of the Prince Consort: Court of Queen Victoria." There was more than one passage here that might offend Her Majesty, and Gladstone chose to use the pseudonym "Etonensis." Gladstone's name was supplied in one of Strahan's circulars, however; and within days the issue reached a second edition, not because the article signed "Etonensis" had any great intrinsic interest, but because it was "universally" rumored to be by the former prime minister. "Really," remarked the *Manchester Guardian* of 7 June, "Mr. Gladstone seems destined to make the fortune of the *Contemporary Review*."[66] The mishap did not deter Gladstone from contributing to the July issue the "sequel to the Ritualism paper" which Knowles had long been seeking: in an article entitled "Is the Church of England Worth Preserving?", Gladstone denied that ritualistic practices embodied Romish dogma, and warned that the church would be rent asunder if anti-Ritualists persisted in their attempts to prosecute Ritualist priests in the church courts. Strahan did his best to promote the article by sending a "trumpet blast," as Knowles termed it, to the *Athenaeum* of 19 June.[67] On 3 July, the *Bookseller* reported that "everybody is talking of Mr. Gladstone's article . . . in this month's *Contemporary*, which has already gone into a third edition, and will probably reach a tenth."[68]

Despite the success of the *Contemporary*, however, Strahan was again encountering financial difficulties, partly because his other, cheaper periodicals were not achieving the very high rates of circulation that were necessary before they could earn a profit. Even in the best of times, Strahan, a notoriously bad manager, tended to allow his bills to mount up for months at a time, until the totals far exceeded his capacity to pay; and by now, he was deeply in debt to McCorquodale and Company, among other creditors.

His solution in July 1875 was to take another partner. Robert Mullan (1845?–1881) was the son of William Mullan, a printer and bookseller in Belfast. Mullan brought with him enough cash to purchase one of the two quarter shares in the periodicals that still remained to Strahan; Strahan was careful to retain the single share that had attached to it the right to publish and edit the periodicals. Strahan and Mullan moved into new offices at 34 Paternoster Row.[69] One of their apprentices, G. Thompson Hutchinson, would establish his own publishing house in 1890 at this same address; in an interview published in 1905, Hutchinson would assert that his apprenticeship to Strahan had been "as good a school as anyone could wish for."[70] Mullan and Strahan also got along well together, perhaps because they had interests in common: eventually, when he began publishing on his own, Mullan would specialize in the literature of evangelical social reform.

As for Strahan, if he attended the second conference of Paton's Inner Mission, held in Nottingham in September 1875, what he heard there may have provided the inspiration for yet another of his occasional articles on the interconnections of literature, religion, and social reform, which appeared in the *Contemporary* for November. "Morality cannot live without a religious root," pronounced Strahan in "Bad Literature for the Young," before going on to explain that "the spirit of divine obligation and human service must be everywhere present" in literature as in society: "From all desire to quietly stand by and see this great power of the press falling into the devil's service,

Good Sense deliver us!"[71] Or perhaps Strahan's article was intended as a response to the opinions of W. K. Clifford, who had written in the September issue of the *Contemporary* "On the Scientific Basis of Morals." A few months later, in the May issue, Francis Peek, a wealthy tea merchant who was a member of the London School Board, argued that "Religious Teaching in Elementary Schools" was necessary to ensure that "the next generation" would consist of "law-abiding Christians under the influence of pure and reasonable faith" rather than of "infidel materialists and lawless anarchists."[72] Peek, an evangelical Anglican, was also, like Strahan, an enthusiastic supporter of Paton's Inner Mission.

By this time, James Knowles had assumed much of the responsibility for dealing with many contributors, including that most valued contributor of them all, Gladstone, whose "Hymnus Responsorius" appeared in the issue for December 1875, and whose three-part series on "Homerology" was to appear in the issues for March, April, and July 1876. Early in 1876, Knowles asked Strahan to increase his salary above the £500 per annum guaranteed by the five-year agreement signed in April 1873. As Strahan told the story later, he initially refused Knowles's request, pleading that the *Contemporary* could not afford the expense. But Knowles promised to intensify his efforts to secure not merely articles signed by famous names, but also "serial works" that Strahan might republish in volume form; and by late April, Strahan agreed that Knowles's salary should be increased immediately to £600, with an additional raise of £100 a year until it reached £1,000 in 1880.[73]

Knowles set to work with a will. Gladstone was already in the midst of writing an article on a topic suggested by Knowles—"The Courses of Religious Thought." On 4 May, Knowles wrote to him, "pray do not consider [the article] can be too long for us—why not make it into a series of two articles or as many more as you feel disposed to write?"[74] In fact, Gladstone felt disposed to write only one such article, at least for the time being. But when Knowles sent along the proofs on 14 May, he included several pages of suggestions for further articles on the same subject: "I only wish it were longer but I hope and believe that you may find your sequel expand itself into more than one paper."[75]

"The Courses of Religious Thought," an analysis of the principles, strengths, and weaknesses of what Gladstone took to be the five "principal currents of thought concerning religion," from "Ultramontanism" through "the Negative School" of skeptics, materialists, agnostics, secularists, pantheists, and positivists, appeared in the *Contemporary* for June 1876. Gladstone's attempt to be evenhanded drew letters of protest from representatives of each of these groups. He also received a cheerful note from Strahan, dated 8 June, which reported that two extra editions of the review had already been sold "thanks to your most valuable paper."

> This is a large circulation, but we would have sold more were it not that the newspapers have quoted so largely from the article. The *Guardian*, for instance, has treated its readers to no less than 17 out of 26 pages![76]

One would not have guessed from the jubilant tone of Strahan's letter that once again he was on the brink of financial disaster.

Strahan blamed his troubles on McCorquodale and Company, insisting that the printers and stationers, through the twin "calamities" of poor printing and inefficient distribution arrangements, had caused a dramatic drop in sales of the magazines; Strahan also maintained that for their inferior work, McCorquodale and Company charged Strahan and Company £3,000 a year more than other firms would have charged for good work.[77] Knowles told the other side of the story in a letter to Gladstone: "The whole difficulty arose," as Knowles explained it, "from Mr. Strahan's being in his frequent condition of insolvency—owing . . . his papermakers and printers . . . about £35,000."[78] In late June 1876, McCorquodale and Company placed a receiver in the offices at 34 Paternoster Row, and Strahan's partnership with Robert Mullan was dissolved. Mullan, who remained friendly to Strahan, took as his share of the assets the book list of the now-defunct firm; he also retained, for the time being, his quarter share in the periodicals.

In July, George McCorquodale asked Knowles's assistance in transferring the *Contemporary* to another publisher. Knowles would later claim that he "made every effort to prevent a step so disastrous" to Strahan;[79] Strahan would recall that Knowles came to him and offered to act as his "friend" in negotiating a compromise with McCorquodale and Company.[80] Knowles did persuade Strahan, McCorquodale, and McCorquodale's partner Charles Hamilton to sign on 5 August a memorandum reaffirming the agreement of April 1876 between himself and Strahan. But he was less effective in safeguarding Strahan's interests: at least two of the compromises he proposed came to nothing. And then, as Knowles later told the story, he was approached in late August by McCorquodale and Hamilton, who told Knowles that their accountants had uncovered "certain business transactions" for which Strahan could be held "criminally liable."[81]

Knowles was always to maintain that he deserted Strahan's cause as a result of these revelations. Within days, Knowles wrote McCorquodale and Hamilton, whom he claimed to regard "as virtually and practically proprietors of the Review," to ask that they appoint him, insofar as it was within their legal power to do so, sole editor of the *Contemporary*, "thus superseding the present joint arrangement between myself and Mr. Strahan." "Fortified by this authoritative undertaking on your part," concluded Knowles in a passage that was later to arouse Strahan's personal fury, "I would wait the course of events (which appears to me certain to end in some self-caused catastrophe to Mr. Strahan), and not trouble myself meanwhile as to what course I might ultimately have to adopt."[82]

In fact, it was impossible for McCorquodale and Hamilton to do as Knowles wished so long as Strahan remained in possession of the quarter share in the periodicals that had attached to it the right to publish and edit them. And so, on 4 September, Strahan was summoned to meet with Knowles and Hamilton. There he learned of Knowles's change of course and was persuaded under what he termed "strong pressure"—perhaps the threat of legal prosecution—to surrender the vital share, in exchange for being released from all of his obligations to McCorquodale and Company. Three days later, Hamilton named Knowles "sole and not joint Editor of the *Contemporary* as heretofore."[83] Knowles was also authorized to place all of the periodicals with another publisher, and he turned, naturally enough, to a friend near at hand: the yearly or half-yearly volumes of the *Peepshow*, the *Day of Rest*, and the *Contemporary* that appeared in the autumn of 1876 each bore on its title page the legend, "Published for the Proprietors by Henry S. King."

But although Knowles and King would remain firm allies in the months to come, the concordat between Knowles and McCorquodale and Company was not to survive September. For Strahan, who seems to have been stung as deeply by what he regarded as Knowles's backstabbing as by the loss of the periodicals, was already preparing his offensive; and although his record as an incorrigible debtor would probably have prevented him from finding, as he had in 1863, 1872, and 1874, yet another backer in the London publishing world, he was not yet as entirely friendless as his enemies seem to have assumed.

Soon Strahan was in Nottingham conferring with John Brown Paton, who helped him send off letters explaining his problems to John Chalmers Stuart, the Presbyterian banker in Manchester, and to William Fleming Stevenson, the Presbyterian minister in Dublin whose books had appeared in the past under Strahan's imprint. They also managed to secure promises of assistance from two Anglican friends of the Inner Mission: Paton appealed to Dr. John Percival, headmaster of Clifton College, who in 1895 would become the bishop of Hereford; while Strahan, back in London, successfully approached Francis Peek.[84] It was not long before McCorquodale and Hamilton, who were more interested in recovering at least a portion of the money they had lost than in managing the periodicals themselves, received word that a group of wealthy investors, represented by Strahan, might soon be willing to purchase the three quarter shares in the periodicals now held by McCorquodale and Company. But the prospective purchasers intended to appoint their own editor; and they would not buy if James Knowles and his contract came along as part of the deal.

And so, by 23 September, McCorquodale and Hamilton asked Knowles to release them from the agreements of 5 August and 7 September. They could not have expected Knowles's counterproposals to be entirely agreeable; but they seem to have been staggered when Knowles demanded, in addition to £5,000 in damages, that McCorquodale and Company spend up to £10,000 to purchase or establish a new review to be edited by himself.[85] Unable to meet these demands, the printers and stationers chose to await further overtures from Strahan's friends, leaving the periodicals for the time being with Knowles and King.

They would not have long to wait. For at about this time, John Brown Paton wrote to Samuel Morley, the wealthy hosiery manufacturer who provided much of the funding for Paton's various evangelical endeavors, to explain that he had long been "pleading" with Strahan "to use the splendid unrivalled power he wields in the 'Contemporary Review' and his other magazines more emphatically for Christ and for the cause of Christianity." Strahan, according to Paton, had been "fettered by his surroundings which are not Christian." But now, "at last," his conscience is aroused, and he has decided to free himself from these, by either giving up all to his partners, or by getting them to give up their share to those that are more in sympathy with him. I cannot endure the thought of the 'Contemporary Review' becoming, like the 'Fortnightly Review,' another and the ablest organ for distributing infidelity among our cultured people—all our own sons and daughters.

Paton explained that Strahan's partners might be persuaded to surrender the periodicals if the capital they had invested—about £20,000—were repaid. "And thus," continued Paton,

the opportunity is presented of securing the highest literary force and guide in this country for the highest Christian and social ends by a small expenditure of money. . . . I cannot spare myself any sacrifice to save and use this foremost and mightiest engine of usefulness for the Great King and Captain of Salvation among men.[86]

The stage was being set for a lengthy, bitter, and highly public controversy over the conduct of the *Contemporary Review,* as edited by James Thomas Knowles.

CHAPTER VIII

The Ethics of Belief: The Battle for the *Contemporary,* 1876–77

> Orthodox, Orthodox,
> Wha believe in John Knox,
> Let me sound an alarm to your conscience;
> There's a heretic blast
> Has been blown in the wast,
> That what is not sense must be nonsense.
>
> —Burns, "Kirk's Alarm"

Samuel Hope Morley (1809–86) was a power in business, in politics, and in journalism. The hosiery manufacturing firm he headed, I. and R. Morley, had evolved since its founding by his father and uncle into one of the largest commercial enterprises of Victorian England, with seven factories employing three thousand workers.[1] Morley was also heir to his family's traditional religious beliefs, and although a Nonconformist, he was on excellent terms with his fellow philanthropist, the Anglican Evangelical, Lord Shaftesbury. Either man might have served as a model for Matthew Arnold's *genus Hebraicus (species puritanicus).* According to Arnold, the Puritan's "great danger" was that he imagined himself to be "in possession of a rule telling him the *unum necessarium,* or one thing needful"; Arnold also recorded "that commonplace which Hebraism . . . is so apt to bring out against us . . . in praise of a man's sticking to the one thing needful,—*he knows,* says Hebraism, *his Bible!*"[2] Samuel Morley was in fact a firm believer, according to his biographer, in "the Bible, the whole Bible, and nothing but the Bible"; and he was in complete agreement when Lord Shaftesbury wrote to him in 1864, "While there is a Bible let us proclaim it, and stick, by God's grace, more and more to the one simple thing needful . . . 'Jesus Christ and Him CRUCIFIED.'"[3] Morley and Shaftesbury also shared an affinity for Scotland and the Scots: each tended to surround himself with Scottish Calvinists and to pay frequent visits to the North. In 1844, Morley made a special trip to the

Highlands to worship in the newly established Free Church; as the years passed, his already strong interest in "home evangelization"—the attempt to alleviate urban social problems by recalling the lapsed masses to Christ—was intensified by the example of such Free Church leaders as Thomas Chalmers and Thomas Guthrie.[4]

Meanwhile, Morley was on his way to a position of influence within the emerging Liberal party. Morley's concern for the welfare of the people earned him in some circles the title of "Radical"; and despite the fact that he was himself the employer of thousands, he seems to have patronized some of the working-class movements of midcentury.[5] In 1856 Morley was one of the founders of the London *Morning Star,* which sold for only a penny and may have achieved a circulation of as high as twenty thousand among its predominantly lower- to middle-class readers.[6] Morley was only a minor proprietor, and was thus not entirely responsible for making the *Star* into what Matthew Arnold termed a "vile" paper, a "true reflexion of the rancour of Protestant Dissent in alliance with all the vulgarity, meddlesomeness, and grossness of the British multitude."[7] But years later, "One Who Knew Him" would write in the *Pall Mall Gazette* that Morley "always considered the responsibility attaching to proprietorship was in the editorial appointment,"[8] and it may be significant that the editor who seems to have lasted the longest at the *Morning Star* was Henry Richard (1812–88), a Congregational minister from South Wales who was the son of a Calvinist Methodist minister.[9]

In 1858, Morley became treasurer of the Congregational Home Missionary Society. In the same year John Brown Paton began his three-year stint as coeditor, along with R. W. Dale, of the *Eclectic Review,* a Congregational periodical owned in part by Morley; and in 1863, the same year in which Paton seems to have become a friend of Alexander Strahan's, Morley put up much of the money to establish the Nottingham Congregational Institute, which trained "Home Missionaries and Evangelists."[10] Paton was to be principal of the institute for its first thirty-five years; Morley would serve as its chairman until his death.

Morley was elected member of Parliament for Nottingham in 1865, and although he was soon unseated through no fault of his own as a result of voting irregularities, he returned to Parliament in 1868 as the member for Bristol, a seat he would fill for seventeen years. Morley also became, in about 1868, a major proprietor of what was perhaps the most influential of all Liberal organs: the *Daily News,* which had already delighted Matthew Arnold by gravely asserting that the middle class was responsible for "all the great things that have been done in all departments."[11] It was Morley who pressed to reduce the price of the *Daily News* from threepence to one penny, and who arranged for the *News* to absorb the *Morning Star;* its middle- to upper-middle-class readers were thus augmented by the poorer and more radical readers of the *Star,* and its circulation eventually climbed to a peak of about one hundred fifty thousand during the Franco-Prussian war, stabilizing afterward at about ninety thousand.[12] Morley threatened more than once to discontinue his connection with the *News* were it to persist in taking any stand in opposition to Gladstone's policies. It is said that on one occasion, when informed of exceptionally large dividends, Morley replied, "I am almost disappointed. I went into the *Daily News* not to make money, but to advance principles."[13] Small wonder that in 1876, Prime Minister Disraeli would refer to the *News* as "the real opposition journal."[14]

In addition to being a prominent member of the Liberal party, Morley could also claim to be a force within that bastion of liberalism, the Congregational Union of England and Wales. He dedicated vast amounts of time, energy, and money to all manner of Congregationalist activities: in addition to being the mainstay of all Home Missionary endeavors, he is said to have spent nearly £15,000 on chapel building between 1864 and 1870.[15] Yet in the 1860s and 1870s, English Congregationalism as a whole was moving away from belief in several dogmas—such as the inerrancy of Scripture, the certainty of eternal punishment for the unregenerate, and the penal substitutionary nature of the Atonement—that Morley held dear; and he began to be concerned, along with other like-minded believers, by what they perceived as the spread of "rationalism" even within their own denomination. Many of the more traditional thinkers were Scots by birth, and it was natural that they should envy the Presbyterians their more efficient system of church discipline; some went so far as to suggest that the time had come for the Congregational Union to replace "non-credalism" with "neo-credalism" by drawing up a list of beliefs deemed common to all member churches. The union was a voluntary organization, with no power to discipline individual members or congregations; but the very idea of a creed formulated and handed down from on high struck at the basis of Congregational polity, and theological innovators within the union were joined by many traditionalists in denying that orthodoxy could be guaranteed by verbal formulas. Nor did John Brown Paton, a man proud of his descent from Scottish Covenanters, calm the troubled waters when he presented at a regional meeting in October 1869 a paper "On a Possible Basis of Union with Presbyterians." Paton suggested that union might be possible if the Congregationalists would institute a system of church discipline; and he expressed the opinion that even if such a system failed to result in union with the (English) Presbyterians, it would still be a boon in that it would enable "our Churches . . . to secure the advantages which are attributed to Presbyterian organization."[16]

More typical than Paton's, however, was the approach of such strategists as the Reverend Edward White, who sought to minimize the "great danger to popular faith from some of the results of modern inquiry" by suggesting that "the ship may be saved by throwing overboard the worthless part of the cargo."[17] His companions within the progressive mainstream of English Congregationalism included J. Guinness Rogers, whose pastorate in the 1870s was in Clapham; J. Baldwin Brown, who in 1874 and again in 1875 explained his own highly unorthodox views concerning the afterlife in volumes published by Henry S. King; and R. W. Dale, whose opinions had evolved dramatically since his days as coeditor with Paton of the *Eclectic Review*. In the 1870s, Dale agreed with White, Brown, and Rogers, among others, that the "demonstration of the historical untrustworthiness of a few chapters here and there in the Old Testament" was of no great importance; he declared at the May 1874 meetings of the Congregational Union his disbelief in eternal punishment; and he delivered in 1875 a series of lectures on the Atonement that proved highly offensive to traditional believers.[18] In November 1876, in an address that triggered much controversy, Dale approvingly heralded "the general disappearance of Calvinism" within Congregationalism; he also suggested that the indigenous tradition of English Congregationalism, a tradition tending toward a "mild" or "moderate" form of Calvinism, had been severely strained, in the preceding half century, by a massive influx of Scots trained in the more extreme traditions of Presbyterianism.[19] There was little need, then, for the *Congregationalist* to remark in 1885 that no man's views were "more distinctly anti-Presbyterian" than Dale's.[20]

It could not have pleased Samuel Morley, John Brown Paton, and friends that by the 1870s, the theologically progressive, anti-Calvinist faction was firmly in control of three of the periodicals circulating widely among Congregationalists. The first of these, the *Christian World*, began life in 1857 as a voice of orthodoxy. But all that changed when in 1859 it was taken over by the publisher James Clarke; and although the Presbyterian *Weekly Review* was soon railing against the *Christian World*'s habit of dismissing Calvinist dogma as "the theology of blood, brimstone, and fire," these complaints did not prevent Clarke's paper from achieving a circulation of one hundred twenty thousand, to become the most successful religious weekly of the period.[21] Clarke also published the *English Independent*, a four-penny weekly that emerged in January 1867 from the amalgamation of the *Patriot* and the *British Standard*. Paton had been a writer of leaders for the *Patriot*, the periodical that, it will be remembered, defended *Good Words* in the face of the *Record* attacks of 1863; but the *English Independent* owed more to the efforts of J. Guinness Rogers, a regular contributor.[22] Rogers was involved as well with the *Congregationalist*, a sixpenny monthly published by Hodder and Stoughton, which appeared in 1872 under the editorship of R. W. Dale. In 1878, Rogers would succeed Dale as editor.[23] The theologically liberal faction, then, had more than one periodical pulpit at its disposal. But Samuel Morley, who in the *Daily News* owned a fit vehicle for the dissemination of his political views, had no comparable platform for the expression of his religious opinions; and he was ready to listen when he learned from Paton, in the autumn of 1876, that Strahan's group of periodicals might be secured "for the highest Christian and social ends by a small expenditure of money."

While Morley considered the merits of Paton's invitation to invest in the periodicals, Paton and Strahan set about enlisting other evangelical funders. Their method, as a disgusted Knowles later explained it to Gladstone, was to argue that unless the *Contemporary* were "rescued and turned to the Service of Heaven," it would be transformed by Knowles into "an atheistic organ";[24] they also charged that on at least one occasion, T. H. Huxley had exerted his influence with Knowles to block publication of a series of articles that challenged the evolutionary theories of Darwin, Tyndall, Spencer, and Huxley himself.[25] Knowles had this information from his Clapham neighbor, J. Guinness Rogers, who would later testify in writing that it was a matter of common notoriety and conversation among Congregationalists and Evengelicals that Mr. Strahan and Mr. Paton were going about . . . endeavouring to get up a Company to buy the *Contemporary Review* in order to give it a more Evangelical (to make it strictly accurate, a less Rationalistic) character.[26]

They were not particularly successful in attracting investors other than those who were already longtime associates of either Strahan or Paton. But by 27 October, the mighty Samuel Morley had decided to join them, and a meeting was held at Morley's London warehouse for the purpose of drawing up articles for the formal enrollment of "Strahan and Company Limited." It was agreed that the company should arrange to purchase all four quarter shares in the periodicals formerly published by the defunct firm of Strahan and Company: the one share in the possession of Robert Mullan, Strahan's former partner, and the three shares, including the share that had attached to it the right to edit and publish the periodicals, in the possession of McCorquodale and Company. The nominal share capital of the new limited company was to be £22,000. Of this amount, Strahan was to receive, in exchange for the use of his name, £7,000 in paid-up shares; he was also to be hired as editorial manager at a yearly salary of £600 plus a share in the profits. But the promoters of the company knew their man better than to make him business manager as well: Strahan would recall eight years later that it was agreed that "I was not to have anything to do with the commercial part of the business."[27] Nor did the promoters overlook Knowles's stake in all this. On the same day as the meeting, Charles Hamilton, who had been present as an observer, tried again to persuade Knowles to retire voluntarily from the *Contemporary*.[28]

Knowles was not to be got rid of so easily. Within the week he managed to meet with Samuel Morley and to report to Gladstone, in a letter dated 2 November, that although their chat had been "as pleasant *personally* as anything could be,"

> he did not scruple to tell me that his own wish was to see an Editor of the C.R. with a strong personal bias in his own direction (ex. gr. as to his own view of the doctrine of the atonement.)[29]

Soon Knowles would be protesting to McCorquodale that he had found the *Contemporary* "a failure (under 2000 in circulation) and by the kindness of my personal friends have made a great success (with a circulation of 8000)."[30] But it was clear that his days with the *Contemporary* were numbered; and already he was planning to launch his own rival review to be called, at Tennyson's suggestion, the *Nineteenth Century*.

Meanwhile, the limited company acquired without difficulty Robert Mullan's quarter share in the periodicals. McCorquodale and Hamilton, however, had begun to think that the prospects of a publishing company directed editorially by Strahan, but commercially by two such well-known businessmen as Peek and Morley, were highly promising, and they decided to retain two of their three quarter shares in the periodicals. It was agreed that they should sell the vital share that carried with it the publishing and editing rights, that they should provide part of the operating capital for the new company, and that they and the company together should each pay half of any damages that might be awarded Knowles in a court of law.[31] The next step was for Francis Peek, in his capacity as chairman of the limited company, to notify James Knowles, on 14 December, that any prior agreements concerning Knowles's connection with the *Contemporary* were now to be regarded as terminated.[32]

Up to this point, readers of the *Contemporary* would have seen no evidence in the review itself of the struggle taking place behind the scenes. Although Knowles would have been minding the store alone from the time of Strahan's dismissal on 4 September to the time of Strahan's restoration in mid-December, the autumn issues would probably have been planned a few months beforehand. There were the usual number of articles by such members of the Metaphysical Society as W. R. Greg and H. E. Manning; Knowles would also have been responsible for obtaining two articles featured in the November issue: "A Psychological Parallel" by Matthew Arnold and "The Song of Brunanburh" by Hallam Tennyson. An article by Gladstone in the same issue—"Russian Policy and Deeds in Turkistan"—had the usual happy effect of attracting widespread comment and thus boosting circulation: on 11 November, Knowles wrote Gladstone to report that "they are printing another edition of the *Contemporary* . . . although a larger number than usual was printed to begin with."[33] The December issue opened with Gladstone's thoughts on "The Hellenic Factor in the Eastern Problem"; it included, as well, a discussion by Francis Peek of "Intemperance: Its Prevalence, Effects, and Remedy."

Knowles would have been gone from the editorial offices by the time of the appearance, in late December, of the *Contemporary* for January 1877, but he may well have been primarily responsible for its contents. The opening article, "Modern Atheism: Its Attitude Towards Morality," was signed by William Hurrell Mallock, whose anonymous satire, *The New Republic: or, Culture, Faith, and Philosophy in an English Country House,* had been serialized in the *Belgravia Magazine* from June through December 1876. In this, his first contribution to the *Contemporary*, Mallock argued that a moral sense not based on belief in God and immortality was an impossibility. He objected to the manner in which periodicals "addressed avowedly to a lay audience" encouraged the mania for "the more and more popular form" of theological speculation; and he named John Tyndall and W. K. Clifford as examples of the type of scientific atheist who would make the world unsafe for morality.[34]

The same issue included a soon-to-be-notorious article by Clifford himself, entitled "The Ethics of Belief," which had already been read before the Metaphysical Society in April 1876. Those historians who have suggested that Knowles was dismissed as a result of the publication of Clifford's article have speculated in ignorance of the complex business maneuverings of June through December 1876.[35] But it is possible that the inclusion of this article, which was certain to offend the religious sensibilities of Paton, Morley, Peek, et al., struck Knowles as an excellent joke at the expense of those earnest believers.

Clifford began with a little parable concerning a shipowner who is about to send to sea a ramshackle vessel, in need of a thorough refitting.

> Doubts had been suggested to him that possibly she was not seaworthy. . . . Before the ship sailed, however, he succeeded in overcoming these melancholy reflections. He said to himself that she had gone safely through so many voyages and weathered so many storms, that it was idle to suppose she would not come safely home from this trip also.

Lest the reader fail to see the connection between the old ship and traditional religious belief, the shipowner is said to have "put his faith in Providence," dismissing from his mind "all ungenerous suspicions about the honesty of builders and contractors."

In such ways he acquired a sincere and comfortable conviction that his vessel was thoroughly safe and seaworthy; . . . and he got his insurance-money when she went down in mid-ocean and told no tales.

Clifford condemned the shipowner as "verily guilty" of the deaths of the passengers, denying that the sincerity of his belief could excuse him, for *"he had no right to believe on such evidence as was before him."* Clifford went on to assert the moral duty of inquiry into every belief, no matter how trivial: "It is not a test, that a thing has been believed for generations. Belief may be founded in fraud and propagated by credulity." Clifford explained also that the genuinely "sacred tradition of humanity consists . . . in questions rightly asked, in conceptions which enable us to ask further questions, and in methods of answering questions." For, announced Clifford sternly, "No evidence can justify us in believing the truth of a statement which is contrary to the uniformity of nature."[36]

Clifford's article triggered a flood of protest. R. H. Hutton, writing anonymously in the *Spectator* of 6 January, complained that Clifford muddied the waters by causing his credulous shipowner to profit commercially by the disaster;[37] the *Saturday Review* as well objected to an argument based upon "supposed instances of credulity prompted by self-interest regardless of the possible or certain injury to others."[38] Clifford's "unnecessary vehemence of language and illustration" offended the far from sanctimonious Edinburgh *Scotsman*.[39] The *Pall Mall Gazette*, although itself unimpressed by "the innocent, not to say trivial character" of Clifford's opinions, remarked that the article "seems to have already been the cause of searchings of heart in more than one quarter": "We are vehemently assured . . . that Professor Clifford's proposition . . . is in some way a dangerous innovation, and strikes at the root of morality."[40]

There was also mounting publicity concerning Knowles's separation from the *Contemporary*. As a result of Strahan's and Paton's fund-raising activities, rumors were already widespread. In a letter dated 1 January 1877, Edward Dowden, whose contributions to the *Contemporary* had been more frequent during Alford's tenure than during Knowles's, wrote from Dublin to his brother John, bishop of Edinburgh, that he had drawn his own conclusions when told of the new limited company by W. F. Stevenson: "The heretics, I guessed, to be less liberally dealt in, or rather their wares—a new editor—and good pay for contributors."[41]

Knowles also was actively spreading the word. Although he had at first been enraged to hear that according to Strahan and friends the *Contemporary* was in danger of being turned by himself into an "atheistic organ," he soon realized that such rumors actually served his own ends by exciting public interest in his forthcoming review, the *Nineteenth Century*. In January he explained to Gladstone that the new owners had informed him of their intention to alter the character of the *Contemporary*.

> What I consider only open and fair discussion they consider partial and unfair to their own favorite opinions. . . . This is surely only one proof the more of the hardening influence of fanatical belief . . . even upon scrupulously upright men![42]

The London press had already been alerted to the story. The *Examiner* of 30 December reported that the *Contemporary* was now the property of Samuel Morley, who intended to hire a new and "properly orthodox" editor;[43] the *Echo* of the same date asserted that Morley required an editor "who believes in the Atonement."[44] It was a piece of privileged information that Knowles may have conveyed to more than one friend in Fleet Street since his interview with Morley, and the editor of the *Examiner*, William Minto, was a friend indeed: his name would soon appear publicly on a list of those who supported Knowles in his new periodical venture.[45] The Presbyterian *Weekly Review* was quick to repeat, on 6 January, the good news that the *Contemporary* would in the future be "conducted on orthodox principles."[46] But the directors of Strahan and Company Limited were not so pleased by such talk: they wrote to the *Athenaeum* to insist that a share in the *Contemporary* had been purchased not by Morley but by the company, and to deny that there was to be any change in editorial policy.[47] Their protests had little effect on public opinion, according to the Edinburgh *Daily Review* of 11 January, which summarized all the fuss and recorded the opinion of its London correspondent that the statement in the *Examiner* was "still held to be substantially, if not verbally accurate."[48]

The directors were alarmed by the adverse publicity because they were finding it far more difficult than they had anticipated to sell

shares in the new company. There had been six original shareholders: Paton, Peek, J. C. Stuart, Strahan, Strahan's brother-in-law
A. P. Watt, and William Gellan, the subeditor of the *Contemporary*,
who had been with Strahan since their days together in Edinburgh as
employees of Johnstone and Hunter. Since November, three more
shareholders had been enrolled: Paton's friend John Percival; J. B.
Lightfoot, whose series on "Supernatural Religion" was still appearing in the *Contemporary;* and Robert Urquhart Strachan, an elder
brother of Strahan's who lived in Glasgow.[49] Samuel Morley's name
was absent from the list, which suggests that he chose to funnel his
cash through Paton, perhaps in a vain attempt to avoid the unpleasant
comment triggered by his reputed connection with the *Contemporary*.
Certainly the directors believed that other investors were being fright-
ened off by persistent rumors that the character of the review was to
be drastically altered. They also believed that no man was more responsible for keeping those rumors alive than James Knowles.

Strahan vented some of his anger in a bitter and lengthy letter to
Knowles dated 10 January. Strahan charged Knowles with many
crimes, including personal treachery toward himself and "deception
and misrepresentation" in his dealing with McCorquodale and Hamilton. He was most enraged, however, at having been assured "by many
persons that you have been going about for several years representing
yourself as Editor of the *Contemporary Review,* and as the person who
made the *Review* the power which it is"; and he insisted that Knowles
had been taken on as assistant to himself only in order to oblige
Tennyson.[50] Strahan could not have known that he received no reply
because Knowles's lawyer deemed the letter "so violent and offensive"
that he would not allow his client to take any notice of it.[51] But within
days, Strahan forced a public exchange of sorts in the columns of the
Times.

The *Times* weighed in on 15 January with its account of the formation of the new company and the concurrent separation of Knowles
from the *Contemporary;* it also published a list of twenty-seven eminent
figures—headed by Tennyson, Huxley, Manning, and Tyndall—who
promised to assist Knowles in launching the *Nineteenth Century*.[52] The
next day's *Times* included a letter from Strahan denying "that there
has been a separation between the *Review* and its late editor": "The
Contemporary Review is now edited and will continue to be edited by the
present writer, who projected the *Review,* established it, and has been

its conductor from the beginning." Strahan also denied that there was to be "any change in the conduct of the *Review*": "The *Contemporary* will keep on its own course . . . free from narrowness, bigotry and sectarianism."[53] The *Times* of 17 January published a rejoinder from Knowles, who maintained, "I have had the name of editor, the work of editor, and the pay of Editor of the 'Contemporary Review' (jointly until recently, and solely of late) from 1870 up to the formation of the new company of Mr. Morley and his friends."[54] Strahan sent off yet another letter to the *Times*, in which he went so far as to say that "it was an error of judgment on my part to give [Knowles] a connection of any kind with the *Review*." This communication the *Times* declined to publish; instead, it turned up on 18 January in the *Publishers' Circular*—one of the few periodicals, along with the *Bookseller*, still willing to give Strahan a hearing.[55] The opinion of trade journals such as these, however, would not have carried much weight in the social circles Strahan sought to impress.

On 20 January, William Minto's *Examiner* took up the cudgel on behalf of Knowles, remarking of the exchange in the *Times* that Knowles's reply was "perfectly convincing."

> It is difficult to believe that the *Review* will hold its old course in the hands of a company of which Mr. Samuel Morley, Mr. Peek, and Mr. Paton are chief members; but the *Nineteenth Century* will probably more than make up for its loss.[56]

On the same date, R. H. Hutton's *Spectator* regretted that in the *Times* correspondence, Strahan had unduly deprecated "the services rendered by Mr. Knowles to the *Contemporary Review*."

> Those who have known that *Review* best and most recently, best know also what those services were; they also will be the persons whose anticipations for the *Nineteenth Century* will be at once the highest and the least likely to be disappointed.[57]

Both the *Examiner* and the *Spectator* repeated the list of Knowles's supporters; remarked the *Spectator*, "It is pretty evident that a considerable number of those whose contributions to the *Contemporary* have attracted the attention of the reading world will be found amongst the writers for the *Nineteenth Century*." Knowles won a third nod of approval on 20 January from the *Academy*, whose editor, Charles Appleton, would soon add his name to Knowles's list; the *Academy* heralded the forthcoming *Nineteenth Century* as "an old friend under a new name."[58] Knowles, delighted by it all, wrote to Tennyson,

> You may have seen what took place in "The Times" & how that little wretch Strahan occupies the position of a pick-pocket detected in public attempting to thieve & prevented.
>
> The little creature with his falsehood has done me all the good in the world—for he has advertised the XIX. Cent. for me in a way which £1000 would not have done![59]

Knowles had already beseeched Tennyson to "send me anything however little for my opening number": "You started the Metaphysical Society," he recalled, "by letting me read your 'higher pantheism' at the first meeting." There was some concern that King might refuse, under the terms of his contract with Tennyson, to allow publication of a new poem; "but," wrote Knowles, perhaps recalling the part he had played in securing that contract, "I think he can hardly have the face to refuse."[60] On 23 January, an elated Knowles was able to convey the news that King had consented to publication of a new poem in the first number of the *Nineteenth Century*, scheduled to appear the end of February: "so I have got Greenwood to record this fact in tonight's *Pall Mall Gazette*."[61]

Meanwhile, Strahan and Knowles competed frantically for the good opinion of W. E. Gladstone. Knowles had been carefully cultivating Gladstone throughout the autumn and had managed to extract the assurance that Gladstone had "not the protoplasm of a thought which could grow into an intention of walking with the *Contemporary Review*" were Knowles to be driven from that periodical.[62] But according to a cryptic letter from Knowles to Gladstone, the presence in the enemy camp of so powerful a member of the Liberal party as Samuel Morley constituted an "obstacle to your invaluable compliance with the request I ventured to make to you."[63] By January Gladstone had decided to "consider carefully" the arguments of each side, a position which brought down upon him a flood of papers and documents.[64] Strahan wrote to invoke the name of Samuel Morley "in the interests of truth and right";[65] Knowles pleaded that if only Gladstone would contribute to the first issue of the new review, "my fortune as an editor would be made."[66] The question was not entirely one of money, however; rather, both editors sought public proof of

Gladstone's moral approbation. As Knowles put it, "the total absence of your name . . . from '*The Nineteenth Century*' would be esteemed so great a tacit reproach to it as it would hardly be able to surmount."[67]

While Gladstone pondered and the London press continued for the most part to support Knowles's cause, Strahan prepared a statement, dated 27 January, in which he attempted to turn back against Knowles and friends the rumors that the range of the *Contemporary* was to be narrowed as a result of the formation of the new company. "On the contrary," wrote Strahan,

> the change will have the effect of preventing the Review from becoming the organ of any sect or party, or otherwise ceasing to be the open platform which it was intended to be from the beginning.

Strahan's statement appeared as part of a paid advertisement, over the list of contributors to the February issue of the *Contemporary*.[68]

It would have been the first issue of the *Contemporary* over which Strahan exercised complete control, and it was noticeably deficient in famous names. The best-known contributor was the historian Edward A. Freeman, who had been approached by Strahan, and who wrote on "The English People in Relation to the Eastern Question."[69] The philanthropist Frances Power Cobbe sent a piece on her favorite subject, vivisection; she was a friend of Paton's. Other articles were signed by such longtime regulars as Edward Dowden, John Hunt, Peter Bayne, and W. B. Rands. There was also a new feature: a concluding section of unsigned "Essays and Notices."

Two of these "Essays," both attributed to Rands by the *Wellesley Index to Victorian Periodicals,* were clearly intended to forestall unfavorable comparison with Knowles's forthcoming review. In "The Higher Controversy and Periodical Literature," Rands argued that "freedom of controversy" must be promoted in the interests of truth; and yet, even in the case of those periodicals that provide an arena for diverse or opposing views, the editor must ensure "that the waters are not poisoned by any influx of bad faith, cynical ethics, persecuting hate, or mere folly."[70] In "Editing," Rands continued his discussion of "the true nature of an editor's duties," declaring that a list of contributors must not "be made up exclusively of 'names to conjure with,' or of 'all the talents.' . . . In literature, as in the drama, the star-system fails upon the whole—is bad in morals, bad in finance, and bad in art." Near the end of the essay came a passage that seems to allude to John Tyndall, or to W. K. Clifford, who was a mathematician.

Professor John is a fine chemist; and Professor George is a great mathematician; but why should their opinions be worth a halfpenny more in ethics or psychology or pure metaphysics than those of anyone else? Have they shown deep and noble sensibilities? Do they write as if they were by nature reverent and tender, or had had much of the higher and more illuminating emotional experience?

It has become "a gravely important portion of an editor's duty," remarks Rands, to check the tendency of his readers to suppose that the opinions of such "stars" have equal validity outside as inside the fields of their special expertise.[71]

Despite such apologies, Strahan was systematically approaching recent contributors to the *Contemporary*, even those who might be expected to strike the pious directors of the limited company as objectionably heretical. He may have intended to demonstrate how "broad" the *Review* still could be when he wrote to George Jacob Holyoake, who in the past had contributed three articles at Knowles's request. Holyoake replied that despite his "very great regard" for Samuel Morley ("His Christian steadfastness I know; his respect for outside sincerity I honour"), he had already promised to support the *Nineteenth Century*.[72]

By this time, however, Strahan had received a far more crucial rebuff than Holyoake's. For Gladstone had finally handed down his decision, in the form of a promise to contribute to the first issue of the *Nineteenth Century;* and when Knowles wrote on 31 January to express his gratitude and relief, he thanked Gladstone also "for what you tell me of your reply to Mr. Strahan."[73]

Strahan's reaction was to launch a desperate new assault. On 8 February, he sent Gladstone two printed leaflets, both entitled "The Contemporary Review" and both labeled "PRIVATE." The first leaflet, which was three pages in length, was signed by Francis Peek, chairman of Strahan and Company Limited; the second, eight-page leaflet was signed by Strahan. Strahan explained in a covering letter that the leaflets were being sent to the contributors to the *Contemporary* in order to explain "the real facts of the case with respect to the *Contemporary*, and Mr. Knowles, so that they may determine their own course of action in the present circumstances."[74]

Peek's part in the new campaign was to explain how he had been involved in the new company by Strahan; how he had investigated Knowles's connection with the *Contemporary* and come to the opinion that the agreement of April 1876 should have been considered binding; how Knowles had instead made another agreement with McCorquodale and Hamilton and then demanded thousands of pounds in compensation when McCorquodale and Hamilton attempted to withdraw from the agreement. Peek also denied "the false rumour . . . that Samuel Morley has taken over the *Review* for the purpose of promoting the views of the school to which he belongs."[75]

Strahan's eight-page leaflet recounted once again the history of his dealings with Knowles, which had commenced at the request of "a distinguished author, whose works I was at that time publishing." Much blame was assigned to Knowles for having betrayed Strahan while pretending to act as his "friend" in the negotiations with McCorquodale and Hamilton, for representing himself as editor of the *Contemporary* when he was no such thing, and for spreading the false rumor that Morley would alter the character of the *Review*.[76]

Although the recital of this story must by now have grown wearisome to the principals, it would have been the first time that many of the names on Strahan's mailing list were made privy to the details. Knowles was not on that list. But within days he received copies of the leaflets from Huxley, Tyndall, Manning, Holyoake, and others. To Tennyson, Knowles complained that Strahan was sending out "privately & *behind my back* . . . a sort of pamphlet full of the grossest libels upon myself."[77] Knowles's response was to rush into print with his own six-page leaflet entitled "The Contemporary Review," in which he denied Strahan's charges and asserted once again that henceforth the *Contemporary* was to be influenced in what the new owners regarded as "the right direction."[78]

Meanwhile there appeared, in both the *Athenaeum* and the *Spectator* of 10 February 1877, an extraordinary advertisement for "THE NINETEENTH CENTURY: A MONTHLY REVIEW. EDITED BY JAMES KNOWLES, LATE OF 'THE CONTEMPORARY REVIEW.'" The first part of the advertisement consisted of a five-paragraph prospectus, which promised that the new periodical would be "conducted on the absolutely impartial and unsectarian principles which governed 'The Contemporary'" during Knowles's connection with it.

The second part of the advertisement consisted of a list of over one hundred illustrious personages said to have "promised their support to the NINETEENTH CENTURY." Many of those listed had not been contributors to the *Contemporary*, nor would they become contributors to the *Nineteenth Century;* others, such as the duke of Argyll, had no intention of abandoning the *Contemporary*. But the list was an impressive indication of Knowles's talent for marshalling friends and well-wishers from varied but for the most part rarefied social circles: headed by Tennyson, Huxley, Manning, and J. H. Newman, it moved on to two bishops (C. J. C. Ellicott of Gloucester and Bristol, W. C. Magee of Peterborough); two deans (Stanley of Westminster and R. W. Church of St. Paul's); Sir James Fitzjames Stephen, who was now acting as one of Knowles's legal advisors; Matthew Arnold; three lords; four members of Parliament; and three canons. The high social tone of the first column was only slightly lowered by the presence of three Congregationalist ministers: R. W. Dale, J. Baldwin Brown, and J. Guinness Rogers—all of whom were, significantly, leaders of the theologically progressive faction within the Congregational Union. Farther down on the list came numerous Anglican ministers; Holyoake turned up near the end. Knowles's connections in the periodical press were represented by a covey of editors: R. H. Hutton and Meredith Townsend of the *Spectator*, Walter Bagehot of the *Economist*, Charles Appleton of the *Academy*, Norman MacCall of the *Athenaeum*, Norman Lockyer of *Nature*, G. Croom Robertson of *Mind*. Most of the members of the Metaphysical Society were on the list. The most notable exception was Gladstone, who perhaps withheld his name out of consideration for Samuel Morley. Still, his name appeared just below the list of "supporters," in a separate list of contributors to the first issue of the *Nineteenth Century*.

But Knowles's advertisement featured yet another name that would prove to be the most disquieting of all to the directors of Strahan and Company Limited: the publisher indicated at the bottom of the page was not, as earlier announcements had said it would be, Longman and Company. It was Henry S. King.[79]

King had his own reasons to be displeased with the directors of the new limited company. They had been trying unsuccessfully for months to persuade him to accept full payment for the debt incurred by Strahan in 1874, and thus relinquish his right to distribute the periodicals; now, they were threatening legal action to achieve this end. According to Strahan, it was "a splendid piece of strategy" for King and Knowles to join forces: for King was in control of the machinery "set up at great cost, for circulating the *Contemporary*," and this same machinery could be used at one and the same time to promote the sale of the *Nineteenth Century,* while destroying that of the elder review.[80]

Faced with this danger, Strahan and Company Limited went to court. All might have been well if they had tried merely to force King to accept his payment. Instead, they sought a threefold injunction to restrain King and Knowles from publishing the *Nineteenth Century* or any other periodical intended to compete with the *Contemporary,* from circulating "certain erroneous representations to the effect that the *Nineteenth Century* was a continuation of the *Contemporary Review,*" and from spreading false rumors concerning the principles governing the conduct of the *Contemporary* following Knowles's separation from it.[81]

Meanwhile, orders for the first issue of the *Nineteenth Century* were pouring into King's office—two thousand by 13 February—and Knowles was being driven "almost off my head" by King's prediction that sales would exceed twenty thousand.[82] Knowles intended the issue to be a blockbuster. Gladstone was to review Sir George Lewis's book *On the Influence of Authority in Matters of Opinion;* Cardinal Manning was to reveal "The True Story of the Vatican Council." Matthew Arnold would eulogize "Falkland"; Bishop Ellicott would discuss "The Church of England, Past, Present, and Future"; J. Baldwin Brown would ask, "Is the Pulpit Losing its Power?" There would be articles by John Lubbock, M. E. Grant Duff, and G. Croom Robertson—all of whom were members of the Metaphysical Society. W. R. S. Ralston, the Russian scholar, would write on "Turkish Story-Books." All was to be capped off by a review of "Recent Science" signed by "The Editor," with a notation that T. H. Huxley had assisted and advised him. But Knowles's excitement was transformed into "a cold perspiration of dismay" when he received the contribution on which he had counted most heavily: Tennyson's "Prefatory Sonnet." It was meant to please, with its opening reference to the separation from the *Contemporary Review,* and its description of Knowles's supporters—particularly those who were members of the Metaphysical Society—as "true co-mates."

> THOSE that of late had fleeted far and fast
> To touch all shores, now leaving to the skill
> Of others their old craft seaworthy still,
> Have charter'd this; where, mindful of the past,
> Our true co-mates regather round the mast,
> Of diverse tongue, but with a common will
> Here, in this roaring moon of daffodil

And crocus, to put forth and brave the blast;
For some, descending from the sacred peak
Of hoar high-templed Faith, have leagued again
Their lot with ours to rove the world about;
And some are wilder comrades, sworn to seek
If any golden harbour be for men
In seas of Death and sunless gulfs of Doubt.

Knowles termed the sonnet, in a letter to Tennyson, "high & fine & noble . . . as perfect & polished as a Greek gem!" But intent as he was on discrediting the *Contemporary,* Knowles waxed frantic over the reference to the "old craft" as "seaworthy still": Strahan, he protested, "would certainly take out the phrase & reprint it as an advertisement by Mr. Tennyson of the Contemporary Review!" Knowles suggested that the line be emended to read "Of others their old craft, adventurous (or 'adventuring') still," in order to convey the idea that the old craft had fallen into "less brave & adventurous hands" than those of the "true co-mates." "This," urged Knowles, "would be precisely & historically accurate."[83]

While Knowles awaited Tennyson's reply ("I shall be in such a fever till I hear from you"), the proprietors of the "old craft" prepared for their day in court, where they would seek an injunction to restrain publication of the *Nineteenth Century.*

When the case was finally heard in Chancery on 22 February, defendant Knowles—represented by Sir James Fitzjames Stephen—proved far more adept at slinging insults than did the plaintiffs, Strahan and Company Limited and Messrs. McCorquodale and Hamilton.[84] Counsel for the plaintiffs summarized their objections to Knowles's advertisements for the *Nineteenth Century,* contending that Knowles had met the famous men whose names he listed as a result of his connection with the *Contemporary,* and that he had secured their "support" for his new venture only by slandering the *Contemporary* unjustly. As for Knowles's assurances that the character of the *Contemporary* was to be altered, Samuel Morley and Francis Peek, in their capacity as directors of the limited company, deposed to the effect that the original plan and object of the *Review* had not been narrowed, and that its platform was as broad and liberal as ever. The presiding judge ventured to remark that if Knowles had in fact first become acquainted with these eminent literary men through his position on the *Contemporary,* it might be considered "bad taste" for him to avail himself of that circumstance to solicit contributions for a rival publication. And then, Sir James took the floor.

Stephen began by reading aloud an affidavit in which Knowles deposed that his acquaintance with the eminent men named in the advertisement was independent of his connection with the *Contemporary;* Stephen remarked that it was not very probable in any case that Mr. Strahan's "personal influence" could have had much to do with the introductions. Stephen asserted that during the time Knowles had been connected with the *Contemporary* its circulation had increased from two thousand to eight thousand; he went on to explain that McCorquodale and Hamilton had appointed Knowles sole editor after a scrutiny of the books revealed that Strahan had "misapplied" funds. Stephen concluded the defense by reasserting that the *Contemporary* had been acquired by a party with strong religious opinions, who would transform it into an evangelical periodical; and he drew appreciative laughter from his courtroom audience when he said that the present position of Morley, Peek, et al. was, "For heaven's sake let it not be known to the world that our opinion will appear in the conduct of the *Review,* for, if you do, it may injure our pockets."

Strahan would soon be making much of the fact that the presiding judge had commented that the plaintiffs had every right to discharge the debt to King and then remove the periodicals to another publisher.[85] But this was not the point at issue on 22 February; and as for the threefold motion to restrain King and Knowles, His Lordship pronounced it failed.

It was a great defeat for Strahan and Company Limited, and not only in legal terms. The state of public opinion was indicated by the *Spectator,* which commented, "Englishmen are so little accustomed to an Index Expurgatorius, that an application to Chancery to prevent the publication of a magazine advertises it throughout the country."[86] The *English Independent*—perhaps in part as a result of the intradenominational conflict between its progressive Congregationalist conductors and the more orthodox faction led by Samuel Morley and his friends—took even greater umbrage, writing that the legal proceedings "were so extraordinary as to be almost incredible."

> Public sympathy was certain to be awakened on behalf of a man who is first dismissed from the conduct of one Review, and then hampered by an attempt to bring the power of the law to prevent him from starting

another. . . . We feel bound to express our opinion as to the ill-judged attempt to deprive Mr. Knowles of what was his manifest and undoubted right.[87]

The *Guardian* commented that the legal proceedings "must prove an extraordinary advertisement" and predicted that the *Nineteenth Century*—now due on the stands any day—"will be sought wholesale."[88]

Strahan had done his best to anticipate the new rival by preparing a particularly hefty issue of the *Contemporary* for March—228 pages, following a previous average of 160 or so. Perhaps because Tennyson's "Prefatory Sonnet" was being advertised so widely, Strahan offered poetry also, as observers in the press were quick to note: "Robert Buchanan supports his friend, the editor" commented the *Academy,* "by publishing in his pages his mythic poem, 'Balder the Beautiful.' "[89] Buchanan was not the only old friend in evidence. John Tulloch contributed an essay on "Progress of Religious Thought in Scotland," an offering perhaps intended to forestall those critics who assumed that the *Contemporary* was to become the vehicle of a theology more reactionary than Tulloch's. John Stuart Blackie, the Scottish nationalist who had been among the earliest contributors to *Good Words,* wrote on "Prussia in the Nineteenth Century." Then there was Richard St. John Tyrwhitt, a clerk in Holy Orders at Oxford who had contributed several times to Alford's *Contemporary,* but not once since; his article on "The Greek Spirit in Modern Literature" took issue with Matthew Arnold's opinions concerning "Hebraism" and "Hellenism." Tyrwhitt would soon become a shareholder in Strahan and Company Limited. Francis P. Verney, who in the past had contributed to Strahan's other periodicals, especially *Saint Pauls Magazine,* wrote on "Turkish Invasions of Europe in 1670–83"; Edward A. Freeman contributed his second article in two months' time, on "Race and Language." There were two completely new names, neither of which would ever again turn up in the *Contemporary*—Maria Catherine Bishop and Arthur Bolles Lee. Their articles may have been included for no better reason than to demonstrate that the "platform" of the review had not been narrowed by a single plank: Bishop wrote in praise of "The Social Methods of Roman Catholicism in England," while Lee celebrated "Spinoza: the Man and the Philosopher."

The center plank of the platform, however, was indicated by what the *Spectator* would slyly term "the most characteristic paper": "Reasonable Faith," by Francis Peek.[90] Peek began by announcing that there was a "manifest fallacy" in the reasoning that led W. K. Clifford to insist, in "The Ethics of Belief," that it was wrong to believe on insufficient evidence, for "the Christian revelation was intended, not only for the wise and learned, but equally for the poor and simple." Peek then illustrated his point by reviewing those extremely simplistic defenses of faith that he, a man engaged in commerce rather than in literature or theology, found particularly convincing.[91] Peek was not the only writer in the March 1877 *Contemporary* to respond to Clifford. The unsigned "Essays and Notices" commenced with a seven-page discussion of "Professor Clifford and His Critics on 'The Ethics of Belief.'" The author was Strahan's close friend W. B. Rands, and if Peek's arguments were all too simple, Rands's were, as was usual with him, more trouble to untangle than they were worth. Rands did eventually come down squarely in the camp of intuitionism, rejecting "a method of testing beliefs" which "throws cold water upon what the intuitions, hopes, fears, or other forecasts of the soul have told us, and still go on telling us."[92] In the next "Essay," a review of George Mac-Donald's recent novel, *Thomas Wingfold, Curate,* the anonymous writer—probably Rands again—seized the opportunity to apply the lessons of the novel "to the questions we have just been considering," and to scold Clifford and other agnostics of his ilk for failing to recognize that, at least in the case of "yon villager," once "a certain primary faith and hope" is destroyed, "duty collapses, and all questions of right and wrong become idle."[93]

The *Contemporary*'s thoroughgoing repudiation of Clifford and his questionable ethics drew praise from at least one commentator. "We rejoice," proclaimed *Dickinson's Theological Quarterly,* "in the vigorous and successful rescue of this splendid review from the grasp and domination of a one-sided sceptical cliquism."[94] *Dickinson's* was in a position to know, not only about the "new regime," but also about cliquism: its editor, William Henry Jellie, was, like Paton, a Congregationalist minister in Nottingham; and soon both he and *Dickinson's* publisher, Richard Duncan Dickinson, would join with Paton in launching a highly orthodox, weekly religious paper. More moderate Congregationalists, in contrast, were lukewarm in their reception of the March *Contemporary*. The *English Independent* suggested that "the maintenance of Evangelical truth" might well have been entrusted to "stronger hands": "What strikes us . . . is the easy way in which Mr. Peek is able to settle points which perplex numbers of intellects not altogether without acuteness or force."[95] But it was the *Spectator,* a periodical with a bias toward High Church Anglicanism, that devoted the greatest amount of space to ridiculing the opinions of Peek, an Evangelical Anglican. The *Spectator,* which was not slow to "presume" that Peek must be "identical with the gentleman mentioned in the Vice-Chancellor's Court as a principal proprietor of the magazine," based its bemused discussion of "A Merchant's Faith" on the tongue-in-cheek observation that in these days

> freedom has been granted not only to scepticism—as it has been granted before—but to orthodoxy, as it never was granted before in sceptical times, and the preacher who has anything to say, whether in the pulpit or the press, never had a fairer field.

Unfortunately, according to the *Spectator,* the orthodox preacher no less than the skeptic "is very often condemned to waste his strength" due to the difficulty of determining which arguments are most effective with a lay audience. And therein lies the peculiar value of Peek's article: he has done a great service for all such preachers by demonstrating that certain "childish" arguments that they would never seriously have dreamed of advancing may after all be the best for persuading men who are only "average in ability."[96]

Some critics compared this issue of the *Contemporary* with the first issue of its rival and found, or claimed to find, little to choose between them. The *Illustrated London News* asserted that "without its wrapper, the *Nineteenth Century* might very well be taken for an average number of the *Contemporary Review*";[97] the *Manchester Guardian* found that "in spirit, character, and appearance the *Nineteenth Century* is a faithful reproduction of the *Contemporary.*"[98] The Baptist *Freeman* pointed out that each review sought "to suit tastes and convictions wide as the Poles asunder" by including, for example, one article for the "Romanist" and one for the "Free-thinker," one article that was weighty and one that was "racy"; the two reviews were even alike in offering "mysterious poetry"—Tennyson's "Prefatory Sonnet" versus Buchanan's "Balder the Beautiful." The *Freeman* joked, surely with a sidelong glance at Strahan, that no properly orthodox follower of

Robert Smith Candlish, the Scottish Free Church leader, could possibly make a case for choosing one over the other: "We can imagine the sturdy descendant of the Candlish school, as he turns from one to the other of these magazines with fierce dissatisfaction, exclaiming, 'Arcades Ambo!'"[99]

Other critics had less difficulty awarding the laurel. The *English Independent,* so cool to the *Contemporary,* announced that "Like Athene full armed from the brain of Jupiter, the new Review, about which we have heard so much in various ways of late, begins its career in all the vigour of maturity"; the *Independent,* although it objected to the "insolence," "intolerance," and "narrow . . . Erastianism" of Matthew Arnold's "Falkland," was, naturally enough, highly gratified by the inclusion of J. Baldwin Brown's article.[100] Brown even drew a backhanded compliment from the *Spectator,* which, fresh from its attack on "A Merchant's Faith," remarked that Brown wrote with a "thoughtful fairness . . . so little expected from Dissenters." The *Spectator* deemed Arnold's piece "most pleasurable reading" and Gladstone's nothing less than "sensational"; all in all, proclaimed the *Spectator,* the *Nineteenth Century* "takes its place at once, and without the usual delay, in the front rank of periodicals."[101] W. G. Ward's *Dublin Review* made much of the fact that "the advent of magazines like the 'Nineteenth Century' has given to Catholic writers a new means of access to the general public," while calling attention to Cardinal Manning's "True Story of the Vatican Council."[102] The *Academy* asserted that "*The Nineteenth Century* has achieved a famous launch";[103] the *Publishers' Circular,* apparently intent on praising the *Contemporary* insofar as it could, remarked that the elder review, despite its "infinitely better name," could offer only Buchanan as against Tennyson, and "Professor Blackie as against the gigantic Gladstone."[104] In fact, Gladstone's essay, which confidently asserted that "a general revolt against authority . . . is a childish or anile superstition," constituted a far more weighty rebuttal to the arguments of such skeptics as Clifford than either Peek or Rands could have managed.[105]

Tennyson's "Prefatory Sonnet," however, attracted the most attention. Evangelical periodicals tended to be hostile. There was, for example, *Evangelical Christendom,* the organ of the Evangelical Alliance, which five years earlier had absorbed Strahan's first periodical, *Christian Work.* Now, *Evangelical Christendom* published a reply "To the Poet Laureate."

Dost thou indeed embark with such a crew
   Of Babel tongues upon a dreary quest
   To find in restlessness the precious rest
And "golden harbour," that, when men eschew
Rashly the coast of Faith, must fade from view,
   For ever sunk beneath the Ocean's crest,
   While they roam starless, chartless, and unblest?
Were it my lot some far course to pursue
Of hope or hazard on a surging sea,
   None but true British tars my bark should steer,
   One language theirs, one flag, one homely faith.
But now, with Pilot good from Galilee,
   And saints true mates, the "Golden Port" we near,
   While our flag rules the gulfs of Doubt and Death.[106]

The *Rock*—a penny paper that catered to the most extreme of Anglican Evangelicals—was shrill in its denunciation of the "mutinous crew of the old *Contemporary*," which it deemed "a motley crew" indeed. The *Rock* classified many of the names on Knowles's list of supporters under such headings as "Broad Church" (Stanley), "Papists" (Manning), and "Infidels" (Huxley, Tyndall). "We are no believers in these or any other 'mixed' missions," declared the *Rock*. "As for those who, like the dignitaries of the Church of England, are supposed to have found the Truth and Light, what right have *they* to embark with Infidels and Papists on a cruise in 'seas of Death or sunless gulfs of Doubt'?"[107]

Theirs was definitely a minority opinion. The *English Independent* was one of several periodicals that praised Tennyson's sonnet at length, concentrating on the very line that had alarmed Knowles, and which now appeared without his emendations: "Kindly is the reference to the *Contemporary* as 'their old craft seaworthy still,' which the 'true co-mates' who form the crew of the new barque are 'now leaving to the skill of others.'"[108] The praise of the *Independent* may have been more delicious to the "true co-mates" than outsiders realized. For although no correspondence survives to prove the theory, it may be that Tennyson insisted on retaining the phrase "seaworthy still" for a reason that Knowles's intense anxiety would have prevented him from recognizing in mid-February: far from being a gracious compliment, the phrase would have reminded members of the Metaphysical Society, who had discussed Clifford's paper on "The Ethics of Belief" months prior to its publication and were thus doubly familiar with its contents, of the credulous shipowner and his "old" but supposedly "seaworthy" vessel, which set out on its journey—and promptly sank.[109]

With such star attractions as Tennyson, Gladstone, Manning, and Arnold, and helped along by the publicity attending Strahan's protests and the motion for an injunction, the *Nineteenth Century* could hardly have failed to make a dramatic debut. Soon Knowles knew that King's predictions had not been overly sanguine: as early as 7 March, he could report to Gladstone, "we are printing a 5th edition of my first number! Although the first edition was 9,000 strong."[110] By the end of the month, even so unsympathetic an observer as the *Weekly Review* was reporting that sales of the *Nineteenth Century* had exceeded twenty thousand.[111] Brilliant issues were already in the works for the months to come. Tennyson would contribute "Montenegro: A Sonnet" (May), "To Victor Hugo" (June), and "Achilles over the Trench" (August); Gladstone would send five more articles by the end of the year. The issues for April and May would also feature "A Modern Symposium," which was, as Knowles wrote Gladstone, "simply a printed debate such as we have at the Metaphysical Society."[112] The topic of the first "Symposium" may have been chosen in order to steal the (presumed) thunder of the *Contemporary:* it was "The Influence upon Morality of a Decline in Religious Belief," and although every one of the eleven participants was a member of the Metaphysical Society, only Clifford would stubbornly persist in denying that if Christian belief were to disappear, the moral tone of society would inevitably be lowered.[113] The September and October issues would feature a second, highly publicized "Modern Symposium," this time on "The Soul and Future Life"; again, members of Knowles's society would predominate, although J. Baldwin Brown, the liberal Congregationalist, would vie with the likes of T. H. Huxley in expressing opinions sure to be highly objectionable to many of his brethren within the Congregational Union.[114]

In the midst of all this excitement, little or no attention seems to have been paid to Strahan's continuing efforts to reverse the general consensus of public opinion against his claims always to have been the guiding genius behind the *Contemporary*. In mid-March of 1877 he distributed yet another printed leaflet, eight pages in length, in which he reviewed his past quarrels with McCorquodale and Hamilton, with

King, and with Knowles; contradicted the various statements made in court on Knowles's behalf; and ridiculed Knowles's insinuations that the *Contemporary* was now to be, in Strahan's words, "perverted, abused, and degraded, by the minions of a base and bigoted obscurantism."[115] Certainly a deliberate attempt was made throughout 1877 to demonstrate, as the *Spectator* remarked, that the *Contemporary* had "in no way rejected intellectual aid from unbelievers."[116] Ernest Renan, whose *Vie de Jésus* (1863) had so angered traditional believers, wrote on "Spinoza" for the April issue; the highly unorthodox F. W. Newman became a contributor at Paton's request;[117] Alexander Bain, a staunch skeptic who in 1860 assumed his post as professor of Logic and English at Aberdeen only over the vigorous opposition of the faithful, responded to Strahan's plea that a contribution from him would help to refute charges that the *Contemporary* was "committed to a reactionary pietism."[118] Two other new contributors, whose opinions would have been more to Strahan's personal taste, were Edward Caird, the well-known "neo-Hegelian" who was professor of Moral Philosophy at Glasgow, and Caird's close friend T. H. Green, professor of Moral Philosophy at Oxford, who drew upon Kant in formulating his own brand of socially committed evangelicalism.

Valuable as such names were under the circumstances, it is likely that Strahan was more excited by his success in wheedling a contribution from Gladstone for the July 1877 issue. But the topic—"Piracy in Borneo and the Operations of July 1849"—was hardly one to send a review into extra editions. And although the *Contemporary* made a respectable showing, the *Nineteenth Century*, which featured many former contributors to the *Contemporary*, was, month after month, the more brilliant of the two periodicals.

Their bitter competition was complicated by the fact that during most of 1877, both were distributed by Henry S. King. King finally agreed in March to accept full payment of the debt secured by the mortgage of April 1874, thereby creating much confusion in the camp of Strahan and Company Limited, where no one was quite sure whether Strahan should pay off the debt himself, or whether the company should accept that responsibility. Technically, the debt was attached to the quarter share in the periodicals that Strahan had surrendered to McCorquodale and Company in September 1876 and that had been sold by them in turn to the limited company. The directors, however, argued that Strahan should be responsible for the debt to King because he had incurred it in the first place. Finally it was decided that £4,000 of the £7,000 in shares in the company held by Strahan personally should be mortgaged to raise the money, and that Morley, Peek, and Stuart should serve as the mortgagees.[119]

It was by no means the end of the matter. For even as he accepted the money, King argued that the original loan would not have been made had he not been granted the right to distribute the periodicals until 1880, and that he thus retained that right whether or not the debt was discharged. Strahan and Company Limited went to court again, and in July 1877 King was directed to surrender the distribution apparatus.[120] For months King dragged his feet, declaring his intention to appeal the ruling, and Strahan was undoubtedly correct in charging that King and Knowles were using for the distribution of the *Nineteenth Century* the same apparatus that had been developed for the *Contemporary*.[121] In October, however, King, who was in poor health, sold his publishing company to his manager, C. Kegan Paul; and it may have been as a result of this change that the periodicals began finally to be distributed from the office at 34 Paternoster Row that now housed both Strahan and Company Limited, and the London branch of William Mullan and Son, who had taken over the book list of the defunct firm of Strahan and Company.[122]

Not all of the periodicals survived. *Evening Hours* became the property of Robert Mullan, perhaps in partial payment for his quarter share; *Good Things for the Young* came to an end in the autumn of 1877. Only the *Peep-show*, the *Day of Rest*, and the *Contemporary* were left to Strahan and Company Limited.

By the end of the year, Knowles's legal claims against McCorquodale and Hamilton were also close to settlement; soon he would be writing to Gladstone that "the shameful little intrigue" against himself had resulted in damages "of £1500—or close thereabouts."[123] Strahan and Company Limited, according to their earlier agreement with George McCorquodale, paid half of this amount.

It would have required a greater setback than this to dampen Strahan's naturally sanguine spirits, now that the *Anchora Spei* was once again appearing on the title page of the *Contemporary*. And so he welcomed the new year by taking a full-page advertisement in the Christmas 1877 *Bookseller* to perorate concerning "the Literature of

the Higher Controversy," and to promise that "in the CONTEMPO-
RARY REVIEW . . . the key-note of all the literature for which I have
ever been personally responsible shall be distinctly heard—'We live
by admiration, hope, and love.'"[124] But already, behind the scenes,
another commercial scandal was in the making.

CHAPTER IX

A Story with a Moral: Strahan and Company Limited, 1877–82

Whoever treats religion, religious discussions, questions of churches and sects, as absorbing, is not in vital sympathy with the movement of men's minds at present.

—Matthew Arnold, March 1881[1]

The problems that were to destroy Strahan and Company Limited were present from its beginnings. Although the nominal operating capital of the firm, as indicated by the face value of the shares issued, was £22,000, it proved impossible in the winter of 1876–77 to raise much more than half this amount through the sale of shares. The money that was raised went immediately in partial payment for the half interest in the periodicals obtained from Robert Mullan and from McCorquodale and Company, leaving nothing other than the income from the firm's publications to cover day-to-day expenses.

By August 1877, the company had run up a number of debts, including one of £1,100 to its bookbinders, the firm of Simpson and Renshaw. Simpson, after making several unsuccessful appeals to the cashier of the company, complained to Strahan; Strahan, although barred from taking any part in the financial management of the firm, placed Simpson's account before Francis Peek and Samuel Morley, who were then serving as "Chairman" and "Vice-Chairman" of the board of directors. Both men seem to have waxed indignant that any doubt should have been cast upon their reputations as trustworthy businessmen; Strahan would later assert that Morley had gone so far as to declaim, "Does he not know that I am here? Tell him that no one shall ever lose a penny by any Company, limited or unlimited, of which I am a Director.[2] A letter to this effect, signed by the solicitor of the company, was sent off to Simpson, who probably would have preferred his money, but who was impressed enough by the evangelical renown of Peek and Morley to continue to bind the company's books and periodicals. He was not the only creditor fobbed off in this manner. As Strahan would later write,

> Here was a Company of limited liability, unable to meet its obligations after only seven months working. What chance had such a Company of getting credit? None, and it would have got none, but would have collapsed there and then had it not been for the personal promises to pay given by the Chairman and Vice-Chairman, and the fact was repeated to every one from whom credit was asked.[3]

And so the company staggered along, running up debts, transferring its custom to new suppliers when the old became too importunate, always on the strength of the names of Messrs. Morley and Peek, "gentlemen," as one disappointed creditor would later put it, "of the highest respectability, of considerable wealth, and of the highest moral rectitude."[4]

Meanwhile Morley, along with John Brown Paton, was preoccupied with a battle developing within the Congregational Union. The trouble began in October 1877, when the union gathered in Leicester for its annual autumnal sessions, and a group of younger ministers who shared progressive and even anti-evangelical opinions called a meeting of their own—the so-called Leicester Conference—for those "who value spiritual religion, and who are in sympathy with the principle that religious communion is not dependent on agreement in theological, critical, or historical opinion."[5]

The outcry that followed was out of all proportion to the event that purportedly triggered it, and can only be explained as a venting of frustration on the part of the theologically conservative "neo-credalists" who found it easier to lecture the young upstarts than to lock horns with such eminent figures as J. Baldwin Brown or R. W. Dale. The actual meeting was disrupted by traditional believers who attended in order to denounce its conveners publicly as "extreme Rationalists"; even before the autumnal sessions were concluded, the chairman of the union for 1877, who was Henry Richard, editor of Samuel Morley's *Daily News,* issued a statement explaining that the meeting on "Religious Communion" had been held independently of the official proceedings and was in no way sanctioned by the union. Despite these disclaimers the Anglican *Record* promptly mounted a shrill campaign against the "gangrene in Congregationalism";[6] within the union, hard-line traditionalists called for a more thoroughgoing repudiation of the ideas expressed by the conveners of the "Leicester Conference." They were opposed by those "non-credalists" who stressed the "Independency" of Congregationalism. But when the controversy continued to mount, and one minister after another reported "widespread uneasiness" among his congregants as to the position of the union, a committee was appointed to recommend, by the time of the annual "May Meetings" in 1878, whether or not some kind of declaration of faith should be issued.

In the interim, theologically progressive Congregationalists, who naturally opposed the formulation of a creed, found a platform in the best-selling religious weekly of the day, the *Christian World*. A few months earlier, the *Christian World* had approvingly quoted W. K. Clifford's opinion that children should not be taught "the dogmas of blood and brimstone theology";[7] now, the paper published many warnings from J. Baldwin Brown, among others, that the Congregationalists were in danger of becoming "a creed-bound community."[8]

It was enough to convince the group of "neo-credalists" connected with Morley's and Paton's Nottingham Congregational Institute that the time had come to launch an orthodox rival to the *Christian World*. On 14 March 1878, a "Memorandum of Association" was drawn up to incorporate the "Christian Signal Publishing Co. Ltd.," a company established, according to the memorandum, in order to edit, print, publish, and sell a newspaper, the *Christian Signal*,

> for the defense and advocacy of the Evangelical faith of the Evangelical churches of England today;—to wit: the authority of Holy Scripture; the divinity and incarnation, the atoning sacrifice, resurrection, ascension, and mediatorial reign of the Lord Jesus Christ; and the work of the Holy Spirit.[9]

The list of shareholders, headed by John Brown Paton, included half a dozen other Congregationalist ministers; a Presbyterian minister; the layman who served as treasurer of the Nottingham Congregational Institute; and a variety of manufacturers, merchants, farmers, and laborers. One of the few shareholders who did not live in Nottingham was Richard Duncan Dickinson, the publisher of *Dickinson's Theological Quarterly;* he was described in the Memorandum of Association as the "publishing manager" of the new company. The editor of the *Christian Signal* was to be William Henry Jellie, who already edited *Dickinson's*, and who was one of the Congregationalist ministers from Nottingham. The address of the Christian Signal Publishing Company—34 Paternoster Row—was the same as that of Strahan and Company Limited; and some of its documents were presented for filing at the Public Record Office by A. P. Watt, Strahan's brother-in-law and a shareholder in Strahan and Company Limited, who had recently begun to operate as an "Advertising Agent" from 34 Paternoster Row.[10]

On 14 March—the same day that the "Memorandum of Association" was drawn up—the *Fountain*, a Congregationalist weekly, reported "a deep laid scheme for the overthrow of our prosperous contemporary the *Christian World*. The plan is ingenious and bold, and we admire the absence of reserve on the part of those who have launched it."[11] The *Christian World* itself was not so amused. Many of its readers would have been thoroughly mystified by an article in the issue for 15 March entitled "The Leaven of the Pharisees," which expended nearly a full column in attacking a "little knot of envious creatures" who were said to have issued "a certain Jesuitical and slanderous Circular" characterized by "the bearing of false witness, and manifold evil speaking." Without naming names, the *Christian World* reported that "these modern successors of those Pharisees who trusted in themselves that they were righteous and despised others" had raised £10,000 for their undertaking—a figure that tallied with the amount of nominal share capital mentioned in the "Memorandum of Association" of the Christian Signal Publishing Company. "These words will, of course, be mysterious to the bulk of our readers," remarked the *Christian World*, "but they are intended only for the initiated."[12]

The uninitiated were not long kept in suspense. Volume 1, Number 1 of the *Christian Signal: A Journal of the Religious World for the Family and Church* appeared on 26 April 1878. It sold for one penny and according to the "Editor's Note" on the first page, two hundred thousand copies had been printed—an optimistic figure, considering that the circulation of the *Christian World* was only about one hundred twenty-five thousand. "Our Meaning and Mission" announced that the *Christian Signal* had been established

to raise a solemn and abiding protest against the danger of a press so-called Christian becoming in effect an unchallenged agency for frittering away all that is essential in the Christian faith. . . . The Christian religion is not to be abandoned at the behest of the dogmatists of science who press their pretensions into a domain which does not belong to them.

A second leading article, "The Basis of Fellowship," discussed "the controversy which has been raised by the recent Conference at Leicester," and pronounced that religious fellowship cannot subsist without "an assumed general acquiescence in the convictions which [our Churches] are notoriously known to maintain. . . . Freedom of thought is one thing, latitude is another."[13] Other features included an attack on the heretical opinions of Professor John Tyndall, and a serial story advocating temperance in the use of alcoholic beverages.

The *Fountain* described the "general standpoint" of the new weekly as being "rather of the old school than the new."[14] A more enthusiastic greeting, two and a half pages in length, appeared in the *Christian's Penny Magazine,* which assailed the *Christian World* as a disparager of "Earnest Evangelical movements" and an advocate of "creedless latitudinarianism"; the *Christian Signal* was hailed as a "defender of the faith" that would supplant the *Christian World.*[15] Such a paean was perhaps to be expected, considering that the editor of the *Christian's Penny Magazine,* Frederick S. Williams, was a tutor at the Nottingham Congregational Institute and a shareholder in the Christian Signal Publishing Company. The response of the *Weekly Review* was equally predictable: it listed those members of the staff of the *Christian Signal* who were natives of Scotland.[16] At the other end of the theological spectrum, the Unitarian *Truthseeker* juxtaposed its notice of the *Christian Signal* with a humorous anecdote intended to demonstrate the ignorance of James Begg, the leader of the most conservative faction within the Free Church of Scotland; commented the *Truthseeker,* "What an evil day it will be for us when we lose these dear, amusing old boys! We shall never replace them."[17]

As far as the majority of Congregationalists were concerned, however, there was little time left for such jesting. In early May, at the spring meetings of the union, the committee that had been appointed to consider the Leicester Conference made its recommendation: that the union pass a resolution asserting that "an essential condition of Religious Communion in Congregational Churches" was "the acceptance of the Facts and Doctrines of Evangelical Faith," including "the Incarnation, the Atoning Sacrifice of the Lord Jesus Christ, His Resurrection, His Ascension and Mediatorial Reign, and the work of the Holy Spirit in the renewal of man"—a credo remarkably similar to that included in the "Memorandum of Association" of the Christian Signal Publishing Company.[18] Non-credalists led by J. Baldwin Brown lobbied hard in an attempt to prevent passage of the resolution; the *Christian World* objected to the "bastard Presbyterianism" that would result if the neo-credalists had their way.[19] But orthodox believers had a powerful spokesman in Samuel Morley, who announced at a meeting of the Home Missionary Society that he was prepared to leave the union should it give an "uncertain sound" on the fundamentals of faith. The news spread quickly: according to one minister, Morley's name was used as an "instrument of terror."[20] When the union convened for the actual vote, one minister referred to rumors "that if the resolution was not passed, some of their great schemes would not have the support of their great givers." Another minister rose to ask whether those who opposed the resolution meant to "drive away" so important a member as Morley, and demanded to know how he was to explain it to his congregation "if such a man as Mr. Morley left them because they were unsound." A few minutes later the Resolution of Faith was carried by an overwhelming majority amid great cheering.[21]

It was a happy outcome for Morley and Paton. But they must have been less gratified by developments at 34 Paternoster Row, where both the *Contemporary Review* and the *Christian Signal* were faring poorly.

In the case of the *Contemporary*, Strahan had begun the year with enthusiasm, taking out a two-page advertisement in the *Publishers' Circular* to announce that for a limited time only the issues for December and January would be available at half price (1s.3d. each) in order to attract new readers; according to the advertisement, the *Contemporary* already enjoyed "a circulation perhaps larger and more influential than was ever enjoyed by a similar publication."[22] Had this been true, Strahan might have been able to attract well-known contributors and to pay the rates necessary to hold them. In fact, given his lackluster list of writers, Strahan could hardly hope to compete successfully against the *Nineteenth Century*, which featured so many former contributors to the *Contemporary*, and which in its early years may have achieved an average circulation of ten thousand.[23] The extraordinary issue for March 1878, which included contributions not only from the "progressive" Congregationalists, R. W. Dale and

IDYLLS OF THE KING

BY ALFRED TENNYSON, D.C.L.

POET LAUREATE

"*Flos Regum Arthurus.*"
JOSEPH OF EXETER

STRAHAN AND CO., PUBLISHERS

56 LUDGATE HILL, LONDON

1869

Title page of the first edition of *Idylls of the King*

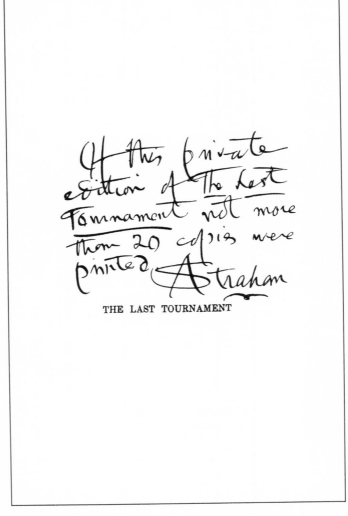

THE LAST TOURNAMENT

Strahan's inscription on the half-title page of one of the
copies of *The Last Tournament* forged by Thomas J. Wise

Alexander Strahan in 1878. This photograph was taken on the
occasion of his marriage to Lisbeth Gooch Séguin, a contributor to
the periodicals.

Cover page, including the contents, of the May 1874, *Saturday Journal*

Strahan in his office on Paternoster Row

Strahan in the early twentieth century

J. Guinness Rogers, but also from Gladstone and Tennyson, sold twenty thousand copies by mid-month;[24] according to the *Publishers' Circular*, Tennyson received, for "The Revenge," the "handsome honorarium of three hundred guineas."[25]

Perhaps Strahan was hoping to enliven the *Contemporary* when in the issues for April, May, and June he imitated Knowles's "Modern Symposiums" by including nineteen short papers on "Future Punishment." Knowles's "Symposium" on "The Soul and Future Life" had been a great success when it appeared in the *Nineteenth Century* in September and October 1877; but Strahan's more narrowly defined discussion attracted less interest, even though he managed to include papers by Edward White and by J. Baldwin Brown, who were not regular contributors. One jaded critic expressed surprise that the *Contemporary* would devote so much space to considering a question that was "no longer a matter for philosophical argument, except . . . in some obscure districts of Scotland."[26] Nor was the prestige of the review enhanced when in the issue for July 1878 Francis Peek argued, in "Aeonian Metempsychosis: A Sequel to the Discussion of Future Punishment," that each individual is destined to reap his due reward and punishment in this world by means of perpetual reincarnation until freed from this process by belief in the truths of Gospel. In November, December, and January there would be another symposiumlike discussion: twelve papers on "The Alcohol Question," which may have been all very interesting for such temperance crusaders as Morley or Peek, but which seems to have put just about everybody else sound asleep. Not that the *Contemporary* ever did become a mere mouthpiece for the expression of the views of its evangelical proprietors. But as its rates of payment fell lower and lower, it came to depend more and more heavily on contributions from shareholders in the limited company, from friends of the shareholders, from longtime cronies of Strahan's, and from others with a special hobbyhorse—Blackie on the Scottish character, Cobbe on vivisection, the duke of Argyll on "natural" and "spiritual" law, for example. By the autumn of 1878 Knowles was boasting to Gladstone that the circulation of the *Nineteenth Century* was triple that of the *Contemporary*;[27] even allowing for some exaggeration on Knowles's part, his claim suggests that circulation of the *Contemporary* may have slumped far below the average of eight thousand that it enjoyed prior to Knowles's departure.

Meanwhile the *Christian Signal*, despite extensive advertising in such friendly periodicals as the Presbyterian *Weekly Review,* had come nowhere near usurping the place of the *Christian World.* The *Christian Signal* continued to appear throughout the summer of 1878, attracting little attention until late August when it advertised the imminent appearance in its pages of a hitherto unpublished poem by Tennyson, "Confessions of a Sensitive Mind." Unfortunately, no one had bothered to ask the poet laureate for permission, and Tennyson lost no time in securing a restraining order against the *Christian Signal.* In court, the defendants could manage no better explanation than that they had found the poem in a manuscript-book of a deceased friend of Tennyson's and had advertised its publication under the misapprehension that no permission was necessary.[28] Soon after, the directors of the Christian Signal Publishing Company agreed, in the face of mounting liabilities, to wind up the concern. The *Weekly Review* made some attempt to put the best light on the demise of the *Christian Signal* by explaining, in February 1879, that the paper's very existence had persuaded the *Christian World,* in order to avoid losing the bulk of its readers, to "mend its manners" toward evangelical Christianity.[29] Two months later, the *Weekly Review* referred again to the "penitent and reforming *Christian World*"—a reference that becomes puzzling when one glances over the *World* itself, for there one finds not a single indication, in the issues for 1879, of any such change in policy or sentiments.[30]

The financial history of Strahan and Company Limited during the same period was nothing short of farcical. The company almost came to an end in July 1878 when George McCorquodale, too much of an insider to be put off by the promises that satisfied some creditors, threatened to apply to Chancery for a winding-up order were he not paid £4,460 that the Company owed him. There was some panic until Strahan, who was after all only one shareholder among several, agreed that if Samuel Morley would advance this amount for McCorquodale, he himself would surrender as security a number of literary copyrights in his possession plus the £3,000 in company shares still remaining to him; the other £4,000 in shares given to Strahan when the company was founded had long since gone to Morley as security for the money used to discharge the debt to Henry S. King. Strahan was told that his situation would be "considered" once the company began to earn a profit.[31] He does not seem to have been worried. In the autumn he was preoccupied with preparing a number of volumes that were to appear under the limited company's imprint, such as "Strahan's Handy Cyclopaedia of Condensed Information for all Readers," which was to be edited by himself. Then there was "Strahan's Books for the People," a series of volumes selling for 2s.6d. each; according to Strahan's signed prospectus to the series, it was intended for "those who, like myself, are workmen."[32] It was in this year, also, that Strahan married Lisbeth Gooch Séguin, a writer of children's stories and travel books who contributed to the company's periodicals; Séguin, who was of Huguenot descent, was the daughter of Henry Séguin, an opera singer, and of Mary Wheatley Gooch Séguin, one of the first female professors of music in England.[33]

Early in 1879, at about the time that the *Christian Signal* ceased publication, Samuel Morley, weary of the incessant demands upon his purse, decreed that Strahan and Company Limited must begin to pay its own way. The *Peep-show* was allowed to die, leaving only the *Day of Rest* and the *Contemporary*. Morley suggested that £4,000 worth of the shares originally promised to Strahan—shares now in Morley's possession—should be sold; the money raised in this manner was used in the summer of 1879 to pay creditors who would wait no longer. Then, in order to raise another £2,500 for the day-to-day expenses of the penniless company, Strahan was persuaded to mortgage several more of his copyrights and to turn over the proceeds. The company operated on these funds until June 1880, when again the coffers were found to be empty.

At this point the board of directors, without consulting Strahan, decided to pawn the company's stock of periodicals and books, a transaction that raised a paltry £1,500, while at the same time making it impossible for the company to fill orders for any works other than newly published ones. A few weeks later, on 16 July, Morley and Peek resigned from the board. Their departure should have served as a warning to all who dealt with the firm; but even though "it was known far and wide throughout the trade that the Company was not successful," a number of businesses continued to extend credit in the innocent belief that, as they would later explain, "whether its trading was carried on at a profit or otherwise, Messrs. Morley and Peek would never allow the creditors to suffer."[34]

Strahan was spending much of his time during this period in the offices of his engravers, the firm of Dalziel Brothers, in order to assist in the production of an elaborate, five-guinea edition of *The Pilgrim's*

Progress that was to include over one hundred drawings by such artists as Fred Barnard, E. F. Brewtnall, William Small, E. G. Dalziel, John Ralston, J. D. Linton, Towneley Green, and Joseph Wolf.[35] Strahan had also been experimenting with methods of color printing; in 1880 he believed that he had invented a new method that would boost the circulation of *Day of Rest* to dizzying heights, solve the financial problems of Strahan and Company Limited, and prove a source of riches to its patentee.

By the end of the year, however, even Strahan recognized—perhaps because the stock of publications remained in pawn, perhaps because payments to authors were more than twelve months in arrears—that the company was close to collapse, and suddenly he began to sound the alarm. He complained to his old friend John Brown Paton, who was still an active director; he addressed a letter of warning to the entire board; he printed up a statement outlining what he knew of the company's problems and mailed it off to the departed directors, Morley and Peek. Strahan's noisy protests were certain to create what he later described as "embitterment" between himself and the directors, even including Paton; and the board seems to have determined to rid themselves of their very embarrassing "Editorial Director" at the earliest opportunity. Soon Paton, who had become vice-chairman, introduced to the board a friend of his own who was elected chairman: Percy William Bunting (1836–1911), grandson of the famous Wesleyan minister Jabez Bunting. Percy Bunting was himself a devout Methodist, a Gladstonian Liberal, and a strong advocate of social reform. He also had some ideas for the reform of the *Contemporary:* high on his list was the need to recruit new contributors who would "write less heavily."[36]

Little could be done, however, as long as Strahan remained on the scene. In August 1881, the directors suggested that if Strahan would sign over to the company his new method for color printing, they would issue to him, in compensation for the color process and for the other properties that he had surrendered to finance the operations of the company, 440 new shares with a nominal value of £50 each. It would take about three months to raise the necessary capital. Meanwhile Strahan was to proceed to Edinburgh, where he would supervise the preparation of *Day of Rest* and a few books to be produced by the new color process; in his absence, Percy Bunting would manage the *Contemporary*. Strahan was wary of the offer of newly financed shares. But he was eager to get to Edinburgh to see the results of his invention, and after some persuasion he acceded to the directors' proposals. He does not seem to have concerned himself with the question of how so much capital was to be raised in so short a time.

He found out how near the end of 1881, when he learned, not from the directors but from the printers in Edinburgh, that £10,000 in debenture claims had been issued against the company. Since the purchasers of debenture claims take precedence over other creditors, this step effectively guaranteed that were the company to collapse, commercial creditors would not see a farthing in payment. Printers, stationers, and bookbinders, now thoroughly alarmed, stopped all supplies and services. In the meantime, Strahan's new color process had come a cropper, and even as advertisements heralded the "novel" color illustrations that were to place *Day of Rest* so far above its competitors, thousands of copies of the magazine were emerging from the presses in repellent shades of turquoise and jaundice. A glance was sufficient to show that few would be sold. Percy Bunting was still writing reassuring letters to Strahan, urging him to stay in Edinburgh and to believe that he might "leave the *Contemporary Review* in my hands safely."[37] But Edinburgh firms were even more adamant than the London ones in refusing any further credit, and soon Strahan was back on Paternoster Row. He was promptly informed that his claims against the company had been considered, and that 440 new shares had been issued in his name. Then he was relieved of his duties as "Editorial Director," a step that had been "in view," according to one director, "for a considerable time."[38] Francis Peek would soon move, at a general meeting of the shareholders, that Strahan should be censured for asserting in the printed statement sent to Peek and to Morley that the company was insolvent and ought to be stopped. But despite Peek's outrage over what he called Strahan's "wicked misrepresentations," the firm collapsed within weeks; and when Samuel Morley, as the chief creditor, petitioned Chancery on 1 April 1882 to wind up the company, it came to light that he and Percy Bunting had been two of the five purchasers of the debenture claims.

The failure of the company rendered Strahan's 440 shares valueless. He was more dismayed at being separated again from the periodicals; and he initiated legal proceedings to argue that the quarter interest in the periodicals that had been purchased by the company from McCorquodale, and that carried with it the right to edit and publish the periodicals, had been acquired by means of his personal property—that is, the copyrights and shares mortgaged to Morley—and should thus rightfully be restored to him. By accepting the 440 new shares, however, Strahan had effectively signed away any further claims against the company, and it was inevitable that his suits would be thrown out of court.

In mid-1882, the *Day of Rest* and the *Contemporary Review* were put up for sale. One prospective purchaser was James Clarke, publisher of the *Christian World*. In the end, however, the periodicals went to Isbister and Company Limited, the successor to the Ludgate Hill firm that Strahan had founded, and from which he had been forced to retire a decade earlier. The managers of Isbister and Company had no intention of welcoming Strahan back. Instead, Percy Bunting was hired to continue as editor of the *Contemporary*, with John Brown Paton as his "Consulting Editor"—the same position Knowles had once filled under Strahan. The *Day of Rest* disappeared, merged into another of the periodicals of Isbister and Company that had been founded by Strahan: the *Sunday Magazine*.

Strahan was left far more destitute than he had been when he departed Ludgate Hill, for in 1872 he had taken with him the *Contemporary*, *Saint Pauls*, and *Good Things for the Young*, as well as a variety of valuable book copyrights. He was not yet quite finished. With much bitterness he repurchased a few of the copyrights which he had surrendered to the limited company; and late in 1883 he began to publish from 25 Henrietta Street, in Covent Garden, under the imprint of "Alexander Strahan." The authors who appeared most regularly on his somewhat scanty lists were the duke of Argyll, George MacDonald, and his wife, L. G. Séguin. It was clearly an uphill struggle, and it seems not to have lasted past October 1884, when Strahan advertised a number of volumes as being "In the Press," including his own autobiographical essays, "Twenty Years of a Publisher's Life," which had been serialized in the *Day of Rest* in 1881.[39] Few of these books appeared. And although Strahan continued to be listed as a publisher in the London Post Office Directory until 1893, he seems to have published little after 1884 aside from elaborately printed and bound editions of his wife's previously published books, or an occasional reprint of the sumptuous *Pilgrim's Progress* first produced under his supervision in 1880.

But even as Strahan's advertisements disappeared, he was more in

the public eye than ever before due to an extraordinary public correspondence, begun by himself in November 1884 in the *Bookseller*,
which by April 1885 would fill dozens of columns with acrimonious
accusations and counteraccusations signed by Strahan, by Francis
Peek, by J. B. Paton, by a solicitor representing Samuel Morley, and
by various creditors of the defunct limited company. Strahan fired the
first volley in an attempt to restore some credibility to his name, which
he asserted had been "dragged through the mire" by Peek's and
Morley's gross mismanagement of the limited company; in fact, explained Strahan, he had never been allowed to take any part in managing the finances of the company, even though £10,000 of his personal property had been "taken" by the company in exchange for
valueless shares.[40]

Strahan's account of the history of Strahan and Company Limited
was partially confirmed by Victor Bauer, the auditor to the company,
who asserted in the *Bookseller* of 13 December, and would assert again
before the correspondence ended, that "The Company has failed,
owing to management which Mr. Strahan had not the power to control, and for which he is made to suffer blame as unfairly as the
creditors suffer loss of money."[41] But other participants in the debate
attempted to shift the blame back to Strahan, or at least to those firms
who had supposed, as Francis Peek put it, that "Mr. Morley and I had
placed our credit at the unlimited disposal of Mr. Strahan." Peek also
denied, in a letter to the *Bookseller* of 7 January 1885, that he had ever
said he would be personally responsible for the debts of the company.
He asserted that the company had been solvent when he and Morley
retired from the board in July 1880, and explained the later collapse
of the company as the result of "some unhappy adventures in colour-
printing and a general deterioration in the quality of the magazines."[42] In a second letter, to the *Bookseller* of 5 March 1885, Peek
would remark that "If Mr. Strahan parted with any of his property,
he must have done so of his own free will and for his own pur-
poses."[43]

Samuel Morley was represented in the debate by his solicitor Henry
Thomas Chambers, who had also served as solicitor to the limited
company. Chambers appeared in the *Bookseller* of 13 December 1884
to label Strahan's account of the firm "misleading." As for the crucial
letter that Chambers himself had written in September 1877 to Simpson the bookbinder, the letter in which Chambers asserted that the

directors "would consider themselves individually compromised if any creditor . . . should sustain any loss," Chambers contended, somewhat lamely, that he had merely been expressing his "personal opinion." Chambers brushed aside Strahan's lamentations concerning the £10,000 he claimed to have lost in the company by remarking that Morley had lost twice that amount.[44] Chambers's letter drew a heated response from Strahan, who in the *Bookseller* of 7 January 1885 described himself as a "scapegoat" for Morley and Peek, arguing that whatever amount Morley may have lost, he had after all been one of those responsible for the mismanagement and consequent collapse of the company. Strahan was also incensed that Morley had told him he was welcome to take his grievances to Chancery: "I don't at all agree with him in this. Let him first give me my £10,000, and then we can meet in the Court of Chancery if he likes on equal terms."[45]

Up to this point in the debate there was consensus on one matter: that the company had been founded, as the auditor put it, "not for profit, but to promote a cause." Strahan had written that the directors had felt "that it was so important to their cause to secure such a well-known review as the *Contemporary,* that it was worth running all the risks involved"; Chambers had agreed that it was well known that "the only object of Mr. Morley and those associated with him . . . was to secure the control of the *Contemporary Review.*"[46] Strahan's formerly close friend John Brown Paton offered a slightly different explanation when he finally made his appearance, in the *Bookseller* of 4 February: Paton asserted that the company had been founded in order to "befriend" Strahan, and that it had failed as a result of Strahan's own color printing process.[47] There followed another round of arguments from Strahan, from Peek, and from the company auditor. But few new details emerged; and in the *Bookseller* of 5 May the correspondence was concluded by a letter from the "Committee of Creditors" of the company.

The creditors had maintained all along that credit had been extended on the basis of Peek's and Morley's "known connection" with the company, and that even when the liquidation was announced, it was assumed by many that these "eminent gentlemen" would step forward and settle all accounts.[48] In December 1884, in the wake of Strahan's initial letter to the *Bookseller,* the creditors had met to censure the directors of the company for half a dozen crimes, such as repeatedly representing the company as solvent when it had been insolvent from the beginning, and issuing the debenture claims at a time when the company was close to collapse.[49] Nothing they had read in the meantime had changed their opinions; now they referred again to the "strong moral obligations" that Peek and Morley, sheltered by the limited liability laws, chose to ignore.[50] They spoke, however, with as little hope of redress as Strahan; for by now it must have been clear to all that, in the words of the *Bookseller,* "Respectability is one thing; business is another."[51]

CHAPTER X

Epilogue

A man of hope and forward-looking mind
Even to the last!

—Wordsworth, the *Excursion*, 7:276–77

In October 1881, the *Spectator* complained of the current issue of the *Contemporary Review*, which included articles by Herbert Spencer, Karl Blind, W. H. Mallock, the Scottish social reformer John Rae, and Alexander Strahan himself ("England and America over the President's Grave"), that it was "a very instructive number, deficient only in entertaining reading. It is a little too gritty with facts."[1] As it happened, Strahan had already set off on his trip to Edinburgh to implement his new color printing method, and Bunting was already casting about for new contributors who would "write less heavily." Neither Strahan nor Bunting is likely to have taken much notice of an event that had occurred only a few days earlier in Manchester, even though this event was destined to mark a new epoch in popular British journalism: the appearance of a soon-to-be-famous sixpenny weekly, *Tit-Bits*, which avoided any such "gritty" dullness by including only the shortest of extracts from books and periodicals. In Manchester alone five thousand copies were sold within two hours. Within a year, circulation climbed to three hundred thousand, and soon the imitators began to appear, including some with such pious titles as *Christian Bits* and *Sunday Bits*.[2] Not that *Tit-Bits* achieved its success through any laxity in the selection of its contents: the founder, owner, and publisher, George Newnes, who was the son of a Congregationalist minister, insisted always on the "purity" of his periodicals.[3] He was also concerned with their profits, and after moving to London in 1884 Newnes hit upon a tactic that boosted the circulation of *Tit-Bits* to seven hundred thousand: he arranged to have each copy serve as an insurance policy against railway accidents.[4]

In London, Newnes met another son of a Congregationalist manse.

This was W. T. Stead (1848–1912), who from earliest childhood venerated Oliver Cromwell as "the uncrowned head of English Puritanism," and who wholeheartedly endorsed the ideal of the priesthood of all believers.[5] In 1883 Stead became editor of the *Pall Mall Gazette*, which he transformed into the prototype of the so-called New Journalism by emphasizing interviews, gossip columns, racy investigative reporting, and dramatic headlines spread across several columns. Within two years circulation increased from 8,360 to 12,250.[6] In 1885, Stead was convicted of kidnapping as a result of his enthusiastic participation in an exposé of the "white slave trade." During his months in prison he formulated a number of theories similar to those expressed by Carlyle more than half a century earlier in "Signs of the Times"; Stead expounded his ideas in two articles in Percy Bunting's *Contemporary Review*. In the first of these, "Government by Journalism" (May 1886), Stead described the journalist as a "preacher," "apostle," and "missionary," entrusted with "the spiritual guidance of mankind." Proclaimed Stead, "We have to write afresh from day to day the only Bible which millions read . . . the only substitute that 'the progress of civilization' has provided for the morning and evening service with which a believing age began and ended the labours of the day."[7] In "The Future of Journalism" (November 1886), Stead compared the ideal newspaper to "a great secular or civic church and democratic university" that was to accomplish "the salvation of the community, the practical realization of the religious idea in national politics and social reform."[8] It was perhaps too much to expect that Stead should combine with such missionary zeal an equal capacity for business. At any rate George Newnes, more concerned with making money than with directing the affairs of nations, soon regretted it when he collaborated with Stead in founding the *Review of Reviews* in 1890.[9] Newnes abandoned that particular pulpit to Stead and went on to launch in 1891 the "magazine with a picture on every page," the famous *Strand*.

As for religious journalism proper, two weighty journals—the *British Quarterly* and the *Congregationalist*—died in 1886. In 1887 they were replaced by a shilling monthly, the *Congregational Review*, edited by J. Guinness Rogers, who in the first issue defined his own position as "Broad Evangelical" and urged a return to the spirit that had prevailed before "the days of creed-building."[10] Meanwhile a "queer, immensely able" young minister of the Free Church of Scotland was succeeding where nearly a decade earlier John Brown Paton and friends had failed: the *British Weekly,* published by Hodder and Stoughton and edited by the Reverend William Robertson Nicoll, was a successful rival to the *Christian World* from the time of its founding in November 1886.[11] Nicoll, like Alexander Strahan a quarter of a century earlier, believed that "much more might be done in the way of uniting religion with literature";[12] and so the *British Weekly* featured serial fiction in each issue, becoming the primary vehicle of the "Kailyard School," which included J. M. Barrie, "Ian Maclaren" (the Reverend John Watson), and the Reverend Samuel Rutherford Crockett. Their work, which has reminded at least one critic of the fiction included in the early volumes of *Good Words,* celebrated pious poverty and rural domesticity in a manner that many readers have found overly maudlin;[13] nonetheless, it was phenomenally popular throughout the 1890s. By then, Nicoll was editor as well of a new journal of the British publishing trade: the *Bookman,* founded in 1891.

Such new favorites did not entirely supplant the older quarterlies and monthlies. E. V. Lucas, writing in the 1930s, believed that by then the weightier periodicals had lost all "authority"; but he recalled that in the 1880s, "the *Nineteenth Century* always had something arresting. . . . So had the *Fortnightly* and the *Contemporary.*" Lucas also recalled a friend who, just before they set off on a short railway journey, "bought at the Victoria bookstall the *Edinburgh* and the *Quarterly,* the *Nineteenth Century,* the *Fortnightly,* the *Contemporary,* and several magazines and illustrated weeklies, in order that I might have 'something to read on the train.'"[14] Percy Bunting's *Contemporary* carved out a sphere for itself by becoming, in contrast to the majority of traditionally Liberal periodicals, more rather than less sympathetic to social reform in the years leading up to 1914, a stance that reflected Bunting's deepest personal convictions: as "Claudius Clear" (Nicoll himself) remarked in the *British Weekly* in 1893, "few magazines are more strongly impressed with the individuality of the editor than the *Contemporary.*"[15] The political views of Bunting's rival editor, James Knowles, grew more and more conservative as the century wore on. Still the *Nineteenth Century* provided a platform for the likes of Keir Hardie, Beatrice Potter, Sidney Webb, and even the anarchist Peter Kropotkin; Knowles also continued, of course, to publish as many contributions as possible from Gladstone and Tennyson.[16]

Knowles certainly prospered personally. In 1884 Sir Edward Walter Hamilton, Gladstone's secretary, was told while at dinner in Knowles's home that the circulation of the *Nineteenth Century* far surpassed that of either the *Fortnightly* or the *Contemporary*, and that Knowles's profits "about equalled the salary of the Prime Minister." Given "the size and contents of the house," Sir Edward was prepared to believe that the review "must be a fine property."[17] The Metaphysical Society had disbanded in 1880, but such an editor did not lack for social or intellectual stimulation: a guest at a "great ball" given by the Knowleses in 1887 recorded that his host "insisted on presenting me to Mr. Gladstone and his daughter, Lord Acton, and Mr. and Mrs. Oscar Wilde, and my hostess introduced me to the Kendals and Mrs. Beerbohm Tree." Later in the evening, Oscar Wilde "stood at the hither end of the room, a little in front of the seats of the mighty, and discoursed to the group of ladies who surrounded him on the splendours of the less-read Elizabethan and Jacobean dramatists."[18] In 1904, the journal *Public Opinion* included a profile of Knowles in its series on "Men Who Make Public Opinion"; much space was devoted to Knowles's friendships with Gladstone, Huxley, and Tennyson.[19] Knowles's political influence prompted the queen of Holland to refer to him as "le quatrième pouvoir de l'Etat Britannique."[20]

There was nothing in the later life of Alexander Strahan to match such glory. At the end of 1888 Strahan, who had belonged to the Reform Club since 1872, allowed his membership to lapse because the club was no longer, in his opinion, "Liberal enough for me."[21] A biography of the publisher William Heinemann describes Strahan in 1889 as "a queer whimsical 'character,' but a man of good intellect and high aims, and with, quite justifiably, no small opinion of his own achievements." Strahan may have been hoping even at this late date to make a comeback as a publisher: he wanted Heinemann to come to work for him, and it was with some chagrin that he learned of the younger man's decision to go into business for himself. "A' we'el," he exclaimed to Heinemann, "A' we'el, ye may mak' a name for yoursel', but ye'll no mak' sic a name as Alexander Strahan!"[22]

In 1890 Strahan issued what seems to have been his last publication: a reprint of the 1880 illustrated edition of the *Pilgrim's Progress* that had been prepared under his direction. In the same year Strahan's wife L. G. Séguin died after eleven years of marriage; from this time on he seems to have devoted himself to raising their three children—two sons and a daughter born in 1880, 1882, and 1884, who as a result of

Séguin's Huguenot background spoke French before they learned English. In 1893—the last year in which his name was included in the list of publishers in the London Post Office Directory—Strahan contributed to Nicoll's *British Weekly* a memoir of his old friend John Pettie, the artist, in which he proudly recalled the early *Good Words*, describing his younger self, with much admiration, in the third person.[23]

So completely did Strahan disappear from public life following the publication of this article that within three years, in the two-volume collection of *Literary Anecdotes of the Nineteenth Century* compiled by Thomas J. Wise, the famous bibliographer, and by W. R. Nicoll, who might have been expected to know better, Strahan was said to have already been "gathered to his fathers."[24] It was a point of vital concern to Wise, who at about this time was forging a number of bogus first editions of the works of famous authors, including one title by Tennyson ("The Last Tournament") that had allegedly appeared under Strahan's imprint.[25]

It is odd that Strahan, who must have seen this premature reference to his passing, did not bother to contradict it, for neither his self-esteem nor his formidable energy seems to have flagged during his long retirement. The descendants of Strahan's brother-in-law A. P. Watt, who after getting his start in Strahan's business went on to amass a fortune as one of the first professional literary agents, believe that Watt assisted Strahan financially for many years; Strahan's own grandchildren recall only that somehow, the family always lived well.[26] Strahan regularly attended art auctions where he purchased dozens of paintings at a time in the hope of discovering a masterpiece. Family legend also has it that he applied unsuccessfully to the College of Heralds to establish a coat of arms that would have depicted a ship in full sail and, in the crest, the *Anchora Spei*. Strahan's two sons— Stuart Séguin Strahan and Geoffrey Bennoch Strahan—attended St. Paul's School and then went on to Oxford, where Stuart was secretary of the Fabian Society. The family also took long journeys through Europe, where they were occasionally stranded through shortages of funds, as when, on one memorable evening, they dropped their entire purse on the gambling tables of Monte Carlo.

On 29 December 1903, the *Inverness Courier* described Strahan's career in an article entitled "A Great Publisher from the North of Scotland." Strahan was said to be living out "the evening of his days" in his London home.[27] It is possible that the article somehow made its way to Thomas J. Wise; at any rate, on 30 January 1904, Wise wrote to Buxton Forman, who had assisted him in perpetrating the Tennyson forgeries, that although he had been "positively assured" some years earlier that Strahan was dead, "I find that he is still very much alive, 74 [*sic*] years of age, & quite lively. He is coming to spend an evening & talk Tennyson in a few days."[28]

No other record of their meeting has come to light. But it is certain that after this date, Wise was able to display a number of copies of works by Tennyson that bore undated inscriptions by Strahan, and that have since been exposed as forgeries. On two of these—"Ode for the Opening of the International Exhibition" (allegedly published by Moxon in 1862) and "A Welcome to Alexandrovna" (King, 1874)—Strahan wrote "To Thos. J. Wise, with best regards, A. Strahan."[29] Even more suspicious are the inscriptions on two bogus "trial" editions allegedly published by Strahan himself in 1868 and in 1871 respectively. On "The Lover's Tale," Strahan wrote that "Of this private edition . . . only two copies were preserved, of which this is one."[30] On "The Last Tournament" Strahan wrote, "Of this private edition . . . not more than twenty copies were printed"—an inscription that pleased Wise so much that he included a facsimile of it in his 1908 bibliography of Tennyson and in the 1925 catalog of his personal library.[31] In the words of John Carter and Graham Pollard, who exposed Wise in their meticulous *Enquiry into the Nature of Certain Nineteenth Century Pamphlets* (1934), if Strahan was not privy to the true nature of these copies, then he was at the least "unusually, almost improbably, careless and obliging"; or perhaps, in the case of "The Last Tournament," "he knew what the book was, and used the word 'private' with a meaning the ordinary reader could not be expected to understand."[32] Perhaps Strahan, still smarting over past humiliations, knowingly inscribed the forgeries, partly out of the vanity involved in reliving for an evening his years of glory as Tennyson's publisher, partly out of some feeling that Wise was perpetrating an excellent practical joke. Wise was sufficiently confident that in September 1906 he wrote to John Henry Wrenn, the American collector who unwittingly purchased many forgeries from Wise over the years, that he had paid Strahan £50 for a privately printed copy of Tennyson's poem "England and America in 1782"—which was, of course, yet another forgery.[33]

Meanwhile William Isbister, Strahan's first business partner, had long since been ousted from Isbister and Company, the successor to the publishing firm founded by Strahan in Edinburgh in the 1850s.[34] The *Contemporary Review,* still edited by Bunting, was published by Isbister and Company until 1900, when it became the property of Columbus Company, Limited. Two of the other periodicals established by Strahan—the *Sunday Magazine* and *Good Words*—continued for a time to appear under the Isbister imprint. In November 1904, Donald Macleod, who had taken over the editorship of *Good Words* upon the death of his much-elder brother Norman in 1872, and who was now about to retire, recalled in "An Editorial Restrospect" how Alexander Strahan had envisioned a magazine that "without being religious in the technical sense . . . would yet be consistent in tone with what is most sacred in Christian conviction." Macleod also described "the change in public taste which has occurred during recent years."

> In spite of the advance of education it must be confessed that there has been a marked tendency towards more sensationalism in much of our periodical literature and art. Literary 'snapshots' and what serves to pass the time without demanding attention are too frequently chiefly sought.

Macleod predicted an imminent return to "the healthier habits of a former time."[35] But he was overly optimistic, and in fact neither *Good Words* nor the *Sunday Magazine* had much longer to live. In 1905 Isbister and Company was absorbed by Pitman and Company, of shorthand fame; *Good Words* and the *Sunday Magazine* were sold to the Amalgamated Press, a conglomerate directed by Alfred Harmsworth.[36] The *Sunday Magazine* disappeared; *Good Words* became a tabloid-size weekly paper. This new *Good Words* was a far cry from the original. It eschewed sermons and weighty devotional essays (although in one issue a Congregational minister explained "Why I do not play golf"), relying instead on third-rate serialized fiction and on solutions to such thorny problems as "When should a girl say 'Yes.' "[37] There seems to have been no comment in the contemporary press when *Good Words* limped to its end in 1910.

Sometime in the 1910s Alexander Strahan, now in his eighties, made one of his rare appearances in London literary society: he dined with a friend at the Authors' Club, where another guest expressed his astonishment at the "resurrection" and "unearthing" of a figure once so well known, but now so long forgotten.[38] In 1912, the centenary year of the birth of Norman Macleod, Strahan was the subject of an article in the *Glasgow Herald* entitled "Norman Macleod's Publisher," which asserted that Strahan's "genius and initiative" had won him a place in "the apostolical succession of the great Scottish publishers," even though, like Archibald Constable before him, he had been ruined by grandiose schemes and his own "reckless generosity."[39]

Already Strahan had outlived his earliest successes by half a century. He had also survived most of his old friends, enemies, and partners. Samuel Morley died in 1886; James Virtue in 1892; George McCorquodale in 1895; Francis Peek in 1899; Robert Buchanan in 1901; George MacDonald and F. R. Daldy in 1905; James Knowles in 1908; Percy Bunting and John Brown Paton in 1911. Strahan's childhood friend from Tain, Alexander Taylor Innes, died in 1912; his brother-in-law A. P. Watt, in 1914. William Isbister survived until 1916.

By then Strahan was living in Reigate, Surrey, in the home of his daughter Mary and her husband, Dr. Ralph Martin Soames, an English medical practitioner. His elder son, Stuart Séguin Strahan, went to Hong Kong in 1915 as a Christian missionary. His younger son, Lieutenant Geoffrey Bennoch Strahan, was killed in 1916 at the Battle of Gallipoli. "It is all over with happiness on this earth so far as I am concerned," Strahan wrote to a relative who had experienced more than one such loss; and yet, "We cannot think that God would send us either suffering or death, if they were not the germ and the earnest of eternal life."[40] Strahan did not live to see the Armistice. He died on 24 May 1918, at the age of eighty-four.

Notice of his death came as a surprise to many. The *Publishers' Circular* explained, "It is so many years since we heard anything of the famous publisher that we thought he was [already] dead."[41] The *Times* recalled that Strahan had been "a power to be reckoned with in the publishing world of the 'sixties and 'seventies."[42] The *Bookseller* suggested that had it not been for Strahan's incapacity for business, his "noble undertaking . . . might very well have taken a permanent place among the great publishing businesses of London."[43]

Long after Strahan's death, a disproportionate number of native-born Scots were still to be counted among the authors, editors, book-sellers, and publishers of London. Many of their internal quarrels were rendered obsolete when in 1929 the Free Church reunited with the established church, bringing together in one communion nearly all the Presbyterians in Scotland. The London-based Scots were mightily alarmed, however, when in the 1950s a Commission of En-quiry was established to study the conditions under which intercom-munion between the Church of England and the Church of Scotland might become possible. When the commission suggested that the Scottish church might bring itself to accommodate some form of epis-copacy, many Scots waxed indignant over what was regarded as yet another attempt on the part of the English to undermine Scottish institutions, the institution in this case being the very shrine of Scot-tish nationhood. One anecdote dating from this period concerns a Scottish journalist in London who was frequently heard to rail bitterly against the proposals. Finally one of his bewildered English colleagues summoned up the courage to ask the Scot, who had often and almost as noisily proclaimed himself to be an atheist, why he took such of-fense over the matter. "An atheist, maybe," came the reply. "But a Presbyterian atheist!"[44]

Although these proposals came to nothing, the Presbyterian churches of England soon proved themselves more amenable to com-promise and assimilation. Since 1945, they had been considering the possibility of union with the much larger Congregational church in England and Wales; and in 1972—more than a century after John Brown Paton's advocacy of such a merger—the Presbyterian Church of England, which had evolved from the "ethnic" chapels filled in the early and mid-nineteenth century by Scottish immigrants, disap-peared into the new United Reformed Church, the first union of churches in Britain to be effected across denominational lines. Only two English Presbyterian congregations, those of the Channel Islands, declined to join the new body, uniting instead with the Church of Scotland.

At the beginning of the new century, James Knowles's review became known as the *Nineteenth Century and After;* "but," quipped Arnold

Bennett, "it ought to call itself the Middle Ages."[45] In 1951 it became, somewhat belatedly, the *Twentieth Century*.

In 1954, the *Fortnightly Review* was absorbed by the *Contemporary Review*.

In 1972, the *Twentieth Century* appeared for the last time.

The *Contemporary Review*—the periodical that Alexander Strahan once termed his "most important literary enterprise"—is still published today.

Notes

Chapter I

1. Alexander Strahan, "Twenty Years of a Publisher's Life," *Day of Rest*, n.s., 3 (1881): 15–16.
2. See the *Congregational Miscellany*, 1 April 1870, 1; and the *Christian*, 9 May 1878, 24.
3. For a discussion of *Saint Pauls Magazine*, see Judith Wittosch Malcolm, "Trollope's *Saint Pauls* Magazine" (Ph.D. diss., University of Michigan, 1984).
4. For a discussion of the *Contemporary Review*, see Donna Lynne Wessel Walker, "The *Contemporary Review* and Contemporary Society, 1866–1877" (Ph.D. diss., University of Michigan, 1984).
5. Mark Pattison, "Books and Critics," *Fortnightly Review*, n.s., 22 (November 1877): 663.
6. In a recent review article, B. E. Maidment has remarked that Strahan filled "a unique and as yet unacknowledged place in the literature of Victorian social concern"; see the *Tennyson Research Bulletin* 3, no. 3 (Summer 1979): 119. Maidment has also discussed Strahan in "Victorian Publishing and Social Criticism: The Case of Edward Jenkins," *Publishing History* 11 (1982): 42–71.
7. Strahan's article on "Bad Literature for the Young," which first appeared in the *Contemporary Review* of November 1875, has been republished, with an introduction by Lance Salway, in *Signal: Approaches to Children's Literature* 20 (May 1976): 83–95.
8. "Good Words," *Saturday Review*, 17 December 1870, 772.
9. The *Literary World* of 17 January 1873; quoted in "A Quarter Century of English Presbyterianism—1848 to 1873," *Weekly Review*, 8 February 1873, 136.
10. R. L. S. [Robert Louis Stevenson], "The Foreigner at Home," *Cornhill Magazine* 45 (May 1882): 537–38.
11. "Literature of the People," *Athenaeum*, 1 January 1870, 14.
12. Alexander Strahan, "Our Very Cheap Literature," *Contemporary Review* 14 (June 1870): 459.

Chapter II

1. *The Works of the Rev. Sydney Smith*, 4 vols. (London: Longman, 1839–40), 1:iii. Smith puns on Vergil *Eclogue* 1.2: *"silvestrem tenui musam meditaris avena"* ("you reflect upon the woodland muse with slender reed").

2. For brief discussions of these and many other editors and periodicals, see John Gross, *The Rise and Fall of the Man of Letters: Aspects of English Literary Life Since 1800* (London: Weidenfeld and Nicolson, 1969), chap. 1; and R. G. Cox, "The Reviews and Magazines," in *From Dickens to Hardy*, vol. 6 of *The Pelican Guide to English Literature*, ed. Boris Ford (Harmondworth: Penguin, 1958; reprint, 1969), 188–204.

3. Richard D. Altick, *The English Common Reader: A Social History of the Mass Reading Public 1800–1900* (Chicago: University of Chicago Press, 1957; reprint, Chicago: University of Chicago Press, Phoenix Books, 1963), 268–69; and Henry Curwen, *A History of Booksellers: The Old and the New* (London: Chatto and Windus, 1873), 132.

4. *Political Register*, 26 March 1825, quoted by G. D. H. Cole, *The Life of William Cobbett*, 3d rev. ed. (London: Home and Van Thal, 1947), 265.

5. As quoted by Albert Peel, *These Hundred Years: A History of the Congregational Union of England and Wales* (London: Congregational Union of England and Wales, 1937), 138–39.

6. James Grant, *History of the Newspaper Press*, 3 vols. (London: Tinsley Brothers, 1871[–72], 1:vi.

7. [David Masson], "The Union with England and Scottish Nationality," *North British Review* 21 (May 1854): 43. The *Wellesley Index to Victorian Periodicals* attributes this article to Masson.

8. Charles Morgan, *The House of Macmillan (1843–1943)* (London: Macmillan, 1944), 14.

9. Charles Larcom Graves, *Life and Letters of Alexander Macmillan* (London: Macmillan, 1910), 130.

10. Derek Hudson, *Munby: Man of Two Worlds: The Life and Diaries of Arthur J. Munby 1828–1910* (London: John Murray, 1972), entry for 25 September 1869, 276.

11. G. E. Davie, *The Democratic Intellect: Scotland and Her Universities in the Nineteenth Century* (Edinburgh: Edinburgh University Press, 1961), 219.

12. Walter Bagehot, "The First Edinburgh Reviewers," in *The Collected Works of Walter Bagehot*, ed. Norman St John-Stevas, 12 vols. (London: Economist, 1965–74), 1:328. This article was originally published in the *National Review*, October 1855.

13. Walter Bagehot, "The Uses of Scotch Liberalism," *The Collected Works*, 7: 181. This article was originally published in the *Economist*, 17 April 1869.

14. James Boswell, *The Life of Johnson*, many editions, 18 April 1775.

15. "Dr. William Chambers," *Bookseller*, 5 June 1883, 493.

16. Kenneth Scott Latourette, *Christianity in a Revolutionary Age*, vol. 2, *The Nineteenth Century in Europe: The Protestant and Eastern Churches* (New York: Harper and Brothers, 1959), 402.

17. [Masson], "The Union with England and Scottish Nationality," 37.

18. Valentine Cunningham, *Everywhere Spoken Against: Dissent in the Victorian Novel* (Oxford: Clarendon Press, 1975), 9–10. Cunningham names Dickens, Trollope, and Thackeray as English novelists who were repelled by "the way Nonconformists talk."

19. Thomas Hughes, *Memoir of Daniel Macmillan* (London: Macmillan, 1882), 48, 220.

20. Graves, *Life and Letters of Alexander Macmillan*, 36.

21. Information concerning the Strahan family is drawn from the census reports of Tain, Ross-shire, 1841 and 1851, and from the commissary records of Ross and Cromarty, the Scottish Record Office, General Register House, Edinburgh.

22. John Prebble, *The Highland Clearances* (London: Secker and Warburg, 1963); see especially chap. 5, "The Massacre of the Rosses," in which there are references to "the Messenger-at-arms in Tain."

23. William Taylor, ed., *Memorials of the Life and Ministry of Charles Calder Mackintosh* (Edinburgh: Edmonston and Douglas, 1870), 5.

24. Alexander MacRae, *Revivals in the Highlands and Islands in the Nineteenth Century* (Stirling: Eneas MacKay, [1906]), 95.

    As the terms *evangelical* and *Evangelical* will be used frequently in the course of this study, it is necessary to explain that *Evangelical* will designate specific parties or groups; in this chapter, for example, it will refer to the party within the Church of Scotland that spearheaded the struggle against patronage and seceded in 1843 to form the Free Church of Scotland. The term *evangelical* will refer generally to those Protestant Christians who accepted what they took to be the revealed doctrines of sin, grace, and salvation through the atoning sacrifice of Christ; this theology emphasized the personal experience of salvation rather than the efficacy of sacraments or the sufficiency of good works. In this general sense both the established Church of Scotland and the Free Church were evangelical throughout the nineteenth century.

25. Alexander Taylor Innes, *Chapters of Reminiscence* (London: Hodder and Stoughton, 1913), 9–11. Innes, who was born in Tain in 1833, became an Edinburgh advocate, and a controversialist on behalf of the Free Church of Scotland in various periodicals, including those published by Alexander Strahan.

26. William Ferguson, *Scotland: 1689 to the Present* (New York: Praeger, 1968), 313. The Ten Years' Conflict and the Disruption of 1843 have been the subject of many histories, including Thomas Brown, *Annals of the Disruption* (Edinburgh: Macniven and Wallace, 1884); James Bryce, *Ten Years of the Church of Scotland from 1833 to 1843*, 2 vols. (Edinburgh: Blackwood and Sons, 1850); Robert Buchanan, *The Ten Years' Conflict: Being the History of the Disruption of the Church of Scotland*, 2 vols. (Glasgow: Blackie and Son, 1849); and Hugh Watt, *Thomas Chalmers and the Disruption* (Edinburgh: Thomas Nelson, 1943).

27. Christopher Harvie, *Scotland and Nationalism: Scottish Society and Politics, 1707–1977* (London: Allen and Unwin, 1977), 128.

28. George Douglas Campbell, Eighth Duke of Argyll, *Autobiography and Memoirs*, ed. the Dowager Duchess of Argyll, 2 vols. (London: John Murray, 1906), 1:174.

29. *The Letters of Sydney Smith*, ed. Nowell C. Smith, 2 vols. (Oxford: Clarendon Press, 1953), 2:442; letter to Mrs. Crowe dated 31 January 1841.

30. Prebble, *The Highland Clearances*, 216; Ian Carter, "The Changing Image of the Scottish Peasantry, 1745–1980," in *People's History and Socialist Theory*, ed. Raphael Samuel (London: Routledge and Kegan Paul, 1981), 9–15.

31. Jean Munro and Robert William Munro, *Tain Through the Centuries* (Inverness: Tain Town Council, 1966), 119.

32. Duncan Fraser, *The Story of Invergordon Church* (Inverness: n.p., 1946), 9; cited by Kenneth M. Boyd, *Scottish Church Attitudes to Sex, Marriage and the Family 1850–1914* (Edinburgh: John Donald Publishers, 1980), 12.

33. Munro and Munro, *Tain Through the Centuries*, 120.

34. Taylor, *Memorials of the Life and Ministry of Charles Calder Mackintosh*, 57; Munro and Munro, *Tain Through the Centuries*, 120.

35. [Mary Jeune] Lady St. Helier, *Memories of Fifty Years* (London: Edward Arnold, 1909), 31. According to Lady St. Helier, her family were exceptional among the gentry for being members of the Free Church rather than of the Scotch Episcopalian Church, a communion that "the lower classes viewed . . . with grave suspicion as a survival of the ancient Papacy, in fighting against which they had suffered so deeply" (53).

36. [Masson], "The Union with England and Scottish Nationality," 48.

37. Innes, *Chapters of Reminiscence*, 13. The Cameronians, who took their name from their leader, Richard Cameron, were a group of Covenanters who refused to join the reestablished Presbyterian Church of Scotland in the early eighteenth century because they rejected any supremacy of the state in ecclesiastical matters. In 1743 they established the Reformed Presbyterian Church.

38. Altick, *The English Common Reader*, chap. 11, discusses "The Self-made Reader," using Hugh Miller as an example (248). For Miller's friendship with the Innes and Strachan families, see Innes, *Chapters of Reminiscence*, 13–14 and 64, and the sources concerning Alexander Strahan's early life listed in n. 49.

39. The members of the group that brought Miller to Edinburgh to edit the *Witness* are named in Peter Bayne, *The Life and Letters of Hugh Miller*, 2 vols. (London: Strahan, 1871), 2:256.

40. William Garden Blaikie, *An Autobiography: Recollections of a Busy Life* (London: Hodder and Stoughton, 1901), 71.

41. David K. Guthrie and Charles J. Guthrie, eds., *Autobiography of Thomas Guthrie, D. D., and Memoir by His Sons*, 2 vols. (New York: Robert Carter and Brothers, 1875), 2:3.

42. "The Religious Press," *Weekly Review*, 21 March 1863, 754.

43. Hugh Miller, *My Schools and Schoolmasters, or the Story of My Education*, 15th ed. (Edinburgh: William P. Nimmo, 1869), 547–49.

44. Hugh Miller, "A Vision of the Railway," *Witness*, 4 March 1843, cited by Harry Escott, *A History of Scottish Congregationalism* (Glasgow: Congregational Union of Scotland, 1960), 138.

45. Hugh Miller, *First Impressions of England and Its People* (Edinburgh and London: John Johnstone, 1847), 376, 397–98, 403.

46. Innes, *Chapters of Reminiscence*, 64; for the Tain Academy, see Munro and Munro, *Tain Through the Centuries*, 107, 124.
47. Alexander Strahan, "Charles Knight, Publisher," *Good Words* 8 (September 1867): 615. I am also indebted to two of Strahan's grandchildren, Mr. Alexander Strahan and Mr. Ralph Strahan Soames, for their interest and assistance.
48. Innes, *Chapters of Reminiscence*, 75–76; and S. G. Checkland, *The Gladstones: A Family Biography 1764–1851* (Cambridge: Cambridge University Press, 1971), 48, 61–62, 78, 102–3, 129, 222–23.
49. For Alexander Strahan's early career, see "A Great Publisher from the North of Scotland," *Inverness Courier*, 29 December 1903, 3; "Norman Macleod's Publisher," *Glasgow Herald*, 20 April 1912, 4; the obituary notice in the *Times*, 29 May 1918, 9; and scattered references in Strahan's autobiographical essays, "Twenty Years of a Publisher's Life," which were serialized in *Day of Rest*, n.s., 3 (1881).

Chapter III

1. H. J. Hanham, "Mid-Century Scottish Nationalism: Romantic and Radical," in *Ideas and Institutions of Victorian Britain: Essays in Honour of George Kitson Clark*, ed. Robert Robson (London: G. Bell and Sons, 1967), 148.
2. R. L. S. [Robert Louis Stevenson], "The Foreigner at Home," *Cornhill* 45 (May 1882): 539. Stevenson asserts that at the University of Edinburgh, "All classes rub shoulders on the greasy benches. The raffish young gentleman in gloves must measure his scholarship with the plain, clownish laddie from the parish school."
3. "The 'Saturday Review' on Scotch and English Style," *Weekly Review*, 15 November 1862, 466. For the newspapers of Edinburgh, see J. B. S. [J. B. Sutherland]. *Random Recollections and Impressions* (Edinburgh: privately printed, 1903), 36.
4. *Times*, 4 December 1856, quoted by Hanham, "Mid-Century Scottish Nationalism," 174.
5. Hugh Walker, *The Literature of the Victorian Era* (Cambridge: Cambridge University Press, 1910), 519.
6. George J. Worth, *James Hannay* (Lawrence: University of Kansas Press, 1964), 134–35; and see, on this subject generally, Stewart Mechie, *The Church and Scottish Social Development 1780–1870* (London: Oxford University Press, 1960).
7. Blaikie, *An Autobiography*, 124–25.
8. *British and Foreign Evangelical Review* 10 (1861): 527, quoted by William G. Enright, "Urbanization and the Evangelical Pulpit in Nineteenth-Century Scotland," *Journal of Church History* 47 (December 1978): 404.
9. [Sutherland], *Random Recollections*, 125.
10. Blaikie, *An Autobiography*, 124.
11. The fullest account of the firm of Johnstone and Hunter is that in the obituary of John Johnstone, *Bookseller*, 26 May 1860, 283. For a descrip-

tion of the *Christian Treasury* and its contents, see the advertisement in the *Bookseller*, 23 April 1858, 169.

12. See the obituary for William Gellan, *Bookseller*, 4 May 1883, 398.

13. John Hepburn Millar, *A Literary History of Scotland* (London: T. Fisher Unwin, 1903), 637.

14. For the "Broad Church" party within the Scottish Establishment, see Millar, *A Literary History*, 625–27. The thought of Erskine, Campbell, and Maurice is discussed by Bernard M. G. Reardon, *Religious Thought in the Victorian Age: A Survey from Coleridge to Gore* (London: Longman, 1971; reprint, London: Longman, 1980), chaps. 5, 6, and 12.

15. [Sutherland], *Random Recollections*, 107.

16. *Letters of Lady Augusta Stanley: A Young Lady at Court 1849–1863*, edited by the Dean of Windsor [Albert Victor Baillie] and Hector Bolitho (London: Gerald Howe, 1927), 106–7.

17. Mechie, *The Church and Scottish Social Development*, 160.

18. Donald Macleod, *Memoir of Norman Macleod*, 2 vols. (London: Daldy, Isbister and Co., 1876), chap. 2 passim.

19. Sydney Smith, *Donald Macleod of Glasgow: A Memoir and a Study* (London: J. Clarke and Co., 1926), 92.

20. Donald Macleod, *Memoir of Norman Macleod*, 1:183, 203.

21. Ibid., 1:196. For Evangelical hostility to the "Forty Thieves," see Thomas Brown, *Annals of the Disruption*, 84; and Robert Buchanan, *The Ten Years' Conflict*, 2:344.

22. John Hollingshead, *My Lifetime*, 2 vols. (London: S. Low, Marston and Co., 1895), 1:178.

23. Donald Macleod, *Memoir of Norman Macleod*, 1:97.
    An article in the London *Weekly Review*, the organ of Evangelical Presbyterians in England, demonstrates that even at the time of his death in 1872, Macleod was still unforgiven: the *Weekly Review*, offended by the "various splendid panegyrics" pronounced over Macleod's grave, objects that "he was never known as a scholar.... He produced nothing in theology that deserves any serious notice.... He showed himself no hero, no martyr ... nor can the literary character of this distinguished man ... be ranked very high." Rather, charges the *Review*, Macleod's talents lay in being "a favourite at Court." The *Review* was particularly angered by any suggestion that Macleod "contributed to mellow and sweeten rigid Scottish orthodoxy, to liberalise the politics of his Church, and to prepare the way for a state of things in Scotland which English Broad Churchmen desire to see"; for "Scotland ... compared with England, abhors Broad Churchism" ("Norman Macleod," 13 July 1872, 682–84).

24. *Autobiography of Thomas Guthrie*, 2:61.

25. Strahan, "Twenty Years of a Publisher's Life," 16.

26. Alexander Strahan to William Angus Knight, 10 October 1873, the Pierpont Morgan Library, New York.

27. Johnstone and Hunter was eventually reestablished, and managed to

reacquire the copyright to the *Christian Treasury,* which survived until 1906. In 1871, Strahan and Company would publish the *Life and Letters of Hugh Miller,* by Peter Bayne, who succeeded Miller for a time as editor of the *Witness.*

28. Innes, *Chapters of Reminiscence,* 64–65.

29. Alexander Strahan, "Charles Knight, Publisher," *Good Words* 8 (September 1867): 617, 621.

30. Alexander Strahan, "Our Very Cheap Literature," *Contemporary Review* 14 (June 1870): 459.

31. *The Letters of Anthony Trollope,* ed. N. John Hall, with the assistance of Nina Burgis (Stanford: Stanford University Press, 1983), 928. The letter, to Trollope's son Henry Merivale Trollope, is dated 5 October 1881.

32. Blaikie, *An Autobiography,* 188; and Greville MacDonald, *George Mac-Donald and His Wife* (London: G. Allen and Unwin, 1924), 361.

33. This advertisement, the earliest I have found for Strahan and Company, appeared in the *Bookseller,* 29 November 1858, 558. For the status of Beecher's and Holmes's copyrights, see Edward Marston, *After Work: Fragments from the Workshop of an Old Publisher* (London: Heinemann, 1904), 71–72; and J. C. Derby, *Fifty Years Among Authors, Books and Publishers* (London: S. Low, Son and Co., 1884), 464; Derby also says that more than a hundred thousand copies of *The Power of Prayer,* by the Reverend S. Irenaeus Prime, were sold in Great Britain and the United States (608).

34. *Publishers' Circular,* 15 April 1859, 192; O. W. Holmes, *John Lothrop Motley: A Memoir* (Boston: Houghton, Osgood and Co., 1879), 80.

35. *Bookseller,* 30 November 1859, 1377.

36. J. Edwin Orr, *The Second Evangelical Awakening in Britain* (London and Edinburgh: Marshall, Morgan and Scott, 1949); although this work provides valuable detail, it considerably exaggerates the effects of the events it describes.

37. Strahan, "Twenty Years of a Publisher's Life," 15.

38. [Norman Macleod], "Note by the Editor," *Good Words* 1 (December 1860), inside front cover.

39. Strahan, "Twenty Years of a Publisher's Life," 16–17.

40. Ibid., 16.

41. A[rthur] P[enrhyn] Stanley, *The Life and Correspondence of Thomas Arnold,* 2 vols. (London: B. Fellowes, 1844), 1:272, 285; and Donald Macleod, *Memoir of Norman Macleod,* 2:97. The *Edinburgh Christian Magazine* is also discussed in Macleod's *Memoir,* 1:302 and 2:136.

42. See Macleod's "Address" on the reverse of the title page to the first issue of *Good Words,* January 1860.

43. Blaikie, *An Autobiography,* 188.

44. Strahan, "Twenty Years of a Publisher's Life," 16.

45. Ibid., 17.

46. [Norman Macleod], "Note by the Editor," *Edinburgh Christian Magazine* 10 (March 1859): 380.

47. Walter Graham, *English Literary Periodicals* (New York: Thomas Nelson and Sons, 1930), 301.
48. *The George Eliot Letters*, ed. Gordon S. Haight, 7 vols. (New Haven: Yale University Press, 1954–55), 3:208.
49. *Publishers' Circular*, 1 December 1859, 600–601.
50. *Publishers' Circular*, 15 December 1859, 704.
51. Strahan, "Twenty Years of a Publisher's Life," 17.
52. Ibid., 16.
   The titles of Victorian periodicals often suggest a model or competitor. The *Christian Guest* may have been meant to recall the *Welcome Guest*, itself an imitator of Dickens's *Household Words*, which was founded in 1858 under the editorship of G. A. Sala and achieved a circulation of one hundred twenty thousand in its first year. Strahan may well have been thinking of Dickens's periodical when he came up with the title for *Good Words*; soon there would appear a flood of cheap periodicals with such titles as *Kind Words, Christian Words, Winged Words, Plain Words, Welcome Words, Winsome Words,* and *Cheering Words.* After Strahan launched *Good Words for the Young* (1868), a rival publisher began to issue *Faithful Words* and *Faithful Words for the Young.*
53. [James Hannay], "Recollections of a Provincial Editor," *Temple Bar* 23 (May 1868): 337. Hannay, who edited the *Edinburgh Evening Courant* from 1860 to 1864, arrived in London in 1865 to work on the *Pall Mall Gazette.*
54. *Bookseller*, 26 January 1860, 2.
55. For these figures, see the *Bookseller*, 26 January 1860, 3, as corrected in the issue of 24 February 1860, 95.
56. Strahan, "Twenty Years of a Publisher's Life," 15.
57. "Norman Macleod, D.D.," *Contemporary Review* 6 (November 1867): 281.
58. *Bookseller*, 26 January 1860, 3.
59. The illustrations that appeared in the early volumes of *Good Words* have been discussed in Gleeson White, *English Illustration: 'The Sixties': 1855–70* (London: Constable, 1897); in Forrest Reid, *Illustrators of the Eighteen Sixties* (London: Faber and Gwyer, 1928; reprint, New York: Dover, 1975); and in George Dalziel and Edward Dalziel, *The Brothers Dalziel: A Record of Fifty Years Work in Conjunction with Many of the Most Distinguished Artists of the Period 1840–1900* (London: Methuen, 1901). See also Martin Hardie's biography of John Pettie (London: Adam and Charles Black, 1908), an artist who painted portraits of Strahan and many of his relatives, in addition to contributing to *Good Words*. Strahan's obituary notice in the *Times* (29 May 1918, 9) refers to his part in encouraging the work of young artists and in advancing the art of wood engraving.
60. "Lady Somerville's Maidens," *Good Words* 1 (1860): 186.
61. Strahan, "Twenty Years of a Publisher's Life," 324.
62. The *Caledonian Mercury* was quoted at length on the inside title page of *Good Words*, June 1860.

63. *Bookseller,* 29 December 1860, 906.
64. [Norman Macleod], "Note by the Editor," *Good Words* 1 (December 1860): 796.
65. For Thomas Mulock, see Blaikie, *An Autobiography,* 149; and Prebble, *The Highland Clearances,* 240–48, 254–55, 267–69. Dinah Maria Mulock married G. Lillie Craik, advocate of *The Pursuit of Knowledge Under Difficulties* (1831) and a partner in Macmillan and Company, in 1864.
66. Strahan probably alludes to the story of Dives, the rich man in the parable of Lazarus, Luke 16:19–31. Nineteen letters from Strahan to Hollingshead, written in 1860 and 1861, are at the Huntington Library, San Marino, California.
67. *Bookseller,* 6 December 1862, 755.
68. Macleod to Ludlow, 27 February 1860, the Ludlow Papers, Add. 7348/7/1, Cambridge University Library.
69. Macleod to Ludlow, 29 February 1860, the Ludlow Papers, Add. 7348/7/2, Cambridge University Library.
70. Strahan to Hollingshead, 26 December 1860, 1 February 1861, 23 May 1861, the Huntington Library.
71. Macleod to Ludlow, June 1860, the Ludlow Papers, Add. 7348/7/7, Cambridge University Library.
72. Strahan to Ludlow, 22 June 1860, the Ludlow Papers, Add. 7348/11/127, Cambridge University Library.
73. Strahan to Hollingshead, 7 March 1861, the Huntington Library.
74. Blaikie, *An Autobiography,* 188.
75. Hollingshead, *My Lifetime,* 2:175.
76. Donald Macleod, *Memoir of Norman Macleod,* 2:109.
77. "X" [pseud.], "'Good Words,'" *Christian Observer,* July 1863, 504.
78. Advertisement, *Bookseller,* 26 March 1861, 195; Strahan to Hollingshead, 7 March 1861, the Huntington Library.
79. G. N. Ray, *Thackeray: The Age of Wisdom, 1847–1863* (London: Oxford University Press, 1958), 299; *Publishers' Circular,* 1 May 1862, 199.
80. Strahan to Hollingshead, 24 August 1861, the Huntington Library.
81. Macleod to Ludlow, [?] August 1861, the Ludlow Papers, Add. 7348/7/13, Cambridge University Library; cited also in Donald Macleod, *Memoir of Norman Macleod,* 2:113.
82. Donald Macleod, *Memoir of Norman Macleod,* 2:109.
83. Macleod to Ludlow, [?] August 1861.
84. Donald Macleod, *Memoir of Norman Macleod,* 2:114. The letter to Stevenson is dated 14 August 1861.
85. Macleod to Ludlow, [?] August 1861.
86. *Bookseller,* 26 September 1861, 522.
87. [John Brown] and D. W. Forrest, eds., *Letters of Dr. John Brown: With Letters from Ruskin, Thackeray, and Others* (London: A. and C. Black, 1907), 147.
88. Strahan to Hollingshead, 24 December 1861, the Huntington Library.

89. Strahan, "Twenty Years of a Publisher's Life," 474; Strahan recalls meeting Smith in the office of the *Edinburgh Telegraph*, a gathering place for literary men in the early 1860s.
90. Advertisement, *Bookseller*, 31 January 1862, 91.
91. Macleod to Trollope, [? April 1862], Bodleian MS. Don. c. 9, fols. 102–3. Macleod's letter is included in *The Letters of Anthony Trollope*, 177–78.
92. Memorandum in Trollope's hand, Bodleian MS. Don. c. 9, fol. 104. Strahan agreed to pay £600 solely for the right to publish in *Good Words* a novel approximately the length of Thackeray's *Lovel the Widower*, which had filled ninety-seven pages in the *Cornhill*.
93. "Trade Changes and Literary Gossip," *Bookseller*, 30 June 1862, 386.

Chapter IV

1. Alexander Strahan, "A Few Words About an Esteemed Contributor" [Richard Rowe], *Day of Rest*, n.s., 2 (1880): 118.
2. "Adelph" [pseud.], *London Scenes and London People: Anecdotes, Reminiscences, and Sketches of Places, Personages, Events, Customs, and Curiosities of London City, Past and Present* (London: W. H. Collingridge, City Press, 1863), 252–53, 258.
3. *Bookseller*, 30 August 1862, 559.
4. For "Strahan's Family Library," see the prospectus and the list of titles bound in the back of many books published by Strahan in 1863, such as *The Recreations of a Country Parson*. A. K. H. Boyd, who received between £600 and £1,000 each for the volumes of sermons he sold to Strahan in the 1860s, would later write, "I do not know whether Mr. Strahan . . . was the most astute of all publishers; but he certainly was the most liberal I have ever known"; see Boyd, *Twenty-Five Years of St. Andrews*, 2 vols., 4th ed. (London: Longmans, Green and Co., 1893), 1:295.
5. Hardie, *John Pettie*, 59–60.
6. Henrietta Keddie ["Sarah Tytler"], *Three Generations: The Story of a Middle-Class Scottish Family* (London: John Murray, 1911), 295.
7. Isabella Fyvie Mayo, *Recollections of What I Saw, What I Lived Through, and What I Learned, During More than Fifty Years of Social and Literary Experience* (London: John Murray, 1910), 147–48.
8. Boswell, *The Life of Johnson*, many editions, section concerning 1783.
9. [Alexander Strahan and Alexander Pollock Watt], "John Pettie, R.A. By Two Old Friends," *British Weekly*, 9 March 1893, 313–14.
10. Donald Macleod, *Memoir of Norman Macleod*, 2:154.
11. Strahan, "Twenty Years of a Publisher's Life," 256.
12. "The Old Lieutenant and His Son," *Spectator*, 18 October 1862, 1171.
13. "A Scotch Minister's Novel," *London Review*, 18 October 1862, 346–47.
14. Donald Macleod, *Memoir of Norman Macleod*, 2:121.
15. Macleod to Ludlow, "Monday" [20 October 1862], and 28 October 1862, the Ludlow Papers, Add. 7348/7/Items 17 and 18, Cambridge University Library.

16. Strahan to Trollope, 17 November 1862, Bodleian MS. Don. c. 10*, fols. 25–26.
17. Memorandum in Trollope's hand, Bodleian MS. Don. c. 9, fol. 104.
18. *Reader*, 17 January 1863, 80; *Publishers' Circular*, 17 January 1863, 14.
19. *Times*, 28 January 1863, 5; *Publishers' Circular*, 2 February 1863, 56.
20. *Publishers' Circular*, 17 January 1863, 14.
21. For the Innere Mission, see William O. Shanahan, *German Protestants Face the Social Question*, vol. 1, *The Conservative Phase, 1815–1871* (Notre Dame, Ind.: University of Notre Dame Press, 1954), especially 70–94 and 208–38.
22. Strahan, "Twenty Years of a Publisher's Life," 829.
23. Ibid., 830.
24. John Lewis Paton, *John Brown Paton: A Biography* (London: Hodder and Stoughton, 1914), 19.
25. "Last Words from Alexander Strahan About 'The Contemporary Review' and Mr. J. Knowles," an eight-page leaflet dated 15 March 1877, included in the Gladstone Papers, Additional Manuscripts 44453, fols. 204–7, the British Library.
26. G. R. Balleine, *A History of the Evangelical Party in the Church of England* (London: Longmans, Green and Co., 1933), 206; see also Michael Hennell, *Sons of the Prophets: Evangelical Leaders of the Victorian Church* (London: Society for Promoting Christian Knowledge, 1979), 12–15; and Alexander Haldane, *The Lives of Robert Haldane of Airthrey, and of His Brother, James Alexander Haldane* (New York: Robert Carter and Brothers, 1853).
27. *Record*, 1 April 1863, 4. The *Record* articles were republished soon after their appearance in a sixty-eight-page pamphlet entitled *"Good Words": The Theology of its Editor, and of Some of Its Contributors*. The British Library copy lacks its title page.
28. *Record*, 1 April 1863, 4.
29. Ibid.
30. *Record*, 13 April 1863, 4.
31. *Record*, 6 April 1863, 4.
32. The *Record*, 13 April 1863, 4. Trollope was of course not a "sensation-writer" of the type exemplified by a Mrs. Henry Wood or a Mary Elizabeth Braddon.
33. "The 'Record's' Attack on 'Good Words,'" *Weekly Review*, 13 June 1863, 163.
34. Donald Macleod, *Memoir of Norman Macleod*, 2:137.
35. Ibid., 2:148.
36. *Patriot*, 23 April 1863, 265. The *Patriot* articles were republished in a pamphlet entitled *An Exposure of the "Record" Newspaper in its Treatment of "Good Words"* (London: Simpkin, Marshall, and Co., [1863]).
37. *Patriot*, 23 April 1863, 265.
38. Macleod's letter was published in the *Bookseller*, 30 April 1863, 218.
39. Obituary of Thomas Alexander, *Weekly Review*, 17 February 1872, 148;

he was identified as the author of the *Record* articles in the *Weekly Review,* 13 June 1863, 163–64.

40. See *"Good Words": The Theology of Its Editor,* iii–iv.

41. See the appendix to *An Exposure of the "Record."*

42. *Patriot,* 4 June 1863, 374; the *Free Church of Scotland Monthly Record,* 1 July 1863, 281.

43. Donald Macleod, *Memoir of Norman Macleod,* 2:287.

44. R. H. Super, *Trollope in the Post Office* (Ann Arbor: University of Michigan Press, 1981), 101.

45. Trollope's letter to Millais is included in John Guille Millais, *The Life and Letters of Sir John Everett Millais,* 2 vols. (London: Methuen, 1899), 1:283–84, and in *The Letters of Anthony Trollope,* 220–21.

46. Macleod to Trollope, 11 June 1863, Bodleian MS. Don. c. 9, fols. 112–15; included in Donald Macleod, *Memoir of Norman Macleod,* 2:150–53, and in *The Letters of Anthony Trollope,* 222–24.

47. Anthony Trollope, *An Autobiography,* ed. Frederick Page (Oxford: Oxford University Press, 1950), 188.

48. Trollope to Strahan, 10 June 1863, draft copy in Trollope's hand, Bodleian MS. Don. c. 9, fols. 108–9; included in *The Letters of Anthony Trollope,* 221.

49. See Strahan's letters to Trollope, 13 June and 16 June 1863, Bodleian MS. Don. c. 9, fols. 116–17; and, for the agreements with Chapman and Hall, Bodleian MS. Don. c. 9, fols. 105 and 110–11.

50. "A Word of Remonstrance with Some Novelists, by a Novelist," *Good Words* 4 (July 1863): 524–26.

51. Trollope to George Eliot, 18 October 1863, *The Letters of Anthony Trollope,* 238.

52. "The Twa Kirks," *London Review,* 13 June 1863, 629.

53. *Scotsman,* 12 November 1863.

54. "Good Words in the Presbytery of Strathbogie," *London Review,* 21 November 1863, 538.

55. *Bookseller,* 10 December 1863, 712.

56. *London Review,* 21 November 1863, 539; *Bookseller,* 10 December 1863, 711.

57. Strahan, "Twenty Years of a Publisher's Life," 17.

58. The few surviving records of the firm of Spalding and Hodge have been deposited by the Inveresk Paper Company Ltd. at the Greater London Record Office, London County Hall. The assignment of the copyright for *Good Words* dated 10 February 1863 is filed as B/SPL/13.

59. D. C. Coleman, *The British Paper Industry 1495–1860* (Oxford: Clarendon Press, 1958), 245.

60. *Past and Present 1796–1921* (London: Spalding and Hodge, [1921]), [1–16]; and the obituary of Thomas S. Spalding in the *Bookseller,* 5 August 1887, 763–64.

61. Ellen E. Ballou, *The Building of the House: Houghton Mifflin's Formative Years* (Boston: Houghton Mifflin, 1970), 192, 201.

62. Edward Bell, *George Bell, Publisher: A Brief Memoir* (London: Chiswick

Press, 1924), 74; another portion of the sum necessary to purchase "Bohn's Library" was lent by William Clowes and Sons, who printed the books of Bell and Daldy.

63. *Bookseller,* 10 December 1864, 993; Strahan, "Twenty Years of a Publisher's Life," 18.
64. Strahan, "Twenty Years of a Publisher's Life," 69.
65. Ibid., 101.
66. Strahan managed to sell eighty thousand copies of this book by soliciting a lengthy letter in praise of it from Lord Brougham, whose opinions Strahan then "scattered very liberally far and near as an advertisement," according to Blaikie's *Autobiography,* 161.
67. *Bookseller,* 30 July 1864, 445.
68. Spalding and Hodge Records, B/SPL/14, Greater London Record Office, London County Hall.
69. Mayo, *Recollections,* 145.
70. Blaikie, *An Autobiography,* 184.
71. Ibid., 188.
72. Ibid., 184; *Autobiography of Thomas Guthrie,* 2:416; "English Books in America," *Bookseller,* 31 January 1866, 7.
73. Strahan, "Twenty Years of a Publisher's Life," 326–27; but the publisher J. M. Dent, who was raised as a Quaker in the small town of Darlington, vividly recalled, in his *Memoirs,* eagerly awaiting each installment of *Hereward* in *Good Words:* "It was the only way in which I could get at modern fiction, for the 'yellow back,' in the form of the cheap novel of the period, was taboo in our household" (*The Memoirs of J. M. Dent 1849–1926* [London: J. M. Dent and Sons, 1928], 24).
74. *Bookseller,* 30 September 1865, 585.
75. Strahan, "Twenty Years of a Publisher's Life," 21.
76. Walker, *The Literature of the Victorian Era,* 576, 580. However, Matthew Arnold, that admirer of Celtic literature, was unimpressed when in the autumn of 1866 he met the "raw and intemperate Scotch youth" and heard him read his poetry aloud; see *The Letters of Matthew Arnold, 1848–1888,* ed. G. W. E. Russell, 2 vols. (New York: Macmillan, 1895), 1:394, 452. In fact, Buchanan was part English and Welsh as well as Scottish.
77. Buchanan made this claim in the preface to *The Fleshly School of Poetry and Other Phenomena of the Day* (London: Strahan, 1872). For Buchanan's life, see the entry by T. W. Bayne in Leslie Stephen and Sidney Lee, eds., *Dictionary of National Biography (DNB)* (London: Smith, Elder and Co., 1885–1904; reprint, London: Oxford University Press, 1921–); and the biography by his sister-in-law, Harriet Jay, *Robert Buchanan: Some Account of His Life, His Life's Work, and His Literary Friendships* (London: T. Fisher Unwin, 1903).
78. Jay, *Robert Buchanan,* 162.
79. John A. Cassidy, *Robert W. Buchanan* (New York: Twayne, 1973), 38. Cassidy provides a detailed account of the quarrel between Buchanan and Swinburne.
80. For MacDonald, see Greville MacDonald, *George MacDonald and His Wife.*

81. Derrick Leon, *Ruskin the Great Victorian* (London: Routledge and Kegan Paul, 1949; reprint, Hamden, Conn.: Archon Books, 1969), 343. Greville MacDonald devotes an entire chapter to his father's friendship with Ruskin.
82. Greville MacDonald, *George MacDonald and His Wife*, 353.
83. Strahan, "Twenty Years of a Publisher's Life," 256.

Chapter V

1. Kenneth Macleod Black, *The Scots Churches in England* (Edinburgh and London: Blackwood and Sons, 1906), 19.
2. "Hindrances to the Progress of Presbyterianism in England," *Weekly Review*, 4 May 1872, 418.
3. [James Hannay], "The Scot at Home," *Cornhill Magazine* 14 (August 1866): 243.
4. Ian Sellars, *Nineteenth-Century Nonconformity* (London: Edward Arnold, 1977), 10.
5. "Correspondence," *Weekly Review*, 18 May 1872, 483.
6. Peter T. Marsh, *The Victorian Church in Decline: Archbishop Tait and the Church of England 1868–1882* (London: Routledge and Kegan Paul, 1969), 14. According to Marsh, Tait was sometimes termed "the Presbyterian Archbishop" by his Anglican critics (246).
7. For the history of English Congregationalism, see R. Tudor Jones, *Congregationalism in England 1662–1962* (London: Independent Press, 1962).
8. Hugh Miller, *First Impressions of England and Its People*, 406.
9. Escott, *A History of Scottish Congregationalism*, xv.
10. Francis B. Smith, "The Atheist Mission, 1840–1900," in *Ideas and Institutions of Victorian Britain: Essays in Honour of George Kitson Clark*, ed. Robert Robson (London: G. Bell and Sons, 1967), 205.
11. Quoted by John Eros, "The Rise of Organized Freethought in Mid-Victorian England," *Sociological Review*, n.s., 2, no. 1 (July 1954): 109. For Holyoake's activities see also Lee J. Grugel, *George Jacob Holyoake: A Study in the Evolution of a Victorian Radical* (Philadelphia: Porcupine Press, 1976); and Edward Royle, *Radical Politics 1790–1900: Religion and Unbelief* (London: Longman, 1971), 51–53.
12. See John Collins Francis, *Notes by the Way* (London: T. Fisher Unwin, 1909), 17. Bradlaugh's activities are described by Royle, *Radical Politics 1790–1900*, 54–58.
13. Noel Annan, "Science, Religion, and the Critical Mind," in *1859: Entering an Age of Crisis*, ed. Philip Appleman et al. (Bloomington: Indiana University Press, 1959), 37.
14. W. E. H. Lecky, *History of the Rise and Influence of the Spirit of Rationalism in Europe*, 2 vols. (London: Longmans, Green and Co., 1865), 1:xviii–xix.
15. See, for example, the advertisement in the *Saturday Review*, 25 March

1865, 362. For the history of the *Fortnightly*, see Edwin Mallard Everett, *The Party of Humanity: The* Fortnightly Review *and Its Contributors 1865–1874* (Chapel Hill: University of North Carolina Press, 1939), 141; and the *Wellesley Index to Victorian Periodicals*, 2:173–83.

16. Trollope, *An Autobiography*, 191.

17. *Spectator*, 3 February 1866, 137.

18. Everett, *The Party of Humanity*, 141.

19. John Morley, "The Death of Mr. Mill," *Fortnightly Review*, n.s., 13 (June 1873): 669–76.

20. John Morley, *Recollections*, 2 vols. (New York: Macmillan, 1917), 1:100.

21. John Morley, "On Compromise," *Fortnightly Review*, n.s., 15 (April 1874): 438.

22. John Morley, "The Struggle for National Education," *Fortnightly Review*, n.s., 14 (September 1873): 313–14.

23. John Morley, "Valedictory," *Fortnightly Review*, n.s., 32 (October 1882): 518.

24. Alan D. Gilbert, *Religion and Society in Industrial England: Church, Chapel and Social Change, 1740–1914* (London: Longman, 1976), 177. Morley estimated that when the circulation of the *Fortnightly* was at twenty-five hundred, one could assume a readership of thirty thousand, according to Everett, *The Party of Humanity*, 321.

25. Strahan, "Twenty Years of a Publisher's Life," 259.

26. For Alford's life, see Henry Alford, *Life, Journals, and Letters of Henry Alford, D.D., Late Dean of Canterbury*, ed. Fanny Alford (London: Rivingtons, 1873).

27. "Preface," *Dearden's Miscellany* 3 (1840): iii.

28. *Life, Journals, and Letters of Henry Alford*, 177.

29. Ibid., 195–96.

30. Strahan, "Twenty Years of a Publisher's Life," 256, 260.

31. "False Guides," *Saturday Review*, 1 December 1866, 666. In Samuel Butler's *The Way of All Flesh* (begun in 1873 and published posthumously in 1903), Ernest Pontifex is thoroughly disillusioned by his study of Dean Alford's notes to the Greek New Testament, which appear to recommend that "the whole story should be taken on trust."

> How was it that Dean Alford . . . could not or would not see what was so obvious to Ernest himself? Could it be for any other reason than that he did not want to see it? And if so was he not a traitor to the cause of truth? Yes; but was he not also a respectable and successful man? And were not the vast majority of respectable and successful men, such, for example, as all the bishops and archbishops, doing exactly as Dean Alford did? (*Ernest Pontifex, or the Way of All Flesh* [Boston: Houghton Mifflin, 1964], 230, 245.)

32. "Dean Alford," *Spectator*, 14 January 1871, 37.

33. "Dean Alford," *Weekly Review*, 21 January 1871, 61.

34. Strahan, "Twenty Years of a Publisher's Life," 259.

35. Ibid.

36. *Weekly Review,* 13 January 1866, 59.
37. Strahan, "Twenty Years of a Publisher's Life," 259.
38. For the background to Shaw's article, and for Alford's attempts to counteract the spread of rationalism, see M. L. Maddox, "Henry Alford and the *Contemporary Review*" (Ph.D. diss., University of Chicago, 1950), 159–69, and Donna Lynne Wessel Walker, "The *Contemporary Review* and Contemporary Society, 1866–1877" (Ph.D. diss., University of Michigan, 1984), chap. 2.
39. Annan, "Science, Religion, and the Critical Mind," 40. For the philosophy of Hamilton and Mansel, see Reardon, *Religious Thought in the Victorian Age,* 223–42.
40. Mansel, *The Limits of Religious Thought Examined in Eight Lectures,* 4th ed. (London: John Murray, 1859), 10.
41. John Stuart Mill, *Autobiography* (London: Longman, 1873), chap. 7.
42. John Passmore, *A Hundred Years of Philosophy* (London: Duckworth, 1957; reprint, Harmondsworth: Penguin, 1968), 30. Reardon, however, says that "in the light of the present day Mansel stands out as one of the most original religious thinkers of the century" and that to reread his Bampton lectures today "is to encounter a remarkable anticipation of some recent developments in theological thought" (223, 237).
43. *Weekly Review,* 13 January 1866, 59.
44. *Life, Journals, and Letters of Henry Alford,* 258–59.
45. John Wellwood, *Norman Macleod* (Edinburgh and London: Oliphant, Anderson and Ferrier, 1897), 118–24; Donald Macleod, *Memoir of Norman Macleod,* chap. 18.
46. Margaret Oliphant, *A Memoir of the Life of John Tulloch* (Edinburgh: Blackwood and Sons, 1888), 220–23.
47. Ibid., 224.
48. The ballad of "Norman's Blast: A Rejected Contribution to 'Good Words'" appeared in several editions in 1865–66. The stanzas cited appear in a version published in Edinburgh (John Maclaren), Glasgow (Thomas Murray and Son) and Aberdeen (Geo. Davidson) in 1866.
49. The Edinburgh *Scotsman* was nearly as irreverent in its treatment of Evangelical concerns as was its London counterpart, the "Superfine" *Saturday Review.* "Hope" may be either Anthony Beresford-Hope, proprietor of the *Saturday Review,* or James Robert Hope-Scott (1812–73), the standing counsel for nearly every British railway company, who was involved in the struggles of the North British Railway Company to establish Sunday service.
50. Anthony Trollope, "The Fourth Commandment," *Fortnightly Review* 3 (15 January 1866): 529–38.
51. E. H. Plumptre, "Sunday," *Contemporary Review* 1 (January 1866): 168.
52. *Weekly Review,* 13 January 1866, 59.
53. *Guardian,* 31 January 1866, 113.

54. *Spectator*, 10 February 1866, 166.
55. *Spectator*, 3 March 1866, 249.
56. *Spectator*, 5 May 1866, 503.
57. *London Review*, 10 November 1866, 531.
58. Connop Thirlwall, *Letters to a Friend*, ed. A. P. Stanley (London: Richard Bentley and Son, 1881), 78.
59. *Letters of Edward Dowden and His Correspondents* [ed. Elizabeth D. Dowden and Hilda M. Dowden] (London: J. M. Dent and Sons, 1914), 30. The letter, to John Dowden, is dated 2 February 1866; the article in question, "French Aesthetics," appeared in the *Contemporary* of February 1866.
60. Ibid., 42, letter dated 10 November 1869; and 64, letter dated 3 September 1872. Dowden's article, "The Poetry of Democracy: Walt Whitman," was published in the *Westminister Review* of July 1871.
61. Albert Peel, ed., *Letters to a Victorian Editor* [Henry Allon of the *British Quarterly Review*] (London: Independent Press, 1929), 251. The circulation of the *Fortnightly Review* in January 1867 was only about fourteen hundred; it rose to twenty-five hundred or more by 1872, according to the *Wellesley Index to Victorian Periodicals*, 2:175–76.
62. Strahan, "Twenty Years of a Publisher's Life," 479.
63. Quoted in James C. Austin, ed., [*James T.*] *Fields of* The Atlantic Monthly: *Letters to an Editor, 1861–1870* (San Marino, Calif.: Huntington Library, 1953), 391.
64. Lona Mosk Packer, ed., *The Rossetti-Macmillan Letters* (Berkeley: University of California Press, 1963), 60–61; Christina Rossetti's three contributions were "Hero: A Metamorphosis" (January), "Who Shall Deliver Me?" (February), and "If" (later "Hoping Against Hope") (March). Craig's editorship of the *Argosy* is also referred to in Stewart M. Ellis, *Henry Kingsley 1830–1876* (London: Grant Richards, 1931), 143, and in the entry by T. W. Bayne in the *DNB*, where Craig appears under her married name, Mrs. Isa Knox.
65. *Publishers' Circular*, 2 October 1865, 547.
66. Walter C. Phillips, *Dickens, Reade, and Collins: Sensation Novelists. A Study in the Conditions and Theories of Novel Writing in Victorian England* (New York: Columbia University Press, 1919), 116; and Stanley J. Kunitz and Howard Haycraft, eds., *British Authors of the Nineteenth Century* (New York: H. W. Wilson Co., 1936), s.v. "Reade."
67. Austin, *Fields of* The Atlantic Monthly, 392.
68. Strahan to Trollope, 3 April 1866, Bodleian MS. Don. c. 10*, fols. 27[b]– 28; included in *The Letters of Anthony Trollope*, 336–37.
69. Ibid. I have seen no other evidence that Strahan and Dallas knew each other; however, Dallas was something of a *Landsmann* of Strahan's: his mother hailed from Tain, where her father and then her brother were ministers of the Church of Scotland and then the Free Church for a span of over forty years, including the years during which the Strachans

were among the congregants. Unfortunately for Strahan, Trollope had certain misgivings concerning the personal characters of both Dallas and Reade, as recorded in his *Autobiography*.

70. See *The Letters of Anthony Trollope*, 290, letter to George Smith, 9 January 1865.

71. According to a letter from Geoffrey Ashton, librarian, the Garrick Club, 26 February 1982.

72. *Bookseller*, 30 April 1866, 298.

73. "Editor" [G. H. Lewes], "Critical Notices," *Fortnightly Review* 3 (15 December 1865): 375.

74. For information concerning the Virtues and their various businesses, see Curwen, *A History of Booksellers;* Basil Hunnisett, *Steel-Engraved Book Illustration in England* (Boston: David R. Godine, 1980); the entries for George Virtue (1794–1868) and James Sprent Virtue (1829–92) in Frederic Boase, *Modern English Biography*, 6 vols. (Truro: Netherton and Worth, 1892–1921; reprint, London: Frank Cass, 1965), 3:1105; and the entry for James Sprent Virtue in the *Dictionary of National Biography* written by George Clement Boase. When George Virtue bought the *Art Journal* it was the *Art-Union;* he retitled it.

75. "Mortgage of Copyright," 12 July 1866, B/SPL/15, Greater London Record Office, London County Hall.

76. *The Hardman Papers: A Further Selection (1865–1868) from the Letters and Memoirs of Sir William Hardman*, ed. S. M. Ellis (London: Constable, 1930), 174.

77. "Agreement," 10 October 1866, B/SPL/16, Greater London Record Office, London County Hall.

78. For further details, see Patricia Thomas Srebrnik, "Trollope, James Virtue, and *Saint Pauls Magazine*," *Nineteenth Century Fiction* 37, no. 3 (December 1982):443–63.

79. Trollope and Virtue refer to the meetings of the *Fortnightly* editorial board in the correspondence at the Bodleian, MS. Don. c. 10*, fols. 7–8 and 9–10.

80. "Literary Gossip," *London Review*, 11 August 1866, 167.

81. Justin McCarthy, *Reminiscences* (London: Chatto and Windus, 1899), 356, 363.

82. Charles Reade, "The Prurient Prude," *New York Times*, 6 October 1866, 5.

83. "Griffith Gaunt," *New York Times*, 6 November 1866, 5.

84. "Griffith Gaunt," *Spectator*, 27 October 1866, 1198.

85. Quoted in Charles L. Reade and the Rev. Compton Reade, comps., *Charles Reade, Dramatist, Novelist, Journalist: A Memoir*, 2 vols. (London: Chapman and Hall, 1887), 2:181–82.

86. "Griffith Gaunt," *Saturday Review*, 3 November 1866, 551.

87. Malcolm Elwin, *Charles Reade: A Biography* (London: Jonathan Cape, 1931), 186.

88. *Letters of Charles Dickens to Wilkie Collins 1851–1870*, selected by Miss

Georgina Hogarth, edited by Laurence Hutton (London: Osgood, McIlvaine and Co., 1892), 154-55.

89. *New York Times*, 16 February 1867, 3; John Coleman, *Charles Reade as I
Knew Him* (London: Traherne and Co., 1903), 301; and Elwin, *Charles
Reade*, 190.

90. "The Magazines," *Illustrated London News*, 4 May 1867, 439.

91. "The Magazines," *Illustrated London News*, 8 June 1867, 583.

92. Virtue to Trollope, 15 November 1866, Bodleian MS. Don. c. 10*, fols.
1-2; included in *The Letters of Anthony Trollope*, 357.

93. For the *Argosy* as edited by Mrs. Henry Wood, see Malcolm Elwin,
Victorian Wallflowers (London: Jonathan Cape, 1934), 240 ff.

94. Virtue to Trollope, 16 November 1866, Bodleian MS. Don. c. 10*, fols.
3-4; included in *The Letters of Anthony Trollope*, 358.

95. For the history of the firm of Bell and Daldy, see Edward Bell, *George
Bell, Publisher;* and the obituary notices of George Bell in the *Athenaeum*,
6 December 1890, 778, and the *Bookseller*, 13 December 1890, 1375-76.

96. The papers of Bell and Daldy are at the University of Reading.

97. Strahan, "Twenty Years of a Publisher's Life," 260.

98. The *Bookseller* of 2 August 1870 would refer to "the preachy-preachiness which gave great offense formerly" (652).

99. *Life, Journals, and Letters of Henry Alford*, 402-3.

100. Plumptre's letters to Gladstone, dated 1 November 1867, 2 December
1867, 16 December 1867, and 17 December 1867, are included in the
Gladstone Papers, Additional Manuscripts 44413, fols. 213-14, 250-51,
283, and 291-92, the British Library.

101. A. F. Hort, *Life and Letters of Fenton J. A. Hort*, 2 vols. (London: Macmillan,
1896), 2:92-93.

102. For Hunt (1827-1909), see the entry in S. Austin Allibone, *A Critical
Dictionary of English Literature and British and American Authors*, 3 vols.
(Philadelphia: Lippincott, 1858; reprint, Detroit: Gale, 1965).

103. For Bayne (1830-96), see the entry in Boase, *Modern English Biography*,
and the entry in the *DNB* by Ronald Bayne. For his editorship of the
Weekly Review, see James Grant, *History of the Newspaper Press*, 3:146;
for his "neo-evangelism," see Everett, *The Party of Humanity*, 60, 128,
137.

104. For Rands (1823-82), see the entry in the *DNB*, based on information
provided by Strahan and written by George Clement Boase.

105. *Learned Lady: Letters from Robert Browning to Mrs. Thomas Fitzgerald,
1876-1889*, ed. Edward C. McAleer (Cambridge, Mass.: Harvard University Press, 1966), 80. *The Ring and the Book* (1868-69) was brought
out in four monthly parts by Smith, Elder, the firm that succeeded in
replacing Chapman and Hall as Browning's regular publishers. George
Smith initially offered £400 for the work, later raising this amount to
£1,250 for the right to publish *The Ring and the Book* for five years; see
Michael Meredith, "Browning and the Prince of Publishers," *Browning
Institute Studies* 7 (1979): 8, 19.

106. *Times,* 4 November 1867, 10; *Life, Journals, and Letters of Henry Alford,* 402.

107. For Argyll, see *Autobiography and Memoirs,* ed. the Dowager Duchess of Argyll; and Neal C. Gillespie, "The Duke of Argyll, Evolutionary Anthropology, and the Art of Scientific Controversy," *Isis* 68 (March 1977): 40–54. When Gladstone was in doubt as to where to direct his first contribution to *Good Words,* he asked Argyll, who wrote to Strahan; Strahan wrote directly to Gladstone on 2 December 1867 to explain that all correspondence should be directed to himself (Additional Manuscripts 44413, fol. 252, the British Library). This is the earliest surviving correspondence between Strahan and Gladstone.

108. Edwin Hodder, *The Life and Work of the Seventh Earl of Shaftesbury,* 3 vols. (London: Cassell, 1887), 3:164.

109. W. E. Gladstone, *"Ecce Homo," Good Words* 9 (January 1868): 36.

110. Connop Thirlwall, *Letters to a Friend,* 132; the letter is dated 15 January 1868.

111. Strahan to Gladstone, 21 December 1867, Additional Manuscripts 44413, fol. 302, the British Library.

112. Strahan to Gladstone, 18 January 1868, Additional Manuscripts 44414, fol. 36, the British Library.

113. See, for example, the advertisement in the *Publishers' Circular,* 1 February 1868, 72.

114. *Lady Tennyson's Journal,* ed. James O. Hoge (Charlottesville: University Press of Virginia, 1981), 262. In his poem "To the Duke of Argyll" (1881), Tennyson would refer to

> . . . thy voice, a music heard
> Thro' all the yells and counter-yells of feud
> And faction, and thy will, a power to make
> This ever-changing world of circumstance,
> In changing, chime with never-changing law.

115. *Lady Tennyson's Journal,* 267.

116. Ibid., 268.

Chapter VI

1. Alexander Strahan, "English Books in America," a letter to the *Bookseller,* 31 January 1866, 8.

2. For Knowles's life, see Priscilla Metcalf, *James Knowles: Victorian Editor and Architect* (Oxford: Clarendon Press, 1980); the preface by Michael Goodwin to *Nineteenth Century Opinion: An Anthology of Extracts from the First Fifty Volumes of* The Nineteenth Century *1877–1901* (Harmondsworth: Penguin, 1951); and the entry in the *Dictionary of National Biography* by Sidney Lee.

3. E. M. Forster, *Marianne Thornton: A Domestic Biography 1797–1887* (New York: Harcourt Brace Jovanovich, 1956), 241.

4. *The Letters of John Stuart Blackie to His Wife. With a Few Earlier Ones to His Parents,* ed. Archibald Stodart Walker (Edinburgh and London: Blackwood and Sons, 1909), 214.

5. [T. H. S. Escott], *Society in London, by a Foreign Resident* (London: Chatto and Windus, 1885), 290. At the time this anonymous work was published, Knowles was editor and proprietor of the *Nineteenth Century;* Escott was editor of the rival *Fortnightly Review.*

6. *Times,* 14 February 1908, 12.

7. Quoted by Goodwin, *Nineteenth Century Opinion,* 11.

8. Strahan to Knowles, 10 January 1877, copy of the original letter in Strahan's hand, the Gladstone Papers, Additional Manuscripts 44453, fol. 46, the British Library. In the winter of 1876–77, when he and Knowles were quarreling, Strahan sent Gladstone a number of documents, including copies of letters written by himself, in an attempt to win Gladstone's support.

9. "To Our Readers," *Clapham Magazine,* no. 1 (November 1850), 2–3; and see Metcalf, *James Knowles,* 67–71.

10. Quoted by Goodwin, *Nineteenth Century Opinion,* 10.

11. Quoted by Metcalf, *James Knowles,* 191, from a transcript of a letter in the possession of Dr. Gordon Ray.

12. Charles Tennyson, *Alfred Tennyson* (London: Macmillan, 1949), 346; Metcalf, *James Knowles,* 191. Pritchard was also a contributor to *Good Words:* his "Hymn to the New Year" was published in the issue for January 1866.

13. James Knowles, "A Personal Reminiscence," *Nineteenth Century* 33 (January 1893): 164.

14. James Knowles, "Tennyson and Aldworth," in *Tennyson and His Friends,* ed. Hallam Tennyson (London: Macmillan, 1911), 246.

15. *Lady Tennyson's Journal,* 263.

16. Robert Bernard Martin, *Tennyson: The Unquiet Heart* (Oxford: Clarendon Press, 1980), 484.

17. Harold G. Merriam, *Edward Moxon: Publisher of Poets* (New York: Columbia University Press, 1939; reprint, New York: AMS Press, 1966), 193.

18. June Steffensen Hagen, *Tennyson and His Publishers* (London: Macmillan, 1979), 161, 167–68.

19. *The Letters of Emily Lady Tennyson,* ed. James O. Hoge (University Park and London: Pennsylvania State University Press, 1974), 156, letter to Edward Lear dated 15 April 1861.

20. Hagen, *Tennyson and His Publishers,* 114; and Charles Tennyson, *Alfred Tennyson,* 354.

21. Tennyson's letter is included in the catalog of *The Library of Louis J. Haber of New York City: Part III. Literary Autographs and Manuscripts Both English and American . . . to be sold December 9–10, 1909* (New York: Anderson Auction Company, [1909]), 67; see also Merriam, *Edward Moxon,* 186.

22. Emily Tennyson to Margaret Gatty, 7 October 1868, MSS. Acc. 476, the Boston Public Library.

23. *Lady Tennyson's Journal*, 272, entry for 10 March 1868; and *The Letters of Emily Lady Tennyson*, 218, letter to Woolner dated 10 March 1868.

24. For Strahan's rate of payment, see Charles Tennyson, *Alfred Tennyson*, 374; and *The Letters of Emily Lady Tennyson*, 227, letter to Alfred Tennyson dated 20 November 1868.

25. *The Swinburne Letters*, ed. Cecil Y. Lang, 6 vols. (New Haven: Yale University Press, 1959–62), 1:293, letter to Houghton dated 28 March [1868]. Lang records Browning's remark in the footnote.

26. *Parodies of the Works of English and American Authors*, collected and arranged by Walter Hamilton, 6 vols. (London: Reeves and Turner, 1884–89), 1:46–47. For the Tennysons' distress over "ill-natured parodies," see Charles Tennyson, *Alfred Tennyson*, 374.

27. [T. J. Wise], "Tennyson and His Publishers," *Bookman* 3, no. 14 (November 1892): 51–52, reprinted in W. Robertson Nicoll and T. J. Wise, eds., *Literary Anecdotes of the Nineteenth Century*, 2 vols. (London: Hodder and Stoughton, 1896), 2:438–40; and Harold T. Hartley, *Eighty-Eight Not Out: A Record of Happy Memories* (London: Frederick Muller, 1939), 231. Although Charles Tennyson states in the biography of his grandfather that Knowles introduced Strahan to Tennyson, I have seen no evidence that Strahan and Knowles knew each other before meeting as a result of their individual dealings with Tennyson.

28. Tennyson's letter to Macmillan is quoted by Hagen, *Tennyson and His Publishers*, 117.

29. Charles Tennyson, *Alfred Tennyson*, 376; Hagen, *Tennyson and His Publishers*, 118. According to Hagen (112), Moxon paid Tennyson over £8,000 in royalties on *Enoch Arden* in the first year of publication.

30. Charles Tennyson, *Alfred Tennyson*, 376; Nicoll and Wise, *Literary Anecdotes*, 2:438.

31. Strahan to Gladstone, 29 June 1868, Additional Manuscripts 44415, fol. 236, the British Library.

32. Strahan, "Twenty Years of a Publisher's Life," 696.

33. *Authorized Report of the Church Congress Held at Dublin on September 29th, 30th, October 1st, 2nd, 3rd 1868* (Dublin: Hodges, Smith and Foster, 1868), 350–51.

34. *Autobiography and Letters of Mrs. M. O. W. Oliphant*, ed. Mrs. Harry Coghill (Edinburgh and London: Blackwood, 1899; reprint, Leicester: Leicester University Press, 1974), 201. Oliphant's *Madonna Mary* was serialized in *Good Words* during 1866.

35. Ellis, *Henry Kingsley*, 173.

36. *Lady Tennyson's Journal*, 282.

37. Ibid., 283.

38. Tennyson's letter diary of 14 November 1868 is quoted in Hallam Tennyson's *Materials for a Life of A. T.*, 4 vols. (privately printed, [1895]), 3:91.

39. Hallam Tennyson, *Alfred Lord Tennyson: A Memoir,* 2 vols. London: Macmillan, 1897), 2:59.
40. Metcalf, *James Knowles,* 213, quoting from a MS. at the Tennyson Research Centre, Lincolnshire.
41. Hallam Tennyson, *Alfred Lord Tennyson,* 2:59.
42. Most sources—Charles Tennyson, Robert Bernard Martin, and June Steffensen Hagen, for example—state that Strahan paid Tennyson £5,000 a year for the right to republish previous works, and deducted a commission of 10 percent for distributing new works. In fact, the figure of £4,000, which is mentioned in Tennyson's letter diary, is confirmed by a copy of the Tennyson-Strahan contract that has survived in the Spalding and Hodge papers at the Greater London Record Office, London County Hall. The contract specifies that Strahan and Company shall pay £4,300 a year for the right to republish previous works; however, a copy of a letter from Tennyson to Strahan and Company that is filed with the contract specifies that £300 of this sum is intended for Edward Moxon's widow, and that in the event of her death, Strahan and Company will be required to pay only £4,000. The same contract specifies that Strahan and Company will deduct a commission of 5 percent on new works. These documents are filed as B/SPL/17 and 18, the Greater London Record Office.
43. *The Letters of Emily Lady Tennyson,* 227.
44. William Tinsley, *Random Recollections of an Old Publisher,* 2 vols. (London: Simpkin, Marshall, Hamilton, Kent and Co., 1900), 1:237–38.
45. Metcalf, *James Knowles,* 219.
46. J. T. K. [James Thomas Knowles], "Alternation of Science and Art in History," *Contemporary Review* 10 (February 1869): 295.
47. E. M. Forster, *Marianne Thornton,* 260.
48. For a history of this group, see Alan Willard Brown, *The Metaphysical Society: Victorian Minds in Crisis, 1869–1880* (New York: Columbia University Press, 1947).
49. According to Lady St. Helier, *Memories of Fifty Years,* 154.
50. Knowles to Gladstone, 14 May 1876, Additional Manuscripts 44231, fol. 116, the British Library. In 1873 another member of the Metaphysical Society, William Connor Magee, the bishop of Peterborough, referred to Knowles as "the *very* broad Editor of the *Contemporary*"; see J. C. MacDonnell, *Life and Correspondence of William Connor Magee,* 2 vols. (London: Isbister, 1896), 1:284.
51. Wilfrid Ward, *Ten Personal Studies* (London: Longmans, Green and Co., 1908), 70. Ward also records Tennyson's famous remark that "No man ever had his brain in his hand as Knowles had. . . . When we first planned the Metaphysical Society he did not know a 'concept' from a hippopotamus. Before we had talked of it for a month he could chatter metaphysics with the best of us" (70–71).
52. Pollock, *For My Grandson: Remembrances of an Ancient Victorian* (London: John Murray, 1933), 93.

53. Virtue to Trollope, 2 April 1869, Bodleian MS. Don. c. 9, fol. 250.

54. The inside front cover of a forty-seven-page book list published by Strahan and Company in May 1869 explains that Strahan and Company has taken over the publications of Virtue Brothers; *Saint Pauls Magaine* is also included in this list, which is in the Bell and Hyman archives at the University of Reading.

55. Strahan to Trollope, 7 March 1867, with draft of Trollope's reply, Bodleian MS. Don. c. 9, fols. 175–76; included in *The Letters of Anthony Trollope*, 372.

56. Edward Bell, *George Bell*, 80–81.

57. Strahan and Company to Bell and Daldy, 3 September 1869, archives of Bell and Hyman, University of Reading.

58. Agreement between Strahan and Company and Bell and Daldy, 30 September 1869, archives of Bell and Hyman, University of Reading.

59. *The Letters of Emily Lady Tennyson*, 246, letter to Hallam Tennyson dated 5 November 1869.

60. Hagen, *Tennyson and His Publishers*, 119.

61. Knowles's draft of this letter, seen by Priscilla Metcalf, is quoted in *James Knowles*, 235.

62. Brown, *The Metaphysical Society*, 319.

63. "Literature of the People," *Athenaeum*, 1 January 1870, 14.

64. *Saturday Review*, 12 June 1869, 774–75.

65. Strahan to Gladstone, 7 January 1874, Additional Manuscripts 44442, fols. 6–7, the British Library.

66. Greville MacDonald, *George MacDonald and His Wife*, 361.

67. Virtue to Trollope, 25 January 1870, Bodleian MS. Don. c. 10*, fols. 15–16; included in *The Letters of Anthony Trollope*, 494–95. Trollope's nominal salary had been £1,000, but £250 of this went to pay the salary of his subeditor.

68. Strahan to Trollope, 25 January 1870, Bodleian MS. Don. c. 10*, fols. 17–18; *The Letters of Anthony Trollope*, 495.

69. *The Letters of Anthony Trollope*, 501–3, letter to John Blackwood, 6 March 1870.

70. Henry Alford, "The Church of the Future," *Contemporary Review* 9 (October 1868): 161.

71. F. W. Farrar, "The Church and Her Younger Members," *Fortnightly Review*, n.s., 4 (November 1868): 572–79; and Farrar, "The Attitude of the Clergy Towards Science," *Contemporary Review* 9 (December 1868): 600–620.

72. T. H. Huxley, "On the Physical Basis of Life," *Fortnightly Review*, n.s., 5 (February 1869): 129–45; and see William Irvine, *Apes, Angels, and Victorians: Darwin, Huxley, and Evolution* (Cleveland and New York: World Publishing Co., 1955; reprint, New York: Meridian Books, 1959), 248–50.

73. John Young, "Professor Huxley and 'The Physical Basis of Life,'" *Contemporary Review* 11 (June 1869): 244, 253.

74. *Weekly Review*, 3 July 1869, 640.

75. *Literary Churchman*, 22 January 1870, 56.
76. *Guardian*, 28 February 1877, 289.
77. Peel, *Letters to a Victorian Editor*, 260.
78. Strahan to Knowles, 10 January 1877, copy in Strahan's hand, Additional Manuscripts 44453, fols. 45–47, the British Library.
79. Priscilla Metcalf counts 156 contributions to the *Contemporary* between April 1870 and January 1877 signed by members of the Metaphysical Society; 27 of these had already been read at meetings of the society (see *James Knowles*, 236).
80. *Illustrated London News*, 9 July 1870, 46.
81. *Bookseller*, 2 August 1870, 652.
82. References to Strahan in Mazzini's letters to Emilie Ashurst Venturi, who placed all his periodical contributions, indicate that Venturi dealt with Strahan rather than with Knowles: see *Mazzini's Letters to an English Family 1861–1872*, ed. E. F. Richards, 3 vols. (London: John Lane, Bodley Head, 1920–22), especially the letters in vol. 3 dating from 1871.
83. Knowles to Huxley, 22 September 1871, the Imperial Library of Science and Technology, London.
84. For details concerning Buchanan's quarrels, see Cassidy, *Robert W. Buchanan*, 36–58; and Christopher D. Murray, "D. G. Rossetti, A. C. Swinburne and R. W. Buchanan. The Fleshly School Revisited," *Bulletin of the John Rylands Library* 65 (Autumn 1982): 206–34, and 66 (Spring 1983): 176–207.
85. See *The Diary of W. M. Rossetti 1870–1873*, ed. Odette Bornand (Oxford: Clarendon Press, 1977), entries for 21 October 1871, 20 November 1871, and 29 November 1871, also cited in the *Letters of Dante Gabriel Rossetti*, ed. Oswald Doughty and John Robert Wahl, 4 vols. (Oxford: Clarendon Press, 1965–67), 3:1018, 1033, 1034.
86. *Letters of Dante Gabriel Rossetti*, 3:1024, letter to Franz Huffer dated 2 November 1871.
87. *Athenaeum*, 2 December 1871, 174.
88. For the letters of Buchanan and of "Strahan and Co.," see the *Athenaeum*, 16 December 1871, 794; "The Stealthy School of Criticism" appeared on 792–94.
89. "Mr. Buchanan and the Fleshly Poets," *Saturday Review*, 1 June 1873, 700.
90. B. E. Maidment, "Victorian Publishing and Social Criticism: The Case of Edward Jenkins," *Publishing History* 11 (1982): 46; and see the *Weekly Review*, 29 July 1876, 738.
91. For Samuel Spalding's partnership with Virtue, see the obituary notices of Virtue in the *Times*, 7 April 1892, 10; the *Bookseller*, 6 April 1892, 312; and the *Publisher's Circular*, 9 April 1892, 407.
92. Three years later, Strahan would complain to Gladstone that "in 1871 Mr. James S. Virtue became a partner of my firm on unfair and deceitful representations. His conduct as a partner was such as I could not sanction or endorse . . ."; see Strahan to Gladstone, 7 January 1874, Additional Manuscripts 44442, fols. 6–7, the British Library.

93. Mayo, *Recollections,* 146–48.
94. For Watt, see James Hepburn, *The Author's Empty Purse and the Rise of the Literary Agent* (London: Oxford University Press, 1968), especially 51–56. Although Hepburn says that Watt moved from Glasgow, his native city, to become a bookseller in Edinburgh before entering Strahan's firm, the Glasgow Post Office Directory lists an A. P. Watt in 1869–70.
95. Blaikie, *An Autobiography,* 188.
96. Strahan, "Twenty Years of a Publisher's Life," 20–21. This letter is not included in Donald Macleod's *Memoir of Norman Macleod.*
97. Greville MacDonald, *George MacDonald and His Wife,* 361.
98. George MacDonald, "The Vicar's Daughter," *Sunday Magazine* 8 (September 1871): 1.
99. Hagen, *Tennyson and His Publishers,* 127; and advertisement in the *Athenaeum,* 23 December 1871, 824.
100. R. W. Dale, "The *Christian Witness* and the *Congregationalist,*" *Christian Witness and Congregational Magazine,* n.s., 7 (December 1871): 595.
101. George Bell to F. R. Daldy, 24 December 1871, Bell and Hyman archives, University of Reading.
102. Alexander Strahan to Bell and Daldy, 5 March 1872, Bell and Hyman archives, University of Reading.
103. Strahan, "A Personal Explanation," letter to the *Bookseller,* 2 December 1873, 1106.
104. Tennyson to Knowles, March 1872, quoted by Metcalf, *James Knowles,* 258.
105. *The Letters of John Stuart Blackie to His Wife,* 210.
106. See the correspondence between Virtue (on behalf of Strahan and Company), Thomas Spalding, and George Bell between April and August 1872, included in the Bell and Hyman archives, University of Reading.
107. Edward Bell, *George Bell,* 83.
108. *Publishers' Circular,* 16 July 1873, 474; *Bookseller,* 2 August 1873, 635. Howard Spalding, who had been an apprentice in the firm of Bell and Daldy, would eventually become head of the firm of Spalding and Hodge.
109. The papers of Virtue and Company Limited are at the Public Record Office, Kew, BT 31/2141/9875.
110. *Presbyterian,* n.s., 15 (January 1873): 144.
111. Mayo, *Recollections,* 148.
112. Greville MacDonald, *George MacDonald and His Wife,* 474–75.
113. Strahan to Knowles, 10 January 1877, copy of the original letter in Strahan's hand, Additional Manuscripts 44453, fol. 46, the British Library.
114. Knowles to Tennyson, 6 January 1877, the Tennyson Research Centre, Lincolnshire.
115. Strahan, "Norman Macleod," *Contemporary Review* 20 (July 1872): 293, 299.
116. Donald Macleod to J. M. Ludlow, 11 December [1872], the Ludlow Papers, Add. 7348/11/51, Cambridge University Library.

Chapter VII

1. Alexander Taylor Innes, "Dean Stanley at Edinburgh," *Contemporary Review* 19 (March 1872): 447–48, 455; and see Rowland E. Prothero, *The Life and Correspondence of Arthur Penrhyn Stanley,* 2 vols. (New York: Charles Scribner's Sons, 1893), 2:273–77.
2. John Tulloch, "Dean Stanley and the Scotch 'Moderates,'" *Contemporary Review* 20 (October 1872): 709.
3. Alexander Strahan to William Angus Knight, 7 October 1872, the Pierpont Morgan Library, New York.
4. For King's life and career, see Charles Kegan Paul, *Memories* (London: Kegan Paul, Trench, Trubner and Co., 1899), 270–88, and Leonard Huxley, *The House of Smith Elder* (London: privately printed, 1923), 82, 87.
5. Mrs. [Harriet Eleanor] Hamilton King, *Letters and Recollections of Mazzini* (London: Longmans, Green and Co., 1912), 31–32.
6. J. W. Robertson Scott, *The Story of the* Pall Mall Gazette (London: Oxford University Press, 1950), 47, 127, 139.
7. Kegan Paul, *Memories,* 274–75.
8. Kegan Paul, *Memories,* 279–81.
9. *The Swinburne Letters,* letter of 18 November [1871], 2:172; and letter of 12 March [1872], 2:174. The anthology was *Pleasure: A Holiday Book of Prose and Verse,* ed. J. H. Friswell (1870); it included Swinburne's "Prelude. Tristram and Iseult."
10. "Introduction," *The Prayer-Gauge Debate* (Boston: Congregational Publishing Society, 1876), 3; this volume collects and republishes the essays by Thompson, Tyndall, and others in the *Contemporary* and by Francis Galton in the *Fortnightly,* along with two reviews from the *Spectator.* So notorious was the controversy that in Arnold Bennett's *Clayhanger* (1910), young Edwin, in a scene set in 1872, overhears his father and Mr. Shusions discussing "Sir Henry Thompson's ingenious device for scientifically testing the efficacy of prayer."
11. "The Editor's Room," *Sunday Magazine* 9 (September 1872): 66.
12. John Lewis Paton, *John Brown Paton,* 189.
13. Quoted by Karl Pearson, *The Life, Letters and Labours of Francis Galton,* 4 vols. (Cambridge: Cambridge University Press, 1914–30), 2:132.
14. Readers of the *Contemporary* would be treated to three more articles on the subject in January, March, and December 1873: the Reverend William Knight, whose orthodoxy was highly suspect to his fellow clerics within the Free Church of Scotland, would denigrate the efficacy of prayer; the duke of Argyll would champion the cause of more orthodox believers; and Knight would be allowed to have the last word.
15. Hallam Tennyson, *Alfred Lord Tennyson,* 2:116.
16. *Bookseller,* 3 December 1872, 1082.
17. *Bookseller,* 3 December 1872, 1080.
18. *Publishers' Circular,* 8 December 1873, 865.
19. *Presbyterian,* n.s., 15 (1 January 1873): 144.

20. *The Swinburne Letters*, letter to Theodore Watts dated 6 December 1872, 2:204.
21. *The Swinburne Letters*, letter to Thomas Purnell dated 26 November [1873], 2:259–60.
22. *The Swinburne Letters*, letter to Theodore Watts dated 30 January [1874], 2:271. Ironically, after Chatto and Windus became Buchanan's publishers in 1881, Swinburne's and Buchanan's works were advertised in the same lists.
23. Knowles to Mrs. Tennyson, 3 April 1873, the Tennyson Research Centre.
24. James Virtue to Arnold White (Tennyson's solicitor), 3 April 1873, the Tennyson Research Centre; Tennyson to White, quoted by Hagen, *Tennyson's Publishers*, 133. Hagen summarizes all of the correspondence between Knowles, King, Virtue, White, and the Tennysons.
25. Hagen, *Tennyson and His Publishers*, 134.
26. Knowles to Mrs. Tennyson, 3 April 1873.
27. Knowles to Strahan, 20 April 1873, quoted by Strahan in "The Contemporary Review," an eight-page printed circular dated 7 February 1877, Additional Manuscripts 44453, fols. 73–76, the British Library.
28. See Metcalf, *James Knowles*, 257, for evidence of Knowles's authorship; she cites Kathleen Tillotson, "Tennyson's Serial Poem," in Geoffrey and Kathleen Tillotson, *Mid-Victorian Studies* (London: University of London, Athlone Press, 1965), 102 n. 1.
29. See James Marchant, *J. B. Paton, Educational and Social Pioneer* (London: James Clarke and Co., 1909), 119.
30. For the September 1873 Conference, see John Brown Paton, *The Inner Mission: Four Addresses* (London: Isbister, 1888), 2, 14; and John Lewis Paton, *John Brown Paton*, 186–88.
31. Alexander Strahan, "Strahan and Co. versus King," an eleven-page printed circular dated 30 August 1877, Additional Manuscripts 44454, fols. 364–69, the British Library.
32. Strahan, "Preface," *Day of Rest* 1 (1873).
33. Strahan, "Strahan and Co. versus King."
34. Strahan explained his problems in a letter to the editor of the *Bookseller* dated 29 November 1873; it was published in the *Bookseller*, 2 December 1873, 1106.
35. For Gladstone's letter, see the *Contemporary Review* 23 (December 1873): 162–63; Knowles persuaded Gladstone to allow its publication, in a letter dated 9 November 1873, Additional Manuscripts 44231, fol. 28, the British Library.
36. Strahan to Gladstone, 7 January 1874, Additional Manuscripts 44442, fol. 6, the British Library.
37. Strahan to Gladstone, 14 January 1874, Additional Manuscripts 44442, fol. 241, the British Library.
38. Knowles to Gladstone, 14 January 1874, Additional Manuscripts 44231, fols. 35–36, the British Library.

39. Surviving records of Henry S. King and Company show that the number of copies of *Saint Pauls Magazine* received by King for distribution dropped from 8,325 in November 1872 to 5,000 in April 1873. There are no later entries for *Saint Pauls* (or for *Good Things for the Young*, which suffered a decline over the same period, in the number of copies printed, from 17,000 to 11,000); this suggests that the records from May 1873 on were being kept by Strahan on Paternoster Row. For the archives of Routledge and Kegan Paul Ltd.—which include those of Henry S. King and Company—see the "Archives of British Publishers," a microfilm series produced by Chadwyck-Healey Ltd.

40. See Strahan's advertisements for the *Saturday Journal* in the *Publishers' Circular*, 16 March 1874, 180; and in the *Bookseller*, 2 April 1874, 318.

41. Strahan, "Strahan and Co. versus King."

42. For George McCorquodale, see the obituary in the *Times* of 19 July 1895, 5; for Sir Charles Edward Hamilton, who was member of Parliament for Southwark 1885–1892, see *Who Was Who*, and the obituary in the *Times* of 17 November 1928, 14. McCorquodale and Company Limited survives today, as one of the largest limited companies in Great Britain.

43. "Notice of New Books," *Congregationalist* 6 (January 1877): 127.

44. The purchase was announced in the *Bookseller*, 5 January 1875, 4. Lady Barker wandered far from her publishing office on Paternoster Row, contributing a series on her travels in Africa for the 1876 volume of *Evening Hours*.

45. "Magazine Literature," *Church Quarterly Review* 3 (January 1877): 386–87.

46. Strahan described his "Deed of Agreement" with McCorquodale and Hamilton in his circular, entitled "The Contemporary Review," of 7 February 1877.

47. Walter Bagehot, "The Metaphysical Basis of Tolerance," *Contemporary Review* 23 (April 1874): 765.

48. "Dr. Manning in the *Contemporary*," *Weekly Review*, 18 April 1874, 373–74.

49. "Mr. Gregg in the *Contemporary Review*," *Weekly Review*, 12 September 1874, 881.

50. "Magazines," *Publishers' Circular*, 2 October 1874, 664. As recently as July 1872, the *Weekly Review* had referred to Strahan as the "able and indefatigable publisher"; see "Norman Macleod," *Weekly Review*, 13 July 1872, 683.

51. By late 1875, Matthew Arnold was quoting, in the preface to *God and the Bible*, Clifford's famous description of Christianity as "that awful plague which has destroyed two civilisations and but barely failed to slay such promise of good as is now struggling to live amongst men . . . a system which has made its red mark on history and still lives to threaten mankind"; see *The Complete Prose Works of Matthew Arnold*, ed. R. H. Super, 11 vols. (Ann Arbor: University of Michigan Press, 1960–77), 7:380. Clifford originally made these remarks in a lecture that was widely re-

ported in the press; they appear in somewhat different form in his article on "The Unseen Universe," *Fortnightly Review*, n.s., 17 (1 June 1875): 793.

52. Arnold, "Review of Objections to 'Literature and Dogma' (Part 1)," *Contemporary Review* 24 (October 1874): 795. In 1884, Arnold wrote to Percy Bunting, editor of the *Contemporary*, that it had been Knowles who first gave him space in the review; see *The Complete Prose Works of Matthew Arnold*, 10:529–30.

53. Quoted in *The Complete Prose Works of Matthew Arnold*, 7:439.

54. Gladstone, "Ritualism and Ritual," *Contemporary Review* 24 (October 1874): 674. For a discussion of the circumstances that may have prompted Gladstone's attack on the Roman Catholic church, see H. C. G. Matthew, "Gladstone, Vaticanism, and the Question of the East," in *Religious Motivation: Biographical and Sociological Problems for the Church Historian*, vol. 15 of *Studies in Church History*, ed. Derek Baker (Oxford: Ecclesiastical History Society, 1978), 417–42.

55. Quoted in *The Complete Prose Works of Matthew Arnold*, 7:437.

56. *Publishers' Circular*, 2 October 1874, 712.

57. Knowles to Gladstone, 3 October 1874, Additional Manuscripts 44231, fol. 53, the British Library.

58. *Bookseller*, 5 October 1874, 820.

59. *Publishers' Circular*, 2 November 1874, 782.

60. See, for example, Knowles's letters to Gladstone of 28 December 1874 and 21 March 1875, Additional Manuscripts 44231, fols. 70, 72, the British Library.

61. For discussions of the controversy triggered by Cassels's book, see L. E. Elliott-Binns, *Religion in the Victorian Era*, 2d ed. (London: Lutterworth Press, 1946), 279; and Willis B. Glover, *Evangelical Nonconformists and Higher Criticism in the Nineteenth Century* (London: Independent Press, 1954), 67–69. Morley's article, "A Recent Work on Supernatural Religion," was signed "Editor."

62. John Lewis Paton, *John Brown Paton*, 176; Paton drew heavily on Lightfoot's criticism of Cassels's scholarship when he wrote his own account of "Supernatural Religion: The History and Results of Modern Negative Criticism" for the *British and Foreign Evangelical Review* 24 (1875): 344–79.

63. David Duncan, *Life and Letters of Herbert Spencer*, 2 vols. (New York: D. Appleton and Co., 1908), 1:228. For summaries of both Huxley's and Tyndall's papers, see Brown, *The Metaphysical Society*, 55, 139, and 232–37.

64. Leonard Huxley, *Life and Letters of Thomas Henry Huxley*, 2 vols. (London: Macmillan, 1900), 1:424.

65. John Brown Paton, "The Twofold Alternative: Materialism or Religion," *Congregationalist* 4 (1875): 82–92.

66. *Manchester Guardian*, 7 June 1875, 7. On 28 May, Knowles wrote to Gladstone to apologize for "the offending circular" and to enclose "Mr.

Strahan's reply to my note of inquiry"; see Additional Manuscripts 44231, fol. 77, the British Library.

67. Knowles to Gladstone, 18 June 1875, Additional Manuscripts 44231, fol. 83, the British Library. Gladstone's forthcoming article was mentioned in the gossip column of the *Athenaeum*, 19 June 1875, 821.

68. *Bookseller*, 3 July 1875, 568.

69. The partnership of Mullan and Strahan was announced in the *Bookseller*, 3 July 1875, 568; see also, for Mullan, the obituary in the *Bookseller*, 6 January 1881, 9.

70. "Publishers of Today. Messrs. Hutchinson & Co.," *Publishers' Circular*, 13 May 1899, 514–15; and "A Chat with Mr. G. Thompson Hutchinson," *Publisher and Bookseller*, 14 October 1905, 51–52.

71. Alexander Strahan, "Bad Literature for the Young," *Contemporary Review* 26 (November 1875): 981–82, 991. For the second conference of the Inner Mission, see John Lewis Paton, *John Brown Paton*, 190–91.

72. Francis Peek, "Religious Teaching in the Elementary Schools," *Contemporary Review* 27 (May 1876): 944.

73. Alexander Strahan, circular entitled "The Contemporary Review," 7 February 1877.

74. Knowles to Gladstone, 4 May 1876, Additional Manuscripts 44231, fol. 113, the British Library.

75. Knowles to Gladstone, 14 May 1876, Additional Manuscripts 44231, fol. 115, the British Library.

76. Strahan to Gladstone, 8 June 1876, Additional Manuscripts 44450, fols. 141–42, the British Library.

77. Strahan, "Last Words from Alexander Strahan About 'The Contemporary Review' and Mr. J. Knowles," 15 March 1877.

78. Knowles to Gladstone, 3 January 1877, Additional Manuscripts 44231, fol. 149, the British Library.

79. James Knowles, "The Contemporary Review," a six-page printed circular dated 15 February 1877, Additional Manuscripts 44231, fols. 168–70, the British Library.

80. Strahan, "Last Words from Alexander Strahan About 'The Contemporary Review' and Mr. J. Knowles," 15 March 1877.

81. Knowles, "The Contemporary Review," 15 February 1877.

82. Ibid. Strahan quotes the same letter in "Last Words from Alexander Strahan About 'The Contemporary Review' and Mr. J. Knowles."

83. Quoted by Knowles, "The Contemporary Review," 15 February 1877.

84. John Lewis Paton, *John Brown Paton*, 175; and Francis Peek, "The Contemporary Review," a three-page printed circular dated 7 February 1877, Additional Manuscripts 44453, fols. 71–72, the British Library.

85. Strahan described the "Terms" presented by Knowles to McCorquodale and Hamilton in the circular entitled "The Contemporary Review," 7 February 1877.

86. Paton's letter to Morley is quoted by John Lewis Paton, *John Brown Paton*, 175.

Chapter VIII

1. Ian Bradley, *The Optimists: Themes and Personalities in Victorian Liberalism* (London: Faber and Faber, 1980), 51.
2. *Culture and Anarchy* (1869); *The Complete Prose Works of Matthew Arnold*, 5:180, 184.
3. Edwin Hodder, *The Life of Samuel Morley*, 2d ed. (London: Hodder and Stoughton, 1887), 239, 457.
4. Ibid., 79–83; Hodder, *The Life and Work of the Seventh Earl of Shaftesbury*, 1:266.
5. For Morley's involvement in Radical and working-class movements, see the scattered references in John Vincent, *The Formation of the British Liberal Party 1857–68* (London: Constable, 1966) and in Stephen Mayor, *The Churches and the Labour Movement* (London: Independent Press, 1967). Karl Marx described Morley, in a letter to Frederick Engels dated 1 February 1865, as an "old sham City agitator"; see Marx and Engels, *Selected Correspondence*, 2d ed., trans. I. Lasker, ed. S. Ryanzanskaya (Moscow: Progress Publishers, 1965), 159.
6. Estimated by Alvar Ellegard, *The Readership of the Periodical Press in Mid-Victorian Britain*, Goteborgs universitets arsskrift, vol. 63, no. 3 (Goteborg: Acta universitatis gothoburgensis, 1957), 4.
7. Russell, *Letters of Matthew Arnold, 1848–1888*, 1:237, 251.
8. "One Who Knew Him" [pseud.], "Samuel Morley," *Pall Mall Gazette*, 6 September 1886, 2.
9. For Richard, see Charles S. Miall, *Henry Richard, M.P.: A Biography* (London: Cassell, 1889).
10. Hodder, *Samuel Morley*, 159; and the *Congregational Year Book*, 1879, 360.
11. Arnold quotes the *Daily News* of 7 December 1864 in "Porro Unum Est Necessarium"; see *The Complete Prose Works*, 8:352. In "A Word More About America" (1884), Arnold would recall the alarm he felt years earlier "at seeing the *Daily News* and the *Morning Star*, like Zedekiah the son of Chenaanah, thus making horns of iron for the middle class and bidding it 'Go up and prosper!' "; see *The Complete Prose Works*, 10:204.
12. Estimated by Ellegard, *The Readership of the Periodical Press*, 4.
13. Hodder, *Samuel Morley*, 247.
14. According to R. J. Cruikshank, *Roaring Century 1846–1946* (London: Hamish Hamilton, 1946), 269. Cruickshank's book is an informal history of the *Daily News*.
15. David Owen, *English Philanthropy 1660–1960* (London: Oxford University Press, 1965), 404.
16. Paton is quoted in "On the Comprehension of Presbyterian and Independent Churches. Part II," *Christian Witness and Congregational Magazine*, n.s., 6, no. 63 (March 1870): 134. For a discussion of "non-credalism" and "neo-credalism," see the introduction to John Briggs and Ian Sellers, eds., *Victorian Nonconformity* (London: Edward Arnold, 1973), 6–7.

17. Quoted by Frederick Ash Freer, *Edward White: His Life and Work* (London: Elliot Stock, 1902), 132.
18. See R. Tudor Jones, *Congregationalism in England*, 257, 267–68.
19. This address, in which Dale also restated his views concerning the Atonement, eternal punishment, and the inerrancy of Scripture, was delivered on 21 November 1876. Under the title, "On Some Present Aspects of Theological Thought Among Congregationalists," it was published in the *Congregationalist* 6 (January 1877): 2–15.
20. This comment appeared in a review of Dale's *Manual of Congregational Principles, Congregationalist* 14 (January 1885): 45.
21. For the *Christian World*, see Owen Chadwick, *The Victorian Church*, 2 vols. (London: Adam and Charles Black, 1966–70), 2:426; L. E. Elliott-Binns, *Religion in the Victorian Era*, 334; Thomas Herbert Darlow, *William Robertson Nicoll: Life and Letters* (London: Hodder and Stoughton, 1925), 58–59; and "The Christian World's Twenty-First Birthday: A Bit of Editorial Gossip: A Story With a Moral," *Christian World*, 19 April 1878, 308–9. For examples of the *Weekly Review's* attacks upon the *Christian World*, see "The *Christian World*," *Weekly Review*, 14 June 1873, 567; and "'Christian' Journals," *Weekly Review*, 30 December 1876, 1272–73.
22. For the *English Independent*, see Darlow, *William Robertson Nicoll*, 60; and R. Tudor Jones, *Congregationalism in England*, 304.
23. For the *Congregationalist*, see R. Tudor Jones, *Congregationalism in England*, 304.
24. Knowles to Gladstone, 3 January 1877, Additional Manuscripts 44231, fol. 149, the British Library.
25. See the letter from D. W. Simon, principal of Spring Hill College, Birmingham, to Gladstone, 11 April 1877, Additional Manuscripts 44454, fols. 37–39, the British Library.
26. Knowles quoted from Rogers's letter in his printed leaflet, "The Contemporary Review," 15 February 1877.
27. Strahan told the story of the meeting in Morley's warehouse in "Publishing by Limited Liability. Some Facts About Strahan and Co., Limited. A Letter to the Editor of the *Bookseller*," *Bookseller*, 6 November 1884, 1181.
28. Knowles, "The Contemporary Review," 15 February 1877, fol. 170.
29. Knowles to Gladstone, 2 November 1876, Additional Manuscripts 44231, fol. 129, the British Library.
30. Knowles to McCorquodale, 2 January 1877, copy in Knowles's hand, enclosed in a letter to Gladstone dated 3 January 1877, Additional Manuscripts 44231, fols. 155–56, the British Library.
31. These events are recounted by Strahan, "The Contemporary Review," 7 February 1877; and see Paton, "Strahan and Company, Limited. A Letter to the Editor of the *Bookseller*," *Bookseller*, 4 February 1885, 105.
32. Knowles, "The Contemporary Review," 15 February 1877, fol. 170.
33. Knowles to Gladstone, 11 November 1876, Additional Manuscripts 44231, fol. 138, the British Library.

34. W. H. Mallock, "Modern Atheism: Its Attitude Towards Morality," *Contemporary Review* 29 (January 1877): 169, 171–72.

35. See, for example, Brown, *The Metaphysical Society*, 180–81; Metcalf, *James Knowles*, 272; and the *Wellesley Index to Victorian Periodicals*, 1:211.

36. W. K. Clifford, "The Ethics of Belief," *Contemporary Review* 29 (January 1877): 289–90, 302–3, 308.

37. [R. H. Hutton], "Professor Clifford on the Sin of Credulity," *Spectator*, 6 January 1877, 10–11. This essay was included in Hutton's *Aspects of Religious and Scientific Thought* (1899).

38. "The Ethics of Unbelief," *Saturday Review*, 13 January 1877, 41.

39. "The Magazines," *Scotsman*, 11 January 1877, 3.

40. "The Ethics of Belief," *Pall Mall Gazette*, 17 January 1877, 10.

41. *Letters of Edward Dowden and His Correspondents*, 104.

42. Knowles to Gladstone, 3 January 1877, Additional Manuscripts 44231, fol. 148, the British Library.

43. "Variorum Notes," *Examiner*, 30 December 1876, 1475.

44. "Art and Literary Gossip," *Echo*, 30 December 1876, 4.

45. For Knowles's list of supporters, see below, n. 79.

46. *Weekly Review*, 6 January 1877, 10.

47. *Athenaeum*, 6 January 1877, 19.

48. "General News," (Edinburgh) *Daily Review*, 11 January 1877, 8.

49. The shareholders are named in the "Memorandum of Association" of Strahan and Co., Ltd., the Public Record Office, Kew BT 31/2293/11057.

50. A copy of this letter in Strahan's hand was sent to Gladstone on 17 January 1877; see Additional Manuscripts 44453, fols. 45–47, the British Library. In a vain attempt to persuade Gladstone of the justice of his cause, Strahan sent the former prime minister copies of a number of letters written by himself in 1876–77.

51. Knowles to Tennyson, 20 January 1877, the Tennyson Research Centre.

52. *Times*, 15 January 1877, 6.

53. *Times*, 16 January 1877, 6.

54. *Times*, 17 January 1877, 9.

55. *Publishers' Circular*, 18 January 1877, 3–4.

56. "Variorum Notes," *Examiner*, 20 January 1877, 87.

57. *Spectator*, 20 January 1877, 71.

58. *Academy*, 20 January 1877, 50.

59. Knowles to Tennyson, 20 January 1877, the Tennyson Research Centre.

60. Knowles to Tennyson, 6 January 1877, the Tennyson Research Centre.

61. Knowles to Tennyson, 23 January 1877, the Tennyson Research Centre.

62. Metcalf, *James Knowles*, 272; and Knowles to Gladstone, 3 January 1877, Additional Manuscripts 44231, fol. 148, the British Library. Gladstone alludes, of course, to T. H. Huxley's theories concerning "protoplasm."

63. Knowles to Gladstone, 20 October 1876, Additional Manuscripts 44231, fol. 125, the British Library.

64. Knowles to Gladstone, 3 January 1877, Additional Manuscripts 44231, fol. 148; and Strahan to Gladstone, 3 January 1877, Additional Manuscripts 44453, fols. 5–6, the British Library.
65. Strahan to Gladstone, 17 January 1877, Additional Manuscripts 44453, fol. 44, the British Library.
66. Knowles to Gladstone, 3 January 1877, Additional Manuscripts 44231, fol. 148, the British Library.
67. Knowles to Gladstone, 26 January 1877, Additional Manuscripts 44231, fol. 160, the British Library.
68. Strahan's advertisement appeared in the *Bookseller*, 2 February 1877, 111; *Spectator*, 10 February 1877, 195; *Athenaeum*, 10 February 1877, 175.
69. On 18 February 1877, Freeman wrote to Henry Allon, editor of the *British Quarterly Review*,

> Who is Mullan? Etymologically I should take him to be the father of Macmillan. I and u are easily interchanged. In real life he is somehow generated by Strahan, but how I know not. . . . As for Strahan, I knew nothing of the Contemporary row, and I don't know [*sic*, now] fully understand it. But Strahan asked me to write an article and I wrote it. (Peel, *Letters to a Victorian Editor*, 116.)

70. [W. B. Rands], "Essays and Notices. The Higher Controversy and Periodical Literature," *Contemporary Review* 29 (February 1877): 517.
71. [W. B. Rands], "Essays and Notices. Editing," *Contemporary Review* 29 (February 1877): 517–20.
72. Copy, in Holyoake's hand, of Holyoake to Strahan, 27 January 1877. Holyoake enclosed this copy of his reply to Strahan in a letter to Knowles dated 4 February 1877; as Items No. 2380 and 2384, both are now included in the Holyoake Papers, Co-operative Union Ltd., Manchester.
73. Knowles to Gladstone, 31 January 1877, Additional Manuscripts 44231, fols. 164–65, the British Library.
74. Strahan to Gladstone, 8 February 1877, Additional Manuscripts 44453, fols. 69–70, the British Library.
75. Francis Peek, "The Contemporary Review," 7 February 1877.
76. Strahan, "The Contemporary Review," 7 February 1877.
77. Knowles to Tennyson, 13 February 1877, the Tennyson Research Centre.
78. Knowles, "The Contemporary Review," 15 February 1877.
79. *Spectator*, 10 February 1877, 191; *Athenaeum*, 10 February 1877, 205.
80. Strahan, "Last Words from Alexander Strahan About 'The Contemporary Review' and Mr. J. Knowles," 15 March 1877.
81. See "Strahan and Co. versus King."
82. Knowles to Tennyson, 13 February 1877, the Tennyson Research Centre.
83. Ibid.

84. See the account of the court hearing in "The *Contemporary Review* and the *Nineteenth Century*," *Guardian*, 28 February 1877, 289; this account is more detailed than the one that appeared in the *Times*, 23 February 1877, 11.
85. Strahan, "Last Words from Alexander Strahan About 'The Contemporary Review' and Mr. J. Knowles," 15 March 1877.
86. "Some Magazines," *Spectator*, 10 March 1877, 316.
87. "The *Nineteenth Century*," *English Independent*, 1 March 1877, 205.
88. *Guardian*, 28 February 1877, 293.
89. "Reviews and Magazines," *Academy*, 10 March 1877, 206. Buchanan's poem, an odd blending of Christianity and old Norse mythology that managed to puzzle just about everybody, appeared in three parts in the issues for March, April, and May.
90. "Some Magazines," *Spectator*, 10 March 1877, 318.
91. Francis Peek, "Reasonable Faith," *Contemporary Review* 29 (March 1877): 660–78.
92. [W. B. Rands], "Professor Clifford and His Critics on 'The Ethics of Belief,'" *Contemporary Review* 29 (March 1877): 745.
93. "Outworks of Faith," *Contemporary Review* 29 (March 1877): 750. Although the remark quoted suggests that this essay, like the preceding one, is by Rands, the *Wellesley Index*, which attributes articles to Rands on the basis of clippings in the possession of his grandson, does not so attribute this essay.
94. "The Contemporary Review," *Dickinson's Theological Quarterly* 3 (1877): 474.
95. "The *Contemporary* and *Fortnightly Reviews*," *English Independent*, 29 March 1877, 319.
96. "A Merchant's Faith," *Spectator*, 10 March 1877, 306–8.
97. *Illustrated London News*, 10 March 1877, 227.
98. *Manchester Guardian*, 5 March 1877, 7.
99. "The 'Contemporary' Battle," *Freeman*, 23 March 1877, 134. The allusion is to Vergil's seventh Eclogue.
100. "The *Nineteenth Century*," *English Independent*, 1 March 1877, 205.
101. "Some Magazines," *Spectator*, 10 March 1877, 317.
102. "Notices of Books," *Dublin Review*, n.s., 28 (April 1877): 508.
103. "Reviews and Magazines," *Academy*, 10 March 1877, 206.
104. *Publishers' Circular*, 1 March 1877, 164.
105. W. E. Gladstone, "On the Influence of Authority in Matters of Opinion," *Nineteenth Century* 1 (March 1877): 21.
106. "J.S.B.," "To the Poet Laureate," *Evangelical Christendom*, n.s., 18 (1877): 101.
107. *Rock*, 2 March 1877, 164–65.
108. "The *Nineteenth Century*," *English Independent*, 1 March 1877, 205.
109. Professor Cecil Y. Lang, who is preparing an edition of Tennyson's letters, has informed Knowles's biographer that he has no knowledge of any surviving letters written by Tennyson to Knowles in January or February 1877; see Metcalf, *James Knowles*, 279 n. 11.

110. Knowles to Gladstone, 7 March 1877, Additional Manuscripts 44231, fols. 173–74, the British Library.
111. *Weekly Review,* 31 March 1877, 299.
112. Knowles to Gladstone, 26 January 1877, Additional Manuscripts 44231, fol. 161, the British Library.
113. For a discussion of the symposium on "The Influence Upon Morality of a Decline in Religious Belief," see James C. Livingston, *The Ethics of Belief: An Essay on the Victorian Religious Conscience* (Tallahassee, Fl.: American Academy of Religion, 1974), 36–38.
114. For a discussion of the symposium on "The Soul and Future Life," see Geoffrey Rowell, *Hell and the Victorians: A Study of the Nineteenth-Century Theological Controversies Concerning Eternal Punishment and the Future Life* (Oxford: Clarendon Press, 1974), 133–38.
115. Strahan, "Last Words from Alexander Strahan About 'The Contemporary Review' and Mr. J. Knowles," 15 March 1877.
116. "The Magazines," *Spectator,* 7 April 1877, 445.
117. John Lewis Paton, *John Brown Paton,* 176.
118. Alexander Bain, *Autobiography,* ed. W. L. Davidson (London: Longman, 1904), 336.
119. See Strahan, "Publishing by Limited Liability. Some Facts About Strahan and Co., Limited. A Letter to the Editor of the *Bookseller,*" *Bookseller,* 6 November 1884, 1183.
120. "Strahan and Co. (Ltd.) vs. King," *Guardian,* 25 July 1877, 1027; and "Strahan vs. King," *Publishers' Circular,* 2 August 1877, 508.
121. See Strahan, "Strahan and Co. versus King."
122. The sale of King's business was announced in the *Bookseller,* 5 October 1877, 866, and 5 November 1877, 991. Kegan Paul succeeded King as Tennyson's publisher until Tennyson went to Macmillan in 1884; Kegan Paul continued to publish Knowles's *Nineteenth Century* until 1891.
123. Knowles to Gladstone, 6 January 1878, Additional Manuscripts 44231, fols. 220–21, the British Library.
124. The Christmas *Bookseller,* 1877, 146.

Chapter IX

1. *Letters of Matthew Arnold, 1848–1888,* ed. Russell, 2:191; the letter, to M. Fontanès, is dated 25 March 1881.
2. Most of the information in this chapter concerning the history of Strahan and Company Limited is based on a letter from Strahan to the *Bookseller,* 6 November 1884, 1181–87. Strahan's account was contradicted in part by Paton, by Peek, and by a lawyer representing Samuel Morley (see below, nn. 42, 43, 44, and 47), and I have not followed it uncritically.
3. Ibid., 1184.
4. Ibid., 1181; Strahan cites a letter from the Edinburgh firm of W. and A. K. Johnston, dated 24 October 1884.
5. For the "Leicester Conference" and its aftermath, see John Webster Grant, *Free Churchmanship in England, 1870–1940* (London: Independent

Press, 1955), 91–93; Albert Peel, *These Hundred Years*, 266–71; and R. Tudor Jones, *Congregationalism in England*, 263–64. Virtually every Non-conformist periodical of the day devoted one or more articles to the "Leicester Conference"; among the most valuable of these are: "The Autumnal Meetings of the Congregational Union," *Congregationalist* 6 (November 1877): 686–92; "The Leicester Conference," *Congregationalist* 6 (December 1877): 707–23; John Page Hopps, "The Significance of the Congregational Union Debate and Vote Upon the Leicester Conference," *Truthseeker* 16 (June 1878): 153–59; Charles Beard, "The Leicester Conference on Free Communion," *Theological Review* 15 (July 1878): 366–88; "The Congregational View of Religious Communion," *British Quarterly Review* 68 (July 1878): 100–109. In *The Best I Remember* (London: Cassell, 1922), Arthur Porritt, who began his career as a journalist in the religious press in 1890, recalled that even then the "echoes" and "rumblings" of the "Leicester Conference" controversy were still to be heard (172–73).

6. The *Record*'s opinions were repeated in "The 'Gangrene in Congregationalism,'" *Spectator*, 8 June 1878, 725–27.

7. *Christian World*, 13 July 1877, 514.

8. See, for example, Brown's letter to the *Christian World*, 11 January 1878, 26; and the editorial, "On Perilous Ground," in the issue of 25 January 1878, 67.

9. The "Memorandum of Association" and other documents of the Christian Signal Publishing Company are at the Public Record Office, Kew, BT 31/2412/12120.

10. Ibid. Watt sold advertising space in Strahan's periodicals. Watt was also, at about this time, helping George MacDonald sell to other publishers the fiction that Strahan could no longer afford to purchase; in this way Watt began his career as a "literary agent."

11. *Fountain*, 14 March 1878, 895.

12. "The Leaven of the Pharisees," *Christian World*, 15 March 1878, 211.

13. The *Christian Signal* of 26 April 1878 is the only issue of this periodical included in the newspaper collection of the British Library (Colindale), nor have I been able to discover issues in other collections, although it is evident from advertisements in the press that the *Christian Signal* survived at least until the autumn of 1878.

14. "Magazines for the Month," *Fountain*, 9 May 1878, 89.

15. "Church News," *Christian's Penny Magazine and Friend of the People* 14 (June 1878): 140–42. The *Christian World* informed its readers that "the person really and solely responsible for the little bit of theological slander is the Rev. F. S. Williams, of the Nottingham Congregational Institute"; see *Christian World*, 5 July 1878, 562.

16. *Weekly Review*, 26 October 1878, 1027; the *Weekly Review* also named those Scots who worked on the *Christian World* and on the *Fountain*.

17. "Notes by the Way," *Truthseeker* 16 (July 1878): 188.

18. "The Congregational View of Religious Communion," *British and Foreign Evangelical Review* 27 (1878): 202.

19. *Christian World*, 10 May 1878, 385.
20. For Morley's comments, see *Christian World*, "Special May Meeting Number," 15 May 1878, 5; *Christian World*, 17 May 1878, 400; and *Christian World*, 24 May 1878, letter from Frederic Wagstaff, 424.
21. See the report of the vote in the *Christian World*, 17 May 1878, 400. According to another Congregational periodical, the union was in severe financial difficulty in 1877; see "The Funds of the Union," *Advance and Congregational Miscellany* 5, no. 3 (March 1877).
22. *Publishers' Circular*, 18 January 1878, 62–63.
23. Editor, "Our Thousandth Number," *Twentieth Century* 167 (June 1960): 504.
24. Charles Wordsworth to W. A. Knight, 14 March 1878, the Pierpont Morgan Library, New York; also quoted in the *Wellesley Index to Victorian Periodicals*, 2:624.
25. *Publishers' Circular*, 1 April 1878, 219.
26. This remark is said to have appeared in *Light: A Journal of Criticism and Belles Lettres*, a sixpenny journal that according to the *Waterloo Directory to Victorian Periodicals* was published from 6 April 1878 through 26 October 1878; the anonymous critic was quoted by the *Christian World*, 12 April 1878, 288. The papers on "Future Punishment" that appeared in the *Contemporary* have been discussed by one of the participants, John Hunt, in *Religious Thought in England in the Nineteenth Century* (London: Gibbings and Co., 1896), 280–84, and more recently by Geoffrey Rowell, *Hell and the Victorians*, 140–41.
27. Knowles to Gladstone, 6 September 1878, Additional Manuscripts 44231, fol. 248, the British Library; Knowles was attempting to dissuade Gladstone from sending to the *Contemporary* his article entitled "The Sixteenth Century Arraigned Before the Nineteenth: A Study on the Reformation," which opened the *Contemporary* of October 1878.
28. "Law Reports—Chancery," *Times*, 5 September 1878, 12; and 12 September 1878, 10. The *Athenaeum* of 14 September 1878 reported that in fact Tennyson's poem had already been published in the United States, in Harper and Company's 1871 edition of Tennyson's works; see "Literary Gossip," 339.
29. *Weekly Review*, 1 February 1879, 102.
30. *Weekly Review*, 1 April 1879, 367.
31. See Strahan's letter to the *Bookseller*, 6 November 1884, 1183–85. Most of the information that follows concerning the history of the limited company is based upon the correspondence in the *Bookseller*.
32. See the advertisement in the *Bookseller*, 3 October 1878, 981.
33. Information concerning L. G. Séguin and her family has been provided by Mr. Martin Strahan Soames, Alexander Strahan's grandson.
34. "Trade and Literary Gossip: Alexander Strahan and Co., Limited," *Bookseller*, 5 March 1885, 235.
35. For Strahan's edition of the *Pilgrim's Progress*, see George Dalziel and Edward Dalziel, *The Brothers Dalziel*, 264–66.
36. Bunting described his plans concerning the review to a contributor, Vio-

let Paget ("Vernon Lee"); see Peter Gunn, *Vernon Lee: Violet Paget, 1856–1935* (London: Oxford University Press, 1964), 93. Bunting's connection with the *Contemporary* is also discussed by James Marchant, in *J. B. Paton*, 268–69.

37. According to Strahan's letter to the *Bookseller*, 6 November 1884, 1187.
38. Ibid.
39. Strahan's advertisement in the *Publishers' Circular* of 1 October 1884 is the last I have been able to find for him.
40. Strahan, letter to the *Bookseller*, 6 November 1884, 1181–87.
41. Victor Bauer (auditor to Strahan and Company Limited), letter to the *Bookseller*, 13 December 1884, 1361.
42. Francis Peek, letter to the *Bookseller*, 7 January 1885, 5–6; Peek responds to Strahan's letter of 6 November 1884.
43. Francis Peek, letter to the *Bookseller*, 5 March 1885, 238.
44. Henry Thomas Chambers (solicitor to Samuel Morley), letter to the *Bookseller*, 13 December 1884, 1361–62.
45. Strahan, letter to the *Bookseller*, 7 January 1885, 7–9.
46. See the *Bookseller*, 6 November 1884, 1182, and 13 December 1884, 1361–62.
47. John Brown Paton, letter to the *Bookseller*, 4 February 1885, 105.
48. See the *Bookseller*, 5 April 1883, 307; 5 March 1885, 235; and 5 May 1885, 445.
49. "Trade and Literary Gossip," *Bookseller*, 7 January 1885, 3.
50. "Committee of Creditors," letter to the *Bookseller*, 5 May 1885, 445.
51. "Trade and Literary Gossip," *Bookseller*, 5 April 1883, 307.

Chapter X

1. *Spectator*, 8 October 1881, 1282.
2. H. Simonis, *The Street of Ink: An Intimate History of Journalism* (London: Cassell, 1917), 286.
3. "Makers of Public Opinion. The Leading Publishers. No. 22.—Messrs. George Newnes," *Public Opinion*, 19 August 1904, 236.
4. Simonis, *The Street of Ink*, 287.
5. Frederic Whyte, *The Life of W. T. Stead*, 2 vols. (London: Jonathan Cape, 1925; reprint, London: Garland, 1971), 1:18.
6. J. W. Robertson Scott, *The Life and Death of a Newspaper: An Account of the Temperaments, Perturbations and Achievements of John Morley, W. T. Stead, and Other Editors of the* Pall Mall Gazette (London: Methuen, 1952), 237.
7. W. T. Stead, "Government by Journalism," *Contemporary Review* 49 (May 1886): 663–64.
8. W. T. Stead, "The Future of Journalism," *Contemporary Review* 50 (November 1886): 678.
9. Whyte, *The Life of W. T. Stead*, 1:320.
10. J. Guinness Rogers, "Present Day Congregationalism," *Congregational Review* 1 (January 1887): 11.

11. Nicoll is described by George Blake, *Barrie and the Kailyard School* (London: Arthur Barker, 1951), 22; see also Darlow, *William Robertson Nicoll*.
12. Quoted by Cunningham, *Everywhere Spoken Against*, 62.
13. Blake, *Barrie and the Kailyard School*, 30.
14. E. V. Lucas, *Reading, Writing and Remembering: A Literary Record* (London: Methuen, 1932), 57–58.
15. [W. R. Nicoll], "The Correspondence of Claudius Clear," *British Weekly*, 6 July 1893, 169.
16. For Knowles's later career, see Metcalf, *James Knowles*.
17. *The Diary of Sir Edward Walter Hamilton 1880–1885*, ed. Dudley W. R. Bahlman, 2 vols. (Oxford: Clarendon Press, 1972), 2:743; the prime minister's salary was approximately £5,000 a year, according to Metcalf, *James Knowles*, 285.
18. *My World as in My Time: Memoirs of Sir Henry Newbolt 1862–1932* (London: Faber and Faber, 1932), 156–57.
19. "Men Who Make Public Opinion. Sir James Knowles," *Public Opinion*, 29 January 1904, 140.
20. Ward, *Ten Personal Studies*, 76–77.
21. According to the obituaries in the *Times*, 29 May 1918, 9, and the *Bookseller*, June 1918, 272; Mr. R. G. Tennant, secretary of the Reform Club, has informed me in a letter dated 22 February 1982 that Strahan's membership lapsed after December 1888 when he failed to pay his annual subscription.
22. Frederic Whyte, *William Heinemann: A Memoir* (London: Jonathan Cape, 1928), 31.
23. "A. S." and "A. P. W." [Alexander Strahan and Alexander Pollock Watt], "John Pettie, R.A. By Two Old Friends," *British Weekly*, 9 March 1893, 313–14.
24. Nicoll and Wise, *Literary Anecdotes*, 2:258.
25. For Wise and his forgeries, see John Carter and Graham Pollard, *An Enquiry into the Nature of Certain Nineteenth Century Pamphlets* (London: Constable, 1934).
26. Information concerning the Watt and Strahan families has been provided by Mr. Martin Strahan Soames, Mr. Alexander Strahan, and Commander Alexander Strachan Watt.
27. "A Great Publisher from the North of Scotland," *Inverness Courier*, 29 December 1903, 3.
28. Wise's letter to Forman is quoted by Fannie E. Ratchford, *A Review of Reviews* (Austin: University of Texas Press, 1946), 47–48. I am grateful to Mr. John P. Chalmers of the Humanities Research Center, the University of Texas, for providing me with photocopies of this material.
29. Thomas J. Wise, *The Ashley Library*, 11 vols. (privately printed, 1925), 7:123, 137.
30. Ibid., 7:107.
31. Ibid., 7:129–30; and Thomas J. Wise, *A Bibliography of Tennyson*, 2 vols. (privately printed, 1908), 1:194–95.

32. Carter and Pollard, *An Enquiry,* 139.
33. *Letters of Thomas J. Wise to John Henry Wrenn. A Further Inquiry Into the Guilt of Certain Nineteenth-Century Forgers,* ed. Fannie E. Ratchford (New York: Alfred A. Knopf, 1944), 71, 454–55.
34. Isbister, who retired from Isbister and Company in 1883, became a partner in the publishing firm of Charles Burnet and Company; see "Literary Gossip," *Athenaeum,* 13 July 1889, 66, and "Mr. W. Isbister's Bankruptcy," *Bookseller,* 6 February 1890, 142.
35. Donald Macleod, "An Editorial Retrospect," *Good Words* 46 (November 1904): 80.
36. See the *Publisher and Bookseller,* 27 May 1905, 214–15, and 30 September 1905, 13.
37. The *Good Words* of 1906 has been described by Patrick Scott, "Victorian Religious Periodicals: Fragments that Remain," in *The Materials, Sources and Methods of Ecclesiastical History, Papers Read at the Twelfth Summer Meeting and the Thirteenth Winter Meeting of the Ecclesiastical History Society,* vol. 11 of *Studies in Church History,* ed. Derek Baker (Oxford: Clarendon Press, 1975), 336–37.
38. Harold T. Hartley, *Eighty-Eight Not Out,* 229.
39. "Norman Macleod's Publisher," *Glasgow Herald,* 20 April 1912, 4.
40. This letter, dated 19 February 1917, is in the possession of Mr. Martin Strahan Soames.
41. *Publishers' Circular,* 1 June 1918, 453.
42. *Times,* 29 May 1918, 9.
43. *Bookseller,* June 1918, 272.
44. Daniel Jenkins, *The British: Their Identity and Their Religion* (London: SCM Press, 1975), 27.
45. Quoted by John Gross, *The Rise and Fall of the Man of Letters,* 80.

Bibliography

Magazines, Newspapers, Periodicals

For information concerning the dates, prices, publishers, and editors of many of these periodicals, see the *Waterloo Directory of Victorian Periodicals 1824–1900*, Phase I, ed. Michael Wolff, John S. North, and Dorothy Deering (Waterloo, Ontario: Wilfrid Laurier University Press, for the University of Waterloo, [1976]). Periodicals marked with an asterisk (*) are included in the *Wellesley Index to Victorian Periodicals, 1824–1900*, ed. Walter E. Houghton, 3 vols. to date (Toronto: University of Toronto Press, 1966–   ), which provides tables of contents (excluding poetry) and identifies contributors when possible. I have indicated the religious bias of several periodicals in the following list.

PERIODICALS OWNED OR CONDUCTED BY ALEXANDER STRAHAN

Argosy
Christian Guest
**Contemporary Review*
Day of Rest
Evening Hours
Good Words
Good Words for the Young (later *Good Things for the Young*)
News of the Churches and Journal of Missions (later *Christian Work Throughout the World*)
Peep-show
Saturday Journal
**Saint Pauls Magazine*
Sunday Magazine

OTHER PERIODICALS

Academy
Athenaeum
Bookman
Bookseller
British and Foreign Evangelical Review (Nonconformist)
British Quarterly Review (Nonconformist)
British Weekly (Nonconformist)
Christian

Christian Observer (Anglican; Evangelical)
Christian Signal (Nonconformist)
Christian Witness (Congregationalist)
Christian World (Nonconformist)
Christian's Penny Magazine (Congregationalist)
Church Quarterly Review (Anglican; High Church)
Church Times (Anglican; High Church)
Clapham Magazine
Congregational Miscellany
Congregational Review
Congregationalist
*Cornhill Magazine
(Edinburgh) *Daily Review*
Dearden's Miscellany
Dickinson's Theological Quarterly (Nonconformist)
Dublin Review (Roman Catholic)
Echo
Edinburgh Christian Magazine (Church of Scotland)
*Edinburgh Review
English Independent (Congregationalist)
Examiner
*Fortnightly Review
Fountain (Congregationalist)
Freeman (Baptist)
Glasgow Herald
Guardian (Anglican; High Church)
Illustrated London News
Inverness Courier
Literary Churchman (Anglican; High Church)
London Review
Manchester Guardian
New York Times
*Nineteenth Century
*North British Review
Pall Mall Gazette
Patriot (Congregationalist)
(Edinburgh) *Presbyterian*
Public Opinion
Publishers' Circular
Reader
Record (Anglican; Evangelical)
Rock (Anglican; Evangelical)
(New York) *Round Table*
Saturday Review
(Edinburgh) *Scotsman*
Spectator

*Temple Bar
*Theological Review (Unitarian)
Times
Truthseeker
Weekly Review

Archives, Manuscripts, Public Records

Bodleian Library. Business papers of Anthony Trollope, including correspondence with James Virtue and with Alexander Strahan. Many of the letters in this collection have been published in The Letters of Anthony Trollope, ed. N. John Hall.

Boston Public Library. Letters of Alfred Tennyson and Emily Tennyson to various correspondents, including James Knowles and Mrs. Margaret Gatty. Many of Emily Tennyson's letters have been published in The Letters of Emily Lady Tennyson, ed. James O. Hoge.

British Library. The Gladstone papers include letters from James Knowles, Alexander Strahan, and other correspondents, as well as the printed pamphlets circulated by Knowles and Strahan in 1876–77.

Cambridge University Library. Letters of Norman Macleod, Donald Macleod, and Alexander Strahan to James Malcom Ludlow. Many of Norman Macleod's letters have been published in Donald Macleod, Memoir of Norman Macleod.

Co-operative Union Ltd., Holyoake House, Manchester. Letters of James Knowles and Alexander Strahan to George Jacob Holyoake, with copies of some of Holyoake's replies.

Greater London Record Office, London County Hall. Archives of Spalding and Hodge, deposited by the Inveresk Paper Co. Ltd.

Huntington Library, San Marino, California. The John Hollingshead papers include letters from Alexander Strahan.

Imperial College of Science and Technology, London. The T. H. Huxley papers include letters from James Knowles.

National Library of Scotland, Edinburgh. Hugh Miller papers; Blackwood Publishing Archives.

Pierpont Morgan Library, New York. The William Angus Knight papers include letters from James Knowles and Alexander Strahan.

Public Record Office, Kew. Records of Virtue and Co. Ltd. (incorporated 1875); Strahan and Co. Ltd. (incorporated 1876); Isbister and Co. Ltd. (incorporated 1879).

Reading, University of, Library. Archives of Bell and Hyman Ltd., including the records of Bell and Daldy and George Bell and Sons.

Scottish Record Office, General Register House, Edinburgh. Census reports of Tain, Ross-shire; commissary records of Ross and Cromarty.

Tennyson Research Centre, City Library, Lincoln. Correspondence of Alfred Tennyson, Emily Tennyson, Hallam Tennyson, Alexander Strahan, James Knowles; business records of Alfred Tennyson; journal of Emily Tennyson. Emily Tennyson's letters and journal have been published in the volumes edited by James O. Hoge.

University College, London. Archives of Kegan Paul, Trench, Trubner, and Henry S. King, 1853–1912. These have been reproduced by Chadwyck-Healey Ltd. in the series, *British Publishers' Archives on Microfilm*, Part 1 (London, 1976).

Books, Articles, Dissertations

"Adelph" [pseud.]. *London Scenes and London People: Anecdotes, Reminiscences, and Sketches of Places, Personages, Events, Customs, and Curiosities of London City, Past and Present.* London: W. H. Collingridge, City Press, 1863.

Alford, Henry. *Life, Journals, and Letters of Henry Alford, D.D., Late Dean at Canterbury.* Edited by Fanny Alford. London: Rivingtons, 1873.

Allibone, S. Austin. *A Critical Dictionary of English Literature and British and American Authors Living and Deceased from the Earliest Accounts to the Latter Half of the Nineteenth Century.* 3 vols. Philadelphia: Lippincott, 1858. Reprint. Detroit: Gale, 1965.

Altick, Richard D. *The English Common Reader: A Social History of the Mass Reading Public 1800–1900.* Chicago: University of Chicago Press, 1957. Reprint. Chicago: University of Chicago Press, Phoenix Books, 1963.

Annan, Noel. "Science, Religion, and the Critical Mind." In *1859: Entering an Age of Crisis,* edited by Philip Appleman et al., 31–50. Bloomington: Indiana University Press, 1959.

Arnold, Matthew. *The Complete Prose Works of Matthew Arnold.* 11 vols. Edited by R. H. Super. Ann Arbor: University of Michigan Press, 1960–77.

———. *Letters of Matthew Arnold, 1848–1888.* 2 vols. Edited by G. W. E. Russell. New York: Macmillan, 1895.

Austin, James C., ed. *Fields of* The Atlantic Monthly: *Letters to an Editor, 1861–1870.* San Marino, Calif.: Huntington Library, 1953.

Bagehot, Walter. *The Collected Works.* 12 vols. Edited by Norman St John-Stevas. London: *Economist,* 1965–74.

Bain, Alexander. *Autobiography.* Edited by W. L. Davidson. London: Longman, 1904.

Baker, Derek, ed. *Studies in Church History.* Vols. 10, 11, and 15. Oxford: Ecclesiastical History Society, 1973, 1975, 1978.

Balleine, G. R. *A History of the Evangelical Party in the Church of England.* London: Longmans, Green and Co., 1933.

Ballou, Ellen B. *The Building of the House: Houghton Mifflin's Formative Years.* Boston: Houghton Mifflin, 1970.

Bayne, Peter. *The Life and Letters of Hugh Miller.* 2 vols. London: Strahan and Co., 1871.

Bell, Edward. *George Bell, Publisher: A Brief Memoir.* London: privately printed at the Chiswick Press, 1924.

Black, Kenneth Macleod. *The Scots Churches in England.* Edinburgh and London: Blackwood and Sons, 1906.

Blackie, John Stuart. *The Letters of John Stuart Blackie to His Wife. With a Few Earlier Ones to His Parents.* Edited by Archibald Stodart Walker. Edinburgh and London: Blackwood and Sons, 1909.

Blaikie, William Garden. *An Autobiography: Recollections of a Busy Life.* London: Hodder and Stoughton, 1901.

Blake, George. *Barrie and the Kailyard School.* London: Arthur Barker, 1951.

Boase, Frederic. *Modern English Biography.* 6 vols. Truro: Netherton and Worth, 1892–1921. Reprint. London: Frank Cass, 1965.

Boyd, A. K. H. *Twenty-Five Years of St. Andrews.* 4th ed. 2 vols. London: Longmans, Green and Co., 1893.

Boyd, Kenneth M. *Scottish Church Attitudes to Sex, Marriage and the Family 1850–1914.* Edinburgh: John Donald Publishers, 1980.

Bradley, Ian. *The Optimists: Themes and Personalities in Victorian Liberalism.* London: Faber and Faber, 1980.

Briggs, John, and Sellers, Ian, eds. *Victorian Nonconformity.* London: Edward Arnold, 1973.

Brown, Alan Willard. *The Metaphysical Society: Victorian Minds in Crisis, 1869–1880.* New York: Columbia University Press, 1947.

[Brown, John], and Forrest, D. W., eds. *Letters of Dr. John Brown: With Letters from Ruskin, Thackeray, and Others.* London: A. and C. Black, 1907.

Brown, Thomas. *Annals of the Disruption.* Edinburgh: Macniven and Wallace, 1884.

Browning, Robert. *Learned Lady: Letters from Robert Browning to Mrs. Thomas FitzGerald 1876–1889.* Edited by Edward C. McAleer. Cambridge, Mass.: Harvard University Press, 1966.

Bryce, James. *Ten Years of the Church of Scotland from 1833 to 1843.* 2 vols. Edinburgh: Blackwood and Sons, 1850.

Buchanan, Robert, D.D. *The Ten Years' Conflict: Being the History of the Disruption of the Church of Scotland.* 2 vols. Glasgow: Blackie and Son, 1849.

Buchanan, Robert (1841–1901). *The Fleshly School of Poetry and Other Phenomena of the Day.* London: Strahan and Co., 1872.

Campbell, George Douglas, Eighth Duke of Argyll. *Autobiography and Memoirs.* 2 vols. Edited by the Dowager Duchess of Argyll. London: John Murray, 1906.

Carlyle, Thomas. "Signs of the Times." *Edinburgh Review* 49 (June 1829): 439–59.

Carter, Ian. "The Changing Image of the Scottish Peasantry, 1745–1980." In *People's History and Socialist Theory,* edited by Raphael Samuel, 9–15. London: Routledge and Kegan Paul, 1981.

Carter, John, and Pollard, Graham. *An Enquiry into the Nature of Certain Nineteenth Century Pamphlets.* London: Constable, 1934.

Cassidy, John A. *Robert W. Buchanan.* New York: Twayne, 1973.

Chadwick, Owen. *The Victorian Church.* 2 vols. London: Adam and Charles Black, 1966–70.

Checkland, S. G. *The Gladstones: A Family Biography 1764–1851.* Cambridge: Cambridge University Press, 1971.

Church of England. *Authorized Report of the Church Congress Held at Dublin on September 29th, 30th, October 1st, 2nd, 3rd 1868*. Dublin: Hodges, Smith and Foster, 1868.

Cole, G. D. H. *The Life of William Cobbett*. 3d rev. ed. London: Home and Van Thal, 1947.

Coleman, D. C. *The British Paper Industry 1495–1860*. Oxford: Clarendon Press, 1958.

Coleman, John. *Charles Reade as I Knew Him*. London: Traherne and Co., 1903.

Cox, R. G. "The Reviews and Magazines." In *From Dickens to Hardy*, 188–204. Vol. 6. of *Pelican Guide to English Literature*, edited by Boris Ford. Harmondsworth: Penguin, 1958. Reprint. 1969.

Cruikshank, R. J. *Roaring Century 1846–1946*. London: Hamish Hamilton, 1946.

Cunningham, Valentine. *Everywhere Spoken Against: Dissent in the Victorian Novel*. Oxford: Clarendon Press, 1975.

Curwen, Henry. *A History of Booksellers: The Old and the New*. London: Chatto and Windus, 1873.

Dalziel, George, and Dalziel, Edward. *The Brothers Dalziel: A Record of Fifty Years Work in Conjunction with Many of the Most Distinguished Artists of the Period 1840–1900*. London: Methuen, 1901.

Darlow, Thomas Herbert. *William Robertson Nicoll: Life and Letters*. London: Hodder and Stoughton, 1925.

Davie, George Elder. *The Democratic Intellect: Scotland and Her Universities in the Nineteenth Century*. Edinburgh: Edinburgh University Press, 1961.

Dent, J. M. *The Memoirs of J. M. Dent 1849–1926*. London: J. M. Dent and Sons, 1928.

Derby, J. C. *Fifty Years Among Authors, Books and Publishers*. London: S. Low, Son and Co., 1884.

Dickens, Charles. *Letters of Charles Dickens to Wilkie Collins 1851–1870*. Selected by Miss Georgina Hogarth, edited by Lawrence Hutton. London: Osgood, McIlvaine and Co., 1892.

[Dowden, Elizabeth D., and Dowden, Hilda M.], eds. *Letters of Edward Dowden and His Correspondents*. London: J. M. Dent and Sons, 1914.

Duncan, David. *Life and Letters of Herbert Spencer*. 2 vols. New York: D. Appleton and Co., 1908.

Eliot, George. *The George Eliot Letters*. 7 vols. Edited by Gordon S. Haight. New Haven, Conn.: Yale University Press, 1954–55.

Ellegard, Alvar. *The Readership of the Periodical Press in Mid-Victorian Britain*. Goteborgs universitets arsskrift, vol. 63, no. 3. Goteborg: Acta universitatis gothoburgensis, 1957.

Elliott-Binns, L. E. *Religion in the Victorian Era*. 2d ed. London: Lutterworth Press, 1946.

Ellis, S[tewart] M. *Henry Kingsley 1830–1876. Towards a Vindication*. London: Grant Richards, 1931.

Elwin, Malcolm. *Charles Reade: A Biography.* London: Jonathan Cape, 1931.
————. *Victorian Wallflowers.* London: Jonathan Cape, 1934.
Enright, William G. "Urbanization and the Evangelical Pulpit in Nineteenth-Century Scotland." *Journal of Church History* 47 (December 1978): 400–407.
Eros, John. "The Rise of Organized Free Thought in Mid-Victorian England." *Sociological Review,* n.s., 2, no. 1 (July 1954): 98–120.
Escott, Harry. *A History of Scottish Congregationalism.* Glasgow: Congregational Union of Scotland, 1960.
[Escott, T. H. S.] *Society in London, by a Foreign Resident.* London: Chatto and Windus, 1885.
Everett, Edwin Mallard. *The Party of Humanity: The* Fortnightly Review *and Its Contributors 1865–1874.* Chapel Hill: University of North Carolina Press, 1939.
Ferguson, William. *Scotland: 1689 to the Present.* New York: Praeger, 1968.
Forster, E. M. *Marianne Thornton: A Domestic Biography 1797–1887.* New York: Harcourt Brace Jovanovich, 1956.
Francis, John Collins. *Notes by the Way.* London: T. Fisher Unwin, 1909.
Freer, Frederick Ash. *Edward White: His Life and Work.* London: Elliot Stock, 1902.
Gilbert, Alan D. *Religion and Society in Industrial England: Church, Chapel and Social Change, 1740–1914.* London: Longman, 1976.
Gillespie, Neal C. "The Duke of Argyll, Evolutionary Anthropology, and the Art of Scientific Controversy." *Isis* 68 (March 1977): 40–54.
Glover, Willis B. *Evangelical Nonconformists and Higher Criticism in the Nineteenth Century.* London: Independent Press, 1954.
Goodwin, Michael. "Preface" to *Nineteenth Century Opinion: An Anthology of Extracts from the First Fifty Volumes of* The Nineteenth Century *1877–1901.* Harmondsworth: Penguin, 1951.
Graham, Walter. *English Literary Periodicals.* New York: Thomas Nelson and Sons, 1930.
Grant, James. *History of the Newspaper Press: Its Origin, Progress, and Present Position.* 3 vols. London: Tinsley Brothers, 1871 [–72].
Grant, John Webster. *Free Churchmanship in England 1870–1940. With Special Reference to Congregationalism.* London: Independent Press, 1955.
Graves, Charles Larcom. *Life and Letters of Alexander Macmillan.* London: Macmillan, 1910.
Gross, John. *The Rise and Fall of the Man of Letters: Aspects of English Literary Life Since 1800.* London: Weidenfeld and Nicolson, 1969. Reprint. Harmondsworth: Penguin, 1973.
Grugel, Lee E. *George Jacob Holyoake: A Study in the Evolution of a Victorian Radical.* Philadelphia: Porcupine Press, 1976.
Gunn, Peter. *Vernon Lee: Violet Paget, 1856–1935.* London: Oxford University Press, 1964.
Guthrie, David K., and Guthrie, Charles J., eds. *Autobiography of Thomas*

Guthrie, D.D., and Memoir by His Sons. 2 vols. New York: Robert Carter and Brothers, 1875.

Hagen, June Steffensen. *Tennyson and His Publishers.* London: Macmillan 1979.

Haldane, Alexander. *The Lives of Robert Haldane of Airthrey, and of His Brother James Alexander Haldane.* New York: Robert Carter and Brothers, 1853.

Hamilton, Edward Walter. *The Diary of Sir Edward Walter Hamilton 1880–1885.* 2 vols. Edited by Dudley W. R. Bahlman. Oxford: Clarendon Press, 1972.

Hamilton, Walter, collector and arranger. *Parodies of the Works of English and American Authors.* 6 vols. London: Reeves and Turner, 1884–89.

Hanham, H. J. "Mid-Century Scottish Nationalism: Romantic and Radical." In *Ideas and Institutions of Victorian Britain: Essays in Honour of George Kitson Clark,* edited by Robert Robson, 143–79. London: G. Bell and Sons, 1967.

Hardie, Martin. *John Pettie.* London: Adam and Charles Black, 1908.

Hardman, William. *The Hardman Papers: A Further Selection (1865–1868) from the Letters and Memoirs of Sir William Hardman.* Edited by S[tewart] M. Ellis. London: Constable, 1930.

Hartley, Harold T. *Eighty-Eight Not Out: A Record of Happy Memories.* London: Frederick Muller, 1939.

Harvie, Christopher. *Scotland and Nationalism: Scottish Society and Politics, 1707–1977.* London: Allen and Unwin, 1977.

Hennell, Michael. *Sons of the Prophets: Evangelical Leaders of the Victorian Church.* London: Society for Promoting Christian Knowledge, 1979.

Hepburn, James. *The Author's Empty Purse and the Rise of the Literary Agent.* London: Oxford University Press, 1968.

Hodder, Edwin. *Life and Work of the Seventh Earl of Shaftesbury.* 3 vols. London: Cassell, 1887.

———. *The Life of Samuel Morley.* 2d ed. London: Hodder and Stoughton, 1887.

Hollingshead, John. *My Lifetime.* 2 vols. London: S. Low, Marston and Co., 1895.

Holmes, Oliver Wendell. *John Lothrop Motley: A Memoir.* Boston: Houghton, Osgood and Co., 1879.

Hort, Arthur Fenton. *Life and Letters of Fenton J. A. Hort.* 2 vols. London: Macmillan, 1896.

Hudson, Derek. *Munby: Man of Two Worlds: The Life and Diaries of Arthur J. Munby 1828–1910.* London: John Murray, 1972.

Hughes, Thomas. *Memoir of Daniel Macmillan.* London: Macmillan, 1882.

Hunnisett, Basil. *Steel-Engraved Book Illustration in England.* Boston: David R. Godine, 1980.

Hunt, John. *Religious Thought in England in the Nineteenth Century.* London: Gibbings and Co., 1896.

Huxley, Leonard. *The House of Smith Elder.* London: privately printed, 1923.

———. *Life and Letters of Thomas Henry Huxley.* 2 vols. London: Macmillan, 1900.

Hyder, Clyde Kenneth. "Introduction" to *Swinburne Replies: Notes on Poems and Reviews, Under the Microscope, Dedicatory Epistle.* Syracuse, N.Y.: Syracuse University Press, 1966.

Innes, Alexander Taylor. *Chapters of Reminiscence.* London: Hodder and Stoughton, 1913.

Irvine, William. *Apes, Angels and Victorians: Darwin, Huxley and Evolution.* Cleveland and New York: World Publishing Co., 1955. Reprint. New York: Meridian Books, 1959.

Jay, Harriet. *Robert Buchanan: Some Account of His Life, His Life's Work, and His Literary Friendships.* London: T. Fisher Unwin, 1903.

Jenkins, Daniel. *The British: Their Identity and Their Religion.* London: SCM Press, 1975.

Jones, R. Tudor. *Congregationalism in England 1662–1962.* London: Independent Press, 1962.

Keddie, Henrietta. *Three Generations: The Story of a Middle-Class Scottish Family.* London: John Murray, 1911.

King, Mrs. Eleanor Hamilton. *Letters and Recollections of Mazzini.* London: Longmans, Green and Co., 1912.

Knowles, James. "A Personal Reminiscence." *Nineteenth Century* 33 (January 1893): 164–88.

———. "Tennyson and Aldworth." In *Tennyson and His Friends,* edited by Hallam Tennyson, 245–52. London: Macmillan, 1911.

Kunitz, Stanley J., and Haycroft, Howard, eds., *British Authors of the Nineteenth Century.* 1936. Reprint. New York: H. W. Wilson Co., 1955.

Latourette, Kenneth Scott. *Christianity in a Revolutionary Age.* Vol. 2. *The Nineteenth Century in Europe: The Protestant and Eastern Churches.* New York: Harper and Brothers, 1959.

Lecky, W. E. H. *History of the Rise and Influence of the Spirit of Rationalism in Europe.* 2 vols. London: Longmans, Green and Co., 1865.

Leon, Derrick. *Ruskin the Great Victorian.* London: Routledge and Kegan Paul, 1949. Reprint. Hamden, Conn.: Archon Books, 1969.

The Library of Louis J. Haber of New York City. Part III. Literary Autographs and Manuscripts Both English and American . . . to be sold December 9–10, 1909. New York: Anderson Auction Co., [1909].

Livingston, James C. *The Ethics of Belief: An Essay on the Victorian Religious Conscience.* Tallahassee, Fl.: American Academy of Religion, 1974.

Lucas, E. V. *Reading, Writing and Remembering: A Literary Record.* London: Methuen, 1932.

McCarthy, Justin. *Reminiscences.* London: Chatto and Windus, 1899.

MacDonald, Greville. *George MacDonald and His Wife.* With an Introduction by G. K. Chesterton. London: G. Allen and Unwin, 1924.

MacDonnell, John Cotter. *Life and Correspondence of William Connor Magee.* 2 vols. London: Isbister and Co., 1896.

Macleod, Donald. *Memoir of Norman Macleod.* 2 vols. London: Daldy, Isbister and Co., 1876.

MacRae, Alexander. *Revivals in the Highlands and Islands in the Nineteenth Century.* Stirling: Eneas MacKay, [1906].

Maddox, M. L. "Henry Alford and the *Contemporary Review.*" Ph.D. diss., University of Chicago, 1950.

Maidment, B. E. "June Steffensen Hagen, *Tennyson and His Publishers*" (review article). *Tennyson Research Bulletin* 3, no. 3 (Summer 1979): 119.

————. "Victorian Publishing and Social Criticism: The Case of Edward Jenkins." *Publishing History* 11 (1982): 42–71.

Malcolm, Judith Wittosch. "Trollope's 'Saint Pauls' Magazine.'" Ph.D. diss., University of Michigan, 1984.

Mansel, Henry Longueville. *The Limits of Religious Thought Examined in Eight Lectures.* 4th ed. London: John Murray, 1859.

Marchant, James. *J. B. Paton, Educational and Social Pioneer.* London: James Clarke and Co., 1909.

Marsh, Peter T. *The Victorian Church in Decline: Archbishop Tait and the Church of England 1868–1882.* London: Routledge and Kegan Paul, 1969.

Marston, Edward. *After Work: Fragments from the Workshop of an Old Publisher.* London: William Heinemann, 1904.

Martin, Robert Bernard. *Tennyson: The Unquiet Heart.* Oxford: Clarendon Press, 1980.

Marx, Karl, and Engels, Frederick. *Karl Marx and Frederick Engels: Selected Correspondence.* 2d ed. Translated by I. Lasker; edited by S. Ryanzanskaya. Moscow: Progress Publishers, 1965.

Matthew, H. C. G. "Gladstone, Vaticanism, and the Question of the East." In *Religious Motivation: Biographical and Sociological Problems for the Church Historian,* 417–42. Vol. 15 of *Studies in Church History,* edited by Derek Baker. Oxford: Ecclesiastical History Society, 1978.

Mayo, Isabella Fyvie. *Recollections of What I Saw, What I Lived Through, and What I Learned, During More than Fifty Years of Social and Literary Experience.* London: John Murray, 1910.

Mayor, Stephen. *The Churches and the Labour Movement.* London: Independent Press, 1967.

Mazzini, Giuseppe. *Mazzini's Letters to an English Family 1861–1872.* 3 vols. Edited by E. F. Richards. London: John Lane, Bodley Head, 1920–22.

Mechie, Stewart. *The Church and Scottish Social Development 1780–1870.* London: Oxford University Press, 1960.

Meredith, George. *The Letters of George Meredith.* 3 vols. Edited by C. L. Cline. Oxford: Clarendon Press, 1970.

Meredith, Michael. "Browning and the Prince of Publishers." *Browning Institute Studies* 7 (1979): 1–20.

Merriam, Harold G. *Edward Moxon: Publisher of Poets.* New York: Columbia University Press, 1939. Reprint. New York: AMS Press, 1966.

Metcalf, Priscilla. *James Knowles: Victorian Editor and Architect.* Oxford: Clarendon Press, 1980.

Miall, Charles S. *Henry Richard, M.P.: A Biography.* London: Cassell, 1889.

Mill, John Stuart. *Autobiography.* London: Longman, 1873.

Millais, John Guille. *The Life and Letters of Sir John Everett Millais.* 2 vols. London: Methuen, 1899.

Millar, John Hepburn. *A Literary History of Scotland.* London: T. Fisher Unwin, 1903.

Miller, Hugh. *First Impressions of England and Its People.* London and Edinburgh: John Johnstone, 1847.

————. *My Schools and Schoolmasters, or the Story of My Education.* 15th ed. Edinburgh: William P. Nimmo, 1869.

Morgan, Charles. *The House of Macmillan (1843–1943).* London: Macmillan, 1944.

Morley, John. *Recollections.* 2 vols. New York: Macmillan, 1917.

Munro, Jean, and Munro, Robert William. *Tain Through the Centuries.* Inverness: Tain Town Council, 1966.

Murray, Christopher D. "D. G. Rossetti, A. C. Swinburne and R. W. Buchanan. The Fleshly School Revisited." *Bulletin of the John Rylands Library* 65 (Autumn 1982): 206–34; 66 (Spring 1983): 176–207.

Newbolt, Henry. *My World as in My Time: Memoirs of Sir Henry Newbolt 1862–1932.* London: Faber and Faber, 1932.

Nicoll, W. Robertson, and Wise, Thomas J., eds. *Literary Anecdotes of the Nineteenth Century.* 2 vols. London: Hodder and Stoughton, 1895–96.

Oliphant, Margaret. *Autobiography and Letters of Mrs. M. O. W. Oliphant.* Edited by Mrs. Harry Coghill. Edinburgh and London: Blackwood, 1899. Reprint. Leicester: Leicester University Press, 1974.

————. *A Memoir of the Life of John Tulloch.* Edinburgh: Blackwood and Sons, 1888.

Orr, J. Edwin. *The Second Evangelical Awakening in Britain.* London and Edinburgh: Marshall, Morgan and Scott, 1949.

Owen, David. *English Philanthropy 1660–1960.* London: Oxford University Press, 1965.

Packer, Lona Mosk, ed. *The Rossetti-Macmillan Letters.* Berkeley: University of California Press, 1963.

Passmore, John. *A Hundred Years of Philosophy.* London: Duckworth, 1957. Reprint. Harmondsworth: Penguin, 1968.

Past and Present 1796–1921. London: Spalding and Hodge, privately printed, [1921].

Paton, John Brown. *The Inner Mission: Four Addresses.* London: William Isbister, 1888.

Paton, John Lewis. *John Brown Paton: A Biography.* London: Hodder and Stoughton, 1914.

Paul, C[harles] Kegan. *Memories.* London: Kegan Paul, Trench, Trubner and Co., 1899.

Pearson, Karl. *The Life, Letters and Labours of Francis Galton.* 4 vols. Cambridge: Cambridge University Press, 1914–30.

Peel, Albert. *These Hundred Years: A History of the Congregational Union of England and Wales.* London: Congregational Union of England and Wales, 1937.

————, ed. *Letters to a Victorian Editor* [Henry Allon of the *British Quarterly Review*]. London: Independent Press, 1929.

Phillips, Walter C. *Dickens, Reade, and Collins: Sensation Novelists. A Study in the Conditions and Theories of Novel Writing in Victorian England*. New York: Columbia University Press, 1919.

Pollock, Frederick. *For My Grandson: Remembrances of an Ancient Victorian*. London: John Murray, 1933.

Porritt, Arthur. *The Best I Remember*. London: Cassell, 1922.

The Prayer-Gauge Debate. Boston: Congregational Publishing Society, 1876.

Prebble, John. *The Highland Clearances*. London: Secker and Warburg, 1963.

Prothero, Rowland E. *The Life and Correspondence of Arthur Penrhyn Stanley*. 2 vols. New York: Charles Scribner's Sons, 1893.

Ratchford, Fannie E. *A Review of Reviews*. Austin: University of Texas Press, 1946.

Ray, G. N. *Thackeray: The Age of Wisdom, 1847–1863*. London: Oxford University Press, 1958.

Reade, Charles L., and Reade, Compton, compilers. *Charles Reade: Dramatist, Novelist, Journalist: A Memoir*. 2 vols. London: Chapman and Hall, 1887.

Reardon, Bernard M. G. *Religious Thought in the Victorian Age: A Survey from Coleridge to Gore*. London: Longman, 1971. Reprint. London: Longman, 1980.

Reid, Forrest. *Illustrators of the Eighteen Sixties*. London: Faber and Gwyer, 1928. Reprint. New York: Dover, 1975.

Robson, Robert, ed. *Ideas and Institutions of Victorian Britain: Essays in Honour of George Kitson Clark*. London: G. Bell and Sons, 1967.

Rossetti, Dante Gabriel. *The Letters of Dante Gabriel Rossetti*. 4 vols. Edited by Oswald Doughty and J. R. Wahl. Oxford: Clarendon Press, 1965–67.

Rossetti, W. M. *The Diary of W. M. Rossetti, 1870–1873*. Edited by Odette Bornand. Oxford: Clarendon Press, 1977.

Rowell, Geoffrey. *Hell and the Victorians: A Study of the Nineteenth-Century Theological Controversies Concerning Eternal Punishment and the Future Life*. Oxford: Clarendon Press, 1974.

Royle, Edward. *Radical Politics 1790–1900: Religion and Unbelief*. London: Longman, 1971.

St. Helier, Lady [Mary Jeune]. *Memories of Fifty Years*. London: Edward Arnold, 1909.

Samuel, Raphael, ed. *People's History and Socialist Theory*. London: Routledge and Kegan Paul, 1981.

Scott, J. W. Robertson. *The Life and Death of a Newspaper: An Account of the Temperaments, Perturbations and Achievements of John Morley, W. T. Stead, and Other Editors of the* Pall Mall Gazette. London: Methuen, 1952.

————. *The Story of the* Pall Mall Gazette. London: Oxford University Press, 1950.

Sellars, Ian. *Nineteenth-Century Nonconformity*. London: Edward Arnold, 1977.

Shanahan, William O. *German Protestants Face the Social Question*. Vol. 1, *The Conservative Phase, 1815–1871*. Notre Dame, Ind.: University of Notre Dame Press, 1954.

Simonis, H. *The Street of Ink: An Intimate History of Journalism.* London: Cassell, 1917.

Smith, Francis B. "The Atheist Mission, 1840–1900." In *Ideas and Institutions of Victorian Britain: Essays in Honour of George Kitson Clark,* edited by Robert Robson, 205–35. London: G. Bell and Sons, 1967.

Smith, Sydney (1771–1845). *The Letters of Sydney Smith.* 2 vols. Edited by Nowell C. Smith. Oxford: Clarendon Press, 1953.

——. *The Works of the Rev. Sydney Smith.* 4 vols. London: Longman, 1839–40.

Smith, Sydney. *Donald Macleod of Glasgow: A Memoir and a Study.* London: J. Clarke and Co., 1926.

Srebrnik, Patricia Thomas. "Trollope, James Virtue, and *Saint Pauls Magazine.*" *Nineteenth Century Fiction* 37, no. 3 (December 1982): 443–63.

Stanley, A[rthur] P[enrhyn]. *The Life and Correspondence of Thomas Arnold.* 2 vols. London: B. Fellowes, 1844.

Stanley, Lady Augusta. *Letters of Lady Augusta Stanley: A Young Lady at Court 1849–1863.* Edited by the dean of Windsor [Albert Victor Baillie] and Hector Bolitho. London: Gerald Howe, 1927.

Stephen, Leslie, and Lee, Sidney, eds. *Dictionary of National Biography.* 63 vols., plus supplements. London: Smith, Elder and Co., 1885–1904. Reprint. 22 vols., plus supplements. London: Oxford University Press, 1921–

Strahan, Alexander. "Bad Literature for the Young." *Contemporary Review* 26 (November 1875): 981–91. Reprinted in *Signal: Approaches to Children's Literature* 20 (May 1976): 83–95.

——. "Charles Knight, Publisher." *Good Words* 8 (September 1867): 615–21.

——. "Our Very Cheap Literature." *Contemporary Review* 14 (June 1870): 439–60.

——. "Twenty Years of a Publisher's Life. Giving Reminiscences of Well-known Writers." *Day of Rest,* n.s., 3 (1881): 15–21, 100–104, 198–202, 256–61, 324–29, 396–401, 474–82, 543–49, 612–22, 828–34.

Super, R. H. *Trollope in the Post Office.* Ann Arbor: University of Michigan Press, 1981.

Sutherland, J. A. *Victorian Novelists and Publishers.* Chicago: University of Chicago Press, 1976. Reprint. Chicago: University of Chicago Press, Phoenix Books, 1978.

[Sutherland, J. B.] *Random Recollections and Impressions.* Edinburgh: privately printed, 1903.

Swinburne, Algernon Charles. *The Swinburne Letters.* 6 vols. Edited by Cecil Y. Lang. New Haven: Yale University Press, 1959–62.

Taylor, William, ed. *Memorials of the Life and Ministry of Charles Calder Mackintosh of Tain and Dunoon.* Edinburgh: Edmonston and Douglas, 1870.

Tennyson, Charles. *Alfred Tennyson.* London: Macmillan, 1949.

Tennyson, Emily. *Lady Tennyson's Journal.* Edited by James O. Hoge. Charlottesville: University Press of Virginia, 1981.

——. *The Letters of Emily Lady Tennyson.* Edited by James O. Hoge. University Park: Pennsylvania State University Press, 1974.

Tennyson, Hallam. *Alfred Lord Tennyson: A Memoir.* 2 vols. London: Macmillan, 1897.

———, compiler. *Materials for a Life of A. T.* 4 vols. Privately printed, [1895].

———, ed. *Tennyson and His Friends.* London: Macmillan, 1911.

Thirlwall, Connop. *Letters to a Friend* [A. P. Stanley]. Edited by A. P. Stanley. London: Richard Bentley and Sons, 1881.

Tillotson, Kathleen. "Tennyson's Serial Poem." In *Mid-Victorian Studies,* by Geoffrey Tillotson and Kathleen Tillotson, 80–109. London: University of London, Athlone Press, 1965.

Tinsley, William. *Random Recollections of an Old Publisher.* 2 vols. London: Simpkin, Marshall, Hamilton, Kent and Co., 1900.

Trollope, Anthony. *An Autobiography.* Edited by Frederick Page. Oxford: Oxford University Press, 1950.

———. *The Letters of Anthony Trollope.* 2 vols. (consecutive pagination). Edited by N. John Hall, with the assistance of Nina Burgis. Stanford: Stanford University Press, 1983.

Vincent, John. *The Formation of the British Liberal Party 1857–1868.* London: Constable, 1966. Reprint. Harmondsworth: Penguin, 1972.

Walker, Hugh. *The Literature of the Victorian Era.* Cambridge: Cambridge University Press, 1910.

Ward, Wilfrid. *Ten Personal Studies.* London: Longmans, Green and Co., 1908.

Watt, Hugh. *Thomas Chalmers and the Disruption.* Edinburgh: Thomas Nelson, 1943.

Wellwood, John. *Norman Macleod.* Edinburgh and London: Oliphant, Anderson and Ferrier, 1897.

Wessel Walker, Donna Lynne. "The *Contemporary Review* and Contemporary Society." Ph.D. diss., University of Michigan, 1984.

White, Gleeson. *English Illustration: 'The Sixties': 1855–70.* London: Constable, 1897.

Whyte, Frederic. *The Life of W. T. Stead.* 2 vols. London: Jonathan Cape, 1925. Reprint. London: Garland, 1971.

———. *William Heinemann: A Memoir.* London: Jonathan Cape, 1928.

Wise, Thomas J. *The Ashley Library. A Catalogue of Printed Books, Manuscripts and Autograph Letters Collected by Thomas J. Wise.* Vol. 7. London: privately printed, 1925.

———. *A Bibliography of Tennyson.* 2 vols. London: privately printed, 1908.

———. *Letters of Thomas J. Wise to John Henry Wrenn. A Further Inquiry Into the Guilt of Certain Nineteenth-Century Forgers.* Edited by Fannie E. Ratchford. New York: Alfred A. Knopf, 1944.

Worth, George J. *James Hannay.* Lawrence: University of Kansas Press, 1964.

Index